PROBLEM SOLUTIONS MANUAL
for the text

Economic Evaluation and Investment Decision Methods

Eighth Edition

Franklin J. Stermole
and
John M. Stermole

Copyright © 1993

Investment Evaluations Corporation
2000 Goldenvue Drive
Golden, Colorado 80401

Copyright © 1974, 1977, 1980, 1982, 1984, 1987, and 1990
by Investment Evaluations Corporation

All rights reserved. No part of this manual may be reproduced in any form without permission in writing from the publisher.

ISBN 1-878740-04-0
Library of Congress Catalog Card Number 92-075478

Printed in the U.S.A.

CHAPTER 2 PROBLEM SOLUTIONS

2-1 Solution:

```
P₀=$1,000         P₁₀=$2,000
                                              F=?
 0 .............. 10 ............... 20 semi-annual periods
```

The nominal interest rate of 6% compounded semi-annually gives semi-annual period interest, i = 3% per semi-annual period

$$F = \$1,000(F/P_{3,20})^{1.806} + 2,000(F/P_{3,10})^{1.344} = \$4,494$$

For annual periods, use an effective interest rate/yr:

$$E = (1+0.03)^2 - 1 = 0.0609$$

$$F = 1,000(F/P_{6.09,10}) + 2,000(F/P_{6.09,5}) = \$4,494$$

2-2 Solution:

The $500 payments may be considered to be either investments or incomes depending on whether you are the borrower or loaner of money. The solution is the same for either case.

```
              A=500    A=500 ............. A=500
P = ? ─────────────────────────────────────────────
       0       1        2 ................ 20 semi-annual periods
```

i = 4% per semi-annual period for a nominal interest rate of 8% compounded semi-annually

$$P = 500(P/A_{4,20})^{13.590} = \$6,795$$

2-3 Solution:

```
P=5,000    A       A ...................... A
                                                F=10,000
  0        1       2 ....................... 6
```

$$A = 5,000(A/P_{6,6})^{.20336} + 10,000(A/F_{6,6})^{.14336} = \$2,450$$

$$A = [5,000 + 10,000(P/F_{6,6})](A/P_{6,6}) = \$2,450$$

$$A = [5,000(F/P_{6,6}) + 10,000](A/F_{6,6}) = \$2,450$$

2-4 Solution:

```
P=$3,000      A           A ..................... A
─────────────────────────────────────────────────────
    0         1           2 ..................... 36 months
```

nominal interest rate r = 12% compounded monthly,
therefore the period interest rate i = 12%/12 or 1% per month

Mathematically, $A/P_{1,36} = \dfrac{0.01(1+0.01)^{36}}{(1+0.01)^{36} - 1} = 0.03321$

therefore, $A = 3,000(A/P_{1,36}) = \$99.63$
                        .03321

By interpolation:

$A/P_{1,35} = 0.03400$

$A/P_{1,40} = 0.03046$

$A/P_{1,36} = 0.03400 - [(0.03400 - 0.03046)/5]$

$A/P_{1,36} = 0.03329$

$A = 3,000(A/P_{1,36}) = \$99.87$
              .03329

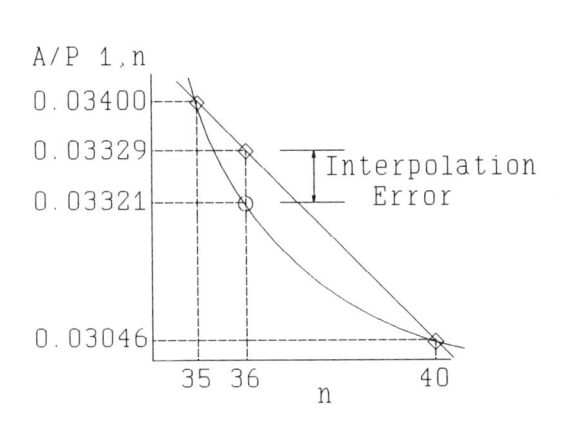

```
A/P 1,n
0.03400 ┤◇
0.03329 ┤   ◇    ┐ Interpolation
0.03321 ┤   ○    ┘ Error
                      
0.03046 ┤              ◇
        └───┬┬───────┬──
           35 36    40
                n
```

2-5 Solution:

```
-         A           A ............... A
─────────────────────────────────────────── F = 10,000
 0        1           2 ............... 20 quarterly periods
```

i = 1.5% per period

$A/F_{1,20} = 0.04542$

$A/F_{2,20} = 0.04116$

interpolating: $(0.04542 - 0.04116)/2 = 0.00213$

$A/F_{1.5\%,20} = 0.04542 - 0.00213 = 0.04329$

$A = 10,000(A/F_{1.5,20}) = 432.90$
              .04329

CHAPTER 2 PROBLEM SOLUTIONS

2-6 Solution:

```
              1,000     1,000  ........  1,000
P=?  ─────────────────────────────────────────
     0         1         2    ..........  10 years
     0    1    2    3    4    ..........  20 semi-annual periods
```

r = 8% compounded semi-annually, so i = 4% per semi-annual period

$$1,000(A/F_{4\%,2}) = \overset{.49020}{} = 490.20$$

```
         490.20  490.20  490.20  490.20  .....  490.20   is an
     ─────────────────────────────────────────────────   equivalent
     0    1       2       3       4    ........  20      time diagram
```

$$P = (1,000(A/F_{4,2}))(P/A_{4,20}) = 6,661.82$$

with factors .4902 and 13.590

or find the effective interest rate, E, per year so

$$P = 1,000(P/A_{E,10})$$

$$E = (1 + 0.04)^2 - 1 = 0.0816, \text{ therefore,}$$

by interpolation between the 8% and 9% table values: (E = 8.16%)

$$P/A_{8.16\%,10} = 6.710 - (6.710 - 6.418)\left(\frac{8.16 - 8.00}{9.00 - 8.00}\right) = 6.710 - 0.0467$$
$$= 6.6633$$

Therefore, $P = 1,000(P/A_{E,10}) = 6,663.30$ (using 6.6633)

Interpolation error in determining $P/A_{E,10}$ accounts for the difference in results.

Explicitly solving for the factor given E = 8.16% yields:

$$P/A_{8.16\%,10} = \frac{(1.0816)^{10}-1}{0.0816(1.0816)^{10}} = 6.6619$$

$$P = 1,000(6.6619) = 6,661.92$$

Alternately, $P = 1,000[P/F_{4,2}+P/F_{4,4}+P/F_{4,6}+ \cdots +P/F_{4,20}] = \$6,662$

with factors .9246+ .8548+ .7903+ ... + .4564

2-7 Solution:

```
$3,000        $6,000        $7,000        $7,000        $4,000
――――――――――――――――――――――――――――――――――――――――――――――――――――――
  0             1             2             3             4
```

$$P = 3{,}000 + 6{,}000(P/F_{12\%,1})^{.8929} + 7{,}000(P/F_{12\%,2})^{.7972} + 7{,}000(P/F_{12\%,3})^{.7118}$$

$$+ 4{,}000(P/F_{12\%,4})^{.6355} = \$21{,}462$$

or

$$= 3{,}000 + 6{,}000(P/F_{12\%,1})^{.8929} + 7{,}000(P/A_{12\%,2})^{1.690}(P/F_{12\%,1})^{.8929}$$

$$+ 4{,}000(P/F_{12\%,4})^{.6355} = \$21{,}462$$

$$F = 3{,}000(F/P_{12\%,4})^{1.574} + 6{,}000(F/P_{12\%,3})^{1.405} + 7{,}000(F/P_{12\%,2})^{1.254}$$

$$+ 7{,}000(F/P_{12\%,1})^{1.120} + 4{,}000 = \$33{,}770$$

where $7{,}000(F/P_{12\%,2}) + 7{,}000(F/P_{12\%,1}) = 7{,}000(F/A_{12\%,2})(F/P_{12\%,1})$

$$A = 21{,}462(A/P_{12\%,4})^{.32923} = \$7{,}066 = 33{,}770(A/F_{12\%,4})^{.20923}$$

2-8 Solution:

```
        1,000      1,000  ............... 1,000
P=? ――――――――――――――――――――――――――――――――――――――――――  F=?
     0    1          2   ................ 20
```

$$F = 1{,}000(F/A_{10,20})^{57.275} = \$57{,}275$$

$$P = 1{,}000(P/A_{10,20})^{8.514} = \$8{,}514$$

Difference due to round-off error in the factors used.

or $P = 57{,}275(P/F_{10,20})^{.1486} = \$8{,}511$

Check answer: $\$8{,}514(F/P_{10,20})^{6.727} = \$57{,}274$ Check OK.

CHAPTER 2 PROBLEM SOLUTIONS

2-9 Solution:

```
$2,000      $1,000      $1,000 ............ $1,000
─────────────────────────────────────────────────── F=?
 0           1           2 .................. 5
```

i = 20% per year

$$F = 2{,}000(F/P_{20,5}) + 1{,}000(F/A_{20,5}) = \$12{,}418$$

with factors 2.488 and 7.442.

Equivalent semi-annual payments for semi-annual compounding

$$= 1{,}000(A/F_{10,2}) = \$476.19$$

(factor = .47619)

```
           -        A=F(A/F_{10,2})           A
                 ────────────────────────── F=1,000
                 0         1         2
                   (semi-annual periods)
                    i = 10% per period
```

```
2,000     476.19     476.19 .............. 476.19
─────────────────────────────────────────────────── F=?
 0          1          2 ................... 10
            (semi-annual periods)
```

$$F = 2{,}000(F/P_{10,10}) + 476.19(F/A_{10,10}) = \$12{,}777 \text{ for semi-annual compounding}$$

(factors 2.594 and 15.937)

2-10 Solution:

$$(1 + 0.05)^4 - 1 = (F/P_{5,4}) - 1 = 1.216 - 1 = 0.216$$

Effective interest rate, E = 21.6%

2-11 Solution:

$$(1 + i)^4 - 1 = 0.20$$

therefore, $(1 + i)^4 = 1.20$

therefore, $1 + i = (1.20)^{0.25}$

$$= 1.0466$$

i = 4.66% per quarterly period:

Nominal rate r = (4.66%/period)(4 periods) = 18.64%

2-12 Solution:

A)
```
      -      1,000    1,000 ........................ 1,000
                                                           F=?
      0        1        2 ........................ 40 years
```

$i = 15\%$ per year

$$F = 1,000(F/A_{15,40}) = 1,779,090$$
with $(F/A_{15,40}) = 1779.09$

B)
```
      -      1,000    1,100 .... gradient +100/yr ........
      0        1        2 ........................ 40
```

$$F = (1,000 + 100(A/G_{15,40}))(F/A_{15,40}) = \$2,938,523$$
with $(A/G_{15,40}) = 6.517$ and $(F/A_{15,40}) = 1779.09$

Using the A\G Factor gives the following time diagram with an equivalent uniform series of values A in years 1-40:

$$A = 1,000 + 100(A/G_{15,40}) = \$1,651.70$$
with $(A/G_{15,40}) = 6.517$

```
      -     1,651.70  1,651.70 ..................... 1,651.70
      0        1         2 ........................ 40
```

$$F = 1,651.7(F/A_{15,40}) = \$2,938,523$$
with $(F/A_{15,40}) = 1779.09$

C) $P = 1,779,090(P/F_{15,40}) = \$6,582$ with $(P/F_{15,40}) = .0037$

or $= 1,000(P/A_{15,40}) = \$6,642$ with $(P/A_{15,40}) = 6.642$

Difference due to round-off error. Note only 2 significant figures on $P/F_{15,40}$

CHAPTER 2 PROBLEM SOLUTIONS   7

2-13 Solution:

–	20,000 tons	19,500	19,000	16,000	15,500	10,500
0	1	2	3 9		10 20	

P = present worth of year 1-9 production @ $6/ton

    + present worth of year 10-20 production @ $8/ton

$$P = (120{,}000 - 3{,}000(\underset{3.491}{A/G_{8,9}}))(\underset{6.247}{P/A_{8,9}})$$

$$+ (124{,}000 - 4{,}000(\underset{4.240}{A/G_{8,11}}))(\underset{7.139}{P/A_{8,11}})(\underset{.5002}{P/F_{8,9}})$$

$$= 684{,}200 + 382{,}200 = \$1{,}066{,}400$$

Equivalent Profit Diagram from the use of $A/G_{8\%,n}$:

P=?	109,527 109,527	107,040 107,040
0	1 9	10 20

Alternate Solution:

P = present worth of 20 years of production @ $8/ton,
     less the present worth of $2/ton for year 1-9 production.

$$P = (160{,}000 - 4{,}000(\underset{7.037}{A/G_{8,20}}))(\underset{9.818}{P/A_{8,20}})$$

$$- (40{,}000 - 1{,}000(\underset{3.491}{A/G_{8,9}}))(\underset{6.247}{P/A_{8,9}})$$

$$= 1{,}294{,}500 - 228{,}100 = \$1{,}066{,}400$$

If the investor requires a 20% rate of return instead of 8%, then:

$$P = (160{,}000 - 4{,}000(\underset{4.464}{A/G_{20,20}}))(\underset{4.870}{P/A_{20,20}})$$

$$- (40{,}000 - 1{,}000(\underset{2.836}{A/G_{20,9}}))(\underset{4.031}{P/A_{20,9}})$$

$$= \$542{,}433$$

2-14 Solution:

```
            $6,000      $6,000 $8,000     $8,000 $10,000      $10,000
P=?    ─────────────────────────────────────────────────────────────
       0     1 ...... 5     6 ........ 9    10 ......... 15
```

$$P = \$6{,}000(P/A_{10,5})_{3.791} + 8{,}000(P/A_{10,4})_{3.170}(P/F_{10,5})_{.6209}$$

$$+ 10{,}000(P/A_{10,6})_{4.355}(P/F_{10,9})_{.4241}$$

$= \$22{,}746 + 15{,}746 + 18{,}469 = \$56{,}961$ which is less than \$70,000

so accept the offer of \$70,000 now to maximize profit.

Alternately: $P = 6{,}000(P/A_{10,5})_{3.791} + 8{,}000(P/A_{10,9}-P/A_{10,5})_{5.759 \; 3.791}$

$$+ 10{,}000(P/A_{10,15}-P/A_{10,9})_{7.606 \; 5.759} = \$56{,}960$$

or $P = 10{,}000(P/A_{10,15}) - 2{,}000(P/A_{10,9}) - 2{,}000(P/A_{10,5}) = \$56{,}960$

Another Alternate Solution (by Comparing Future Values):

$$F = 70{,}000(F/P_{10,15})_{4.177} = \$292{,}390$$

$$F = 6{,}000(F/A_{10,15})_{31.772} + 2{,}000(F/A_{10,10})_{15.94} + 2{,}000(F/A_{10,6})_{7.716} = \$237{,}944$$

or $= 6{,}000(F/A_{10,5})_{6.105}(F/P_{10,10})_{2.594} + 8{,}000(F/A_{10,4})_{4.641}(F/P_{10,6})_{1.772}$

$$+ 10{,}000(F/A_{10,6})_{7.716} = \$237{,}969$$

To maximize future value, accept \$70,000 now.

CHAPTER 2 PROBLEM SOLUTIONS

2-15 Solution:

Equivalent Annual Payments = A = $56,961(A/P_{10,15}^{.13147}) = \$7,488$

Alternate Solution:

A = $237,969(A/F_{10,15}^{.03147}) = \$7,488$

2-16 Solution:

```
$11,000    $500      $550      $600 .......... $950
_____ Salvage = $2,000
   0         1         2         3 ............  10
```

Equivalent
Annual Cost = $11,000(A/P_{8,10}^{.14903}) + 500 + 50(A/G_{8,10}^{3.871}) - 2,000(A/F_{8,10}^{.06903})$

$\qquad = \$1,639.33 + \$500 + \$193.55 - \$138.06 = \$2,194.82$

2-17 Solution:

```
 -     -     - ........ -     $100    $100 ..... $100
_____
 0     1     2 ....... 30     31      32 ....... 48
```

A) Monthly - Discrete Interest, Discrete $:

The monthly discrete interest rate given a nominal interest rate of 15.0% compounded monthly is a period interest rate:

i = 0.15/12 = 0.0125

$(P/A_{i,n}) = [(1+i)^n - 1]/i(1+i)^n$
$(P/F_{i,n}) = 1/(1+i)^n$

$(P/A_{1.25\%,18}) = 16.0295$
$(P/F_{1.25\%,30}) = 0.6889$

P = $\$100(P/A_{1.25\%,18}^{16.0295})(P/F_{1.25\%,30}^{0.6889}) = \$1,104$

B) Yearly - Discrete Interest, Discrete $:

```
-          -          -        $1,200      $600
─────────────────────────────────────────────────
0          1          2          3           4
```

$$P = \$1{,}200(P/F_{15\%,3})^{0.6575} + \$600(P/F_{15\%,4})^{0.5718} = \$1{,}132$$

However, this $1,132 result is incorrect because it should be based on the annual effective discrete interest for a 15% nominal interest rate compounded monthly calculated using Eq. 2-9:

$$E = (1.0125)^{12} - 1 = 0.16075 \text{ or } 16.07\%$$

$$P = \$1{,}200(P/F_{16.07\%,3})^{0.6395} + \$600(P/F_{16.07\%,4})^{0.55096} = \$1{,}098$$

This $1,098 result is very close to the $1,104 result from Case A.

C) Yearly - Effective Continuous Interest, Discrete $

The continuous interest rate "r" that is equivalent to the discrete interest rate of 16.07% is calculated by using Eq. 2-10 as follows:

$$E = e^r - 1 = 0.1607, \quad \text{rearranging gives,} \quad e^r = 1.1607$$
$$r = \ln(1.1607) = 0.1490 \text{ or } 14.9\%$$

$$P = \$1{,}200(P/F_{14.9\%,3})^{0.6395} + \$600(P/F_{14.9\%,4})^{0.5510} = \$1{,}098$$

Note this result is identical to the Case B result. Factors are from Appendix B for continuous interest with discrete dollar values:

$$P/F_{r,n} = 1/e^{rn}, \quad e = \text{the natural log base, } r = 14.9\%,$$
$$\text{and } n = 3 \text{ and } 4 \text{ respectively.}$$

D) Yearly - Continuous Interest, Continuous Flowing $

```
-          -         --$1,200--   --$600--
─────────────────────────────────────────────────
0          1          2          3           4
```

In Case D, we now work with the same continuous interest calculated in Case C assuming the dollars are realized uniformly over the third and fourth years of this analysis as illustrated on the time diagram. In Appendix C, for continuous interest with continuous flowing funds, $P/F^*_{r,n} = [(e^r-1)/r]/e^{rn}$, which is also equivalent to $(e^r-1)/(re^{rn})$ as illustrated in Appendix C.

$$P = \$1{,}200(P/F^*_{14.9\%,3})^{0.6896} + \$600(P/F^*_{14.9\%,4})^{0.5942} = \$1{,}184$$

Continuous flow of money is a different assumption from the discrete dollar value Case B and C assumptions, so a different answer results.

CHAPTER 2 PROBLEM SOLUTIONS 11

2-18 Solution:

```
P=?     600    700 ... gradient ... 1,200  1,200  1,200  1,200
——————————————————————————————————————————————————————————————— F=?
0        1      2 .................. 7      8      9      10
```

A) $P = [600+100(A/G_{12,7})^{2.552}](P/A_{12,7})^{4.564}+1,200(P/A_{12,3})^{2.402}(P/F_{12,7})^{0.4523} = \$5,207$

$\$5,207$ is a rounded solution from $\$5,206.84$

or $P = [600+100(A/G_{12,6})^{2.172}](P/A_{12,6})^{4.111}+1,200(P/A_{12,4})^{3.037}(P/F_{12,6})^{0.5066} = \$5,207$

B) $F = 5,206.84(F/P_{12,10})^{3.106} = \$16,172$

or $F = [600+100(A/G_{12,7})^{2.552}](F/A_{12,7})^{10.089}(F/P_{12,3})^{1.405}+1,200(F/A_{12,3})^{3.374} = \$16,171$

2-19 Solution:

```
              -  .......... -      5,000 ............... 5,000
P=? —————————————————————————————————————————————————————————————
    0          1 ............ 4    5 ................... 14
```

$P = 5,000(P/A_{9,10})^{6.418}(P/F_{9,4})^{.7084} = \$22,733$

If the payments start at the end of year 1 instead of at the end of year 5, the time zero cost is $5,000(P/A_{9,10}) = \$32,090$.

2-20 Solution:

```
6,000      A=?     A=?     A=? .................. A=?
———————————————————————————————————————————————————————
  0         1       2       3 ................... 36
```

A) Simple interest, 10%: principal = 6,000/36 = 166.67
                          interest = 6,000(0.10)/(12) = 50.00

End-of-month payment = A = 166.67 + 50.00 = $ 216.67

B) 10% annual interest compounded monthly.
   Use mathematical definition of $A/P_{i,n}$, where i = 10%/12:

$i = 0.10/12 = 0.00833$
$n = 36$
$A/P_{i,n} = i(1+i)^n/[(1+i)^n-1] = 0.00833(1.00833)^{36}/[(1.00833)^{36}-1] = 0.0322$

End-of-month payments = A = $6,000(A/P_{0.833\%,36})^{0.0322} = \$ 193.49$

Beginning-of-month payments = $193.49(P/F_{0.833\%,1})^{0.9917} = \$ 191.88$

2-21 Solution:

APR of 11.5% compounded monthly is a period interest rate of
0.115/12 = 0.009583 or 0.9583% per month.

End of Month Payments: "A"

$$A_{End} = \$15,000(A/P_{0.9583\%,48})^{0.026088} = \$391.32 \text{ per month.}$$

Beginning of Month Payments: "X" = $391.32(P/F_{0.9583\%,1}) = \$387.61$

An alternate beginning-of-month solution:

$$\$15,000 = X + X(P/A_{.9583\%,47})^{37.6979}$$

$$\$15,000 = X(1+37.6979)$$

$$X = \$387.62$$

2-22 Solution:

```
C=$1,500    OC=$400    OC=$500    OC=$600
                                              L=$300
    0          1          2          3
```

Present Worth Cost @ 15%:

$$P = 1,500 + [400 + 100(A/G_{15,3})^{0.907}](P/A_{15,3})^{2.283} - 300(P/F_{15,3})^{0.6575}$$

$$= 1,500 + 1,120.27 - 197.25 = \$2,423$$

$$\text{or} = 1,500 + 400(P/F_{15,1})^{.8696} + 500(P/F_{15,2})^{.7561} + (600-300)(P/F_{15,3})^{.6575} = \$2,423$$

Future Worth Cost @ 15%:

$$F = 1,500(F/P_{15,3})^{1.521} + [400 + 100(A/G_{15,3})^{0.907}](F/A_{15,3})^{3.472} - 300$$

$$= 2,281.50 + 1,703.71 - 300 = \$3,685$$

$$\text{or} = 2,423(F/P_{15,3})^{1.521} = \$3,685$$

Equivalent Annual Cost @ 15%:

$$A = 2,423(A/P_{15,3})^{0.43798} = \$1,061$$

$$\text{or} = 3,685(A/F_{15,3})^{0.28798} = \$1,061$$

CHAPTER 2 PROBLEM SOLUTIONS

2-23 Solution:

(A)

```
         ---$300---  ---$400---  ---$400---  ---$400---  ---$500---
─────────────────────────────────────────────────────────────────────
    0         1           2           3           4           5
```

$$P = 300(P/F^*_{9,1})^{.9563} + 400(P/F^*_{9,2})^{.8740} + 400(P/F^*_{9,3})^{.7988} + 400(P/F^*_{9,4})^{.7300} + 500(P/F^*_{9,5})^{.6672}$$

$$= \$1,581.61$$

$$\text{or} = 300(P/F^*_{9,1})^{.9563} + 400(P/A^*_{9,3})^{2.6291}(P/F_{9,1})^{.9139} + 500(P/F^*_{9,5})^{.6672} = \$1,581.58$$

Where from Appendix C, $P/F^*_{r,n} = [(e^r-1)/r](1/e^{rn})$

$$P/A^*_{r,n} = [(e^{rn}-1)/r](1/e^{rn})$$

and from Appendix B, $P/F_{r,n} = 1/e^{rn}$

Note that since $400(P/A^*_{9,3})$ is a discrete year 1 sum, the continuous interest single payment present worth factor, $P/F_{9,1}$ from Appendix B, is needed to bring the year 1 sum to year 0. The continuous interest, continuous flow of money factor, $P/F^*_{9,1}$, is NOT valid for this calculation.

Continuously Flowing Yearly Payments, $A = 1,581.61(A/P^*_{9,5})^{0.24836} = \$392.81$

Where from Appendix C, $A/P^*_{r,n} = re^{rn}/(e^{rn}-1)$

Future Value, $F = 1,581.61(F/P_{r=9,5})^{1.5683} = 1,581.61(e^{0.09(5)}) = \$2,480.46$

(B) From Eq 2-10, effective discrete rate $E = 0.09 = e^r - 1$

so $r = \ln(1.09) = 0.0862$
or $r = 8.62\%$

```
              (150+200)  (200+200)  (200+200)  (200+250)
   ---$150---  ---$350---  ---$400---  ---$400---  ---$450---  ---$250---
─────────────────────────────────────────────────────────────────────────
     0           1           2           3           4           5           6
```

$$P = 150(P/F^*_{8.62,1})^{.9581} + 350(P/F^*_{8.62,2})^{.8790} + 400(P/F^*_{8.62,3})^{.8064} + 400(P/F^*_{8.62,4})^{.7398}$$

$$+ 450(P/F^*_{8.62,5})^{.6787} + 250(P/F^*_{8.62,6})^{.6226} = \$1,530.91$$

This result is very similar to the \$1,529 discrete compounding, discrete value result from Example 2-8.

$A = 1,530.91(A/P^*_{8.62,5})^{0.24619} = \$376.89$ flowing continuously each year

$F = 1,530.91(F/P_{8.62,5})^{1.5388} = 1,530.91(e^{0.0862(5)}) = \$2,355.76$

2-23 Solution: Continued

(C) Mid-Period Timing Assumption, Using Effective Discrete Rate

```
-    $300      $400      $400      $400      $500
─────────────────────────────────────────────────────
0    0.5       1.5       2.5       3.5       4.5
```

Effective discrete interest rate equivalent to a 9% continuous rate:

$E = e^r - 1 = e^{0.09} - 1 = 0.0942 = 9.42\%$

$$P = 300(P/F_{9.42\%, 0.5})^{.9560} + 400(P/A_{9.42\%, 3})^{2.5125}(P/F_{9.42\%, 0.5})^{.9560}$$
$$+ 500(P/F_{9.42\%, 4.5})^{.6669} = \$1,581.03$$

Note that this result is nearly equal to the part (A) result.

CHAPTER 3 PROBLEM SOLUTIONS

3-1 Solution:

```
           C=550     C=500     C=500     C=500     C=500
Time   ─────┼─────────┼─────────┼─────────┼─────────┼─────
            0         1         2         3         4

          C=2,250     -         -         -         -
Cash   ─────┼─────────┼─────────┼─────────┼─────────┼─────
            0         1         2         3         4
```

PW Eq: $2{,}250 = 550 + 500(P/A_{i,4})$

$P/A_{i,4} = \dfrac{2{,}250 - 550}{500} = \dfrac{1{,}700}{500} = 3.400$

$P/A_{6,4} = 3.465$

$P/A_{7,4} = 3.387$

$i = 6\% + 1\%\left(\dfrac{3.465 - 3.400}{3.465 - 3.387}\right)$

   = 6.83% compounded annually

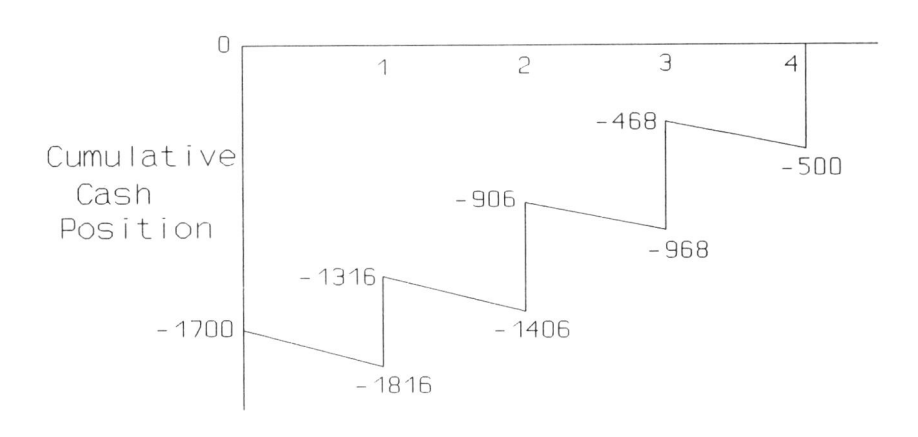

```
         0    1         2         3         4
         ┼────┬─────────┬─────────┬─────────┬──
                                      -468
Cumulative                                  -500
 Cash                            
Position                -906    
                                 -968
               -1316
     -1700            -1406
                -1816
```

The meaning of the 6.83% is that it is the % return on unamortized <u>incremental</u> investment each year as follows:

```
Cash  C=1,700    I=500     I=500     I=500     I=500
-Time ──┼─────────┼─────────┼─────────┼─────────┼─────
        0         1         2         3         4
```

If you pay cash, you put out an extra $1,700 at time zero to save making $500 payments in years 1-4, saving an effective interest cost of 6.83% per year on unamortized incremental investment.

3-2 Solution:

```
P   3,000 ........ 3,000   5,000 ........ 5,000   6,000 .... 6,000
    ─────────────────────────────────────────────────────────────────
    0   1 ........... 5    6 ............ 13    14 ....... 16
```

$$P = 3{,}000\overset{3.993}{(P/A_{8,5})} + 5{,}000\overset{5.747}{(P/A_{8,8})}\overset{.6806}{(P/F_{8,5})} + 6{,}000\overset{2.577}{(P/A_{8,3})}\overset{.3677}{(P/F_{8,13})}$$

$$= 11{,}979 + 19{,}557 + 5{,}685 = \$37{,}221 \text{ at year 0}$$

Value at the end of the 3rd year $= (37{,}221)\overset{1.260}{(F/P_{8,3})} = \$46{,}900$

Alternate Solution:

$$\text{Yr 3 value} = [6{,}000\overset{8.851}{(P/A_{8,16})} - 1{,}000\overset{7.904}{(P/A_{8,13})}$$

$$- 2{,}000\overset{3.993}{(P/A_{8,5})}]\overset{1.260}{(F/P_{8,3})} = \$46{,}900$$

3-3 Solution:

```
              10,000
    50,000    5,000    5,000 ..... 5,000    5,000 .... 5,000
A)  ──────────────────────────────────────────────────────────── L=10,000
    0         1        2 ........ 5         6 ........ 10
```

Using Text Eq. 3-1 (pg. 70 in the textbook):

$$AC_A = 50{,}000\overset{.16275}{(A/P_{10,10})} - 10{,}000\overset{.06275}{(A/F_{10,10})} + 10{,}000\overset{.6209}{(P/F_{10,5})}\overset{.16275}{(A/P_{10,10})}$$

$$+ 5{,}000 = 13{,}520$$

Using Text Eq. 3-2 (pg. 70 in the textbook):

$$AC_A = (50{,}000-10{,}000)(A/P_{10,10}) + 10{,}000(0.10) + 10{,}000(P/F_{10,5})(A/P_{10,10})$$

$$+ 5{,}000 = 13{,}520$$

or $AC_A = (\text{PW Cost A})(A/P_{10,10}) = (83{,}067)(0.16275) = 13{,}520$

```
B)  40,000    8,000    8,500 ........ grad=500 ..... 12,500
    ──────────────────────────────────────────────────────────── L=0
    0         1        2 ......................... 10
```

$$AC_B = 40{,}000\overset{.16275}{(A/P_{10,10})} + 8{,}000 + 500\overset{3.276}{(A/G_{10,10})} = 16{,}373$$

or $AC_B = (\text{PW Cost B})(A/P_{10,10}) = (100{,}598)(0.16275) = 16{,}373$

Select A with smaller annual cost.

CHAPTER 3 PROBLEM SOLUTIONS

3-4 Solution:

```
                    (Profit/Year = 25,000-15,000 = 10,000)
Cost=120,000   10,000      10,000 ................ 10,000   Salvage
                                                             L=70,000
───────────────────────────────────────────────────────────
     0           1           2 .................... 15
```

PW Eq: $0 = -120,000 + 10,000(P/A_{i,15}) + 70,000(P/F_{i,15})$

For investments with relatively long lives of 10 years or more, as a starting "i" value it is usually desireable to start in the neighborhood of i = average profit/initial investment = 10/120 = 8.33% in this case.

i = 8%: 120,000 = 10,000(8.559) + 70,000(.3152) = 107,654
i = 7%: 120,000 = 10,000(9.108) + 70,000(.3624) = 116,448
i = 6%: 120,000 = 10,000(9.712) + 70,000(.4173) = 126,331

$i = 6\% + 1\%\left(\dfrac{126,331 - 120,000}{126,331 - 116,448}\right) = 6.64\%$

3-5 Solution:

```
                       400                        400
             Costs     200                        200
  Cost=50,000          900 ...................... 900
                                                          L=?
  ──────────────────────────────────────────────────
       0                1 ......................... 10

  Rental Costs
                      4,800 ..................... 4,800
                                                          L=0
  ──────────────────────────────────────────────────
       0                1 ......................... 10
```

Annual Cost Equation, Rental Cost = Purchase Cost:

 .1359 .07587

$4,800 = (50,000)(A/P_{6,10}) + 1,500 - L(A/F_{6,10})$

$3,300 = 50,000(0.1359) - L(0.07587)$

$L(0.07587) = 6,795 - 3,300 = 3,495$

$L = 3,495/0.0758 = \$46,066$

PW Cost Equation:

 7.360 7.360 .5584

$4,800(P/A_{6,10}) = 50,000 + 1,500(P/A_{6,10}) - L(P/F_{6,10})$

L = 46,046 with difference due to factor round-off error.

FW Cost Equation:

 13.181 1.791 13.181

$4,800(F/A_{6,10}) = 50,000(F/P_{6,10}) + 1,500(F/A_{6,10}) - L$

L= 46,053   with difference due to factor round-off error.

3-6 Solution: All values are in dollars.

```
C=800       I=40 ............................. I=40
                                                      L=1,000
   0          1 ............................. 40 semi-annual periods
```

PW Eq: $0 = -800 + 40(P/A_{i,40}) + 1{,}000(P/F_{i,40})$

i = semi-annual period ROR = 5.22% by trial and error

The nominal (annual) bond ROR is 10.44% compounded semi-annually. Brokers and bankers refer to the 10.44% as **"yield to maturity"**.

If the bond is callable in 8 years (16 semi-annual periods):

```
C=?         I=40 ........... I=40
                                   L=1,000
   0          1 ............ 16 semi-annual periods to
                                call date
```

$C = 40(P/A_{3,16}) + 1{,}000(P/F_{3,16}) = \$1{,}125.64$

An investor can pay $1,125.64 for this old bond to realize a 6% ROR compounded semi-annually to the call date on this bond investment.

3-7 Solution:

```
C=?         I=40 ................ I=40
                                        L=1,000
   0          1 ................. 40 semi-annual periods to
                                     maturity
```

$$C = 40(P/A_{5,40})^{17.159} + 1{,}000(P/F_{5,40})^{.1420} = \$828.36$$

3-8 Solution:

```
C=5,000      C=200      C=200 ............... C=200
                                                      L=13,000
   0           1          2 ................. 10
```

PW Eq: $5{,}000 = -200(P/A_{i,10}) + 13{,}000(P/F_{i,10})$

Rearranging:
i = 7%: $-200(7.024) + 13{,}000(0.5083) = 5{,}203$
i = 8%: $-200(6.710) + 13{,}000(0.4632) = 4{,}680$

$i = 7\% + 1\%\left(\dfrac{5{,}203-5{,}000}{5{,}203-4{,}680}\right) = 7.39\%$.

Risk considerations for the relative safety of 7% from a bank and 7.39% in land speculation should be considered, but results show slight economic advantage to the land investment.

Alternate FW analysis:

Bank Account FW = $5{,}000(F/P_{7,10})^{1.967} + 200(F/A_{7,10})^{13.816} = \$12{,}598 < \$13{,}000$

so slight advantage to the land investment.

CHAPTER 3 PROBLEM SOLUTIONS

3-9 Solution:

```
             C=100
C=60   I=40  I=40   I=40   I=70 ........... I=70
─────────────────────────────────────────────────── L=0
 0      1     2      3      4  ............  10
```

Yr 0 PW Eq: $60 = -100(P/F_{i,2}) + 40(P/A_{i,3}) + 70(P/A_{i,7})(P/F_{i,3})$

$i=40\%$ = $-100(0.5102) + 40(1.589) + 70(2.263)(0.3644) = +70.26$
$i=50\%$ = $-100(0.4444) + 40(1.407) + 70(1.883)(0.2963) = +50.90$

$i = ROR = 40\% + (50\% - 40\%)\left(\dfrac{70.26 - 60.00}{70.26 - 50.90}\right) = 45.3\%$

3-10 Solution:

```
        C=500  C=500  C=500  C=750  C=750  C=750  C=750   -
Lease   ─────────────────────────────────────────────────
          0      1      2      3      4      5      6     7

        C=2,000   -      -      -   C=600    -      -     -
Purchase ─────────────────────────────────────────────────
           0      1      2      3     4      5      6     7
```

$$PC_{Lease} = [500 + 500\overset{1.528}{(P/A_{20,2})} + 750\overset{2.589}{(P/A_{20,4})}\overset{.6944}{(P/F_{20,2})}] = \$2,612$$

$$AC_{Lease} = 2,612\overset{.27742}{(A/P_{20,7})} = \$724.7$$

$$PC_{Purchase} = [2,000 + 600\overset{.4823}{(P/F_{20,4})}] = \$2,289 \quad \text{Select Smaller}$$

$$AC_{Purchase} = 2,289\overset{.27742}{(A/P_{20,7})} = \$635.1 \quad \text{Select Smaller}$$

Note that using the "replacement-in-kind" assumption for the lease at the end of year 3 would make the year 3, 4, 5 and 6 lease costs 500 instead of 750, making the equivalent annual end-of-year lease cost 600 instead of 724.7. This would make leasing look economically better than purchasing, which is not correct if you think the year 3 to 6 lease costs will actually be 750. Replacement-in-kind often leads to incorrect economic conclusions, and so should not be used.

Alternate Solution by Incremental ROR Analysis:

```
          C=1,500 I=500  I=500  I=750  I=150  I=750  I=750  -
Purchase  ─────────────────────────────────────────────────
-Lease       0      1      2      3      4      5      6   7
```

PW Equation:
$0 = -1,500 + 500(P/A_{i,2}) + 750(P/F_{i,3}) + 150(P/F_{i,4}) + 750(P/A_{i,2})(P/F_{i,4})$

by trial and error, i=incremental ROR=28.0% > i*=20%, so satisfactory
Accept Purchase

$$NPV = -1,500 + 500\overset{1.528}{(P/A_{20,2})} + 750\overset{.5787}{(P/F_{20,3})} + 150\overset{.4823}{(P/F_{20,4})}$$

$$+ 750\overset{1.528}{(P/A_{20,2})}\overset{.4823}{(P/F_{20,4})} = +323.0 > 0, \text{ so purchase}$$

3-11 Solution: All Values in Thousands of Dollars.

```
C=100      C=200           I=90 ................ I=90
                                                        L=150
─────────────────────────────────────────────────────
  0          1               2 ................  10
```

A) Discrete Interest, Discrete Dollar Values

PW Eq: $0 = -100 - 200(P/F_{i,1}) + 90(P/A_{i,9})(P/F_{i,1}) + 150(P/F_{i,10})$

Approximate i = 90 / (100+200) = 0.30 or 30%

i=30% = -100-200(0.7692)+90(3.019)(0.7692)+150(0.0725) = -33.96
i=25% = -100-200(0.8000)+90(3.463)(0.8000)+150(0.1074) = +5.45

i = ROR = 25% + (30%-25%)[(5.45-0)/(5.45+33.96)] = 25.69%

Due to interpolation error the 25.69% result is a little high. The true interpolation error-free ROR is 25.60% which is illustrated below. The PW equation is a non-linear function of i, represented by the curve on the graph below.

$\dfrac{a}{b} = \dfrac{c}{d}$

therefore, $a = b * \dfrac{c}{d}$

substitution gives:

$a = (30\% - 25\%) * \dfrac{(5.45-0)}{(5.45-(-33.96))}$

ROR = 25% + a = 25.69%

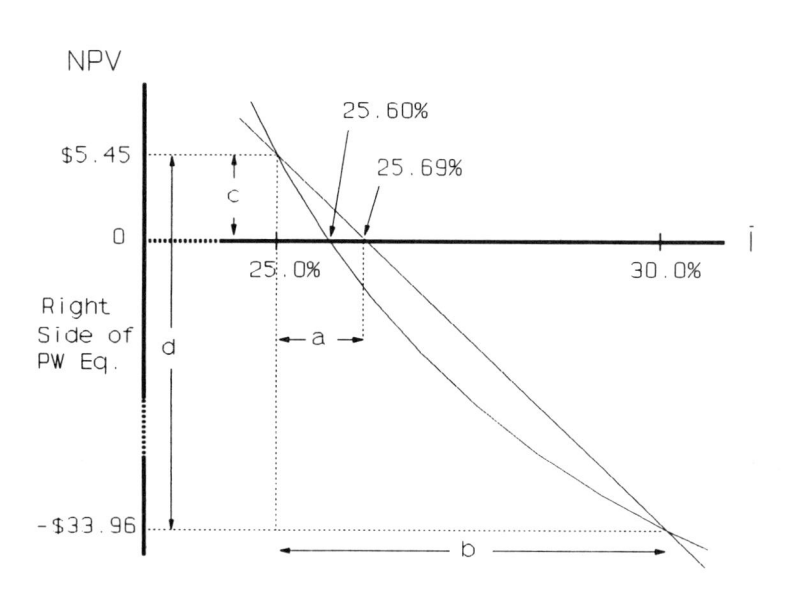

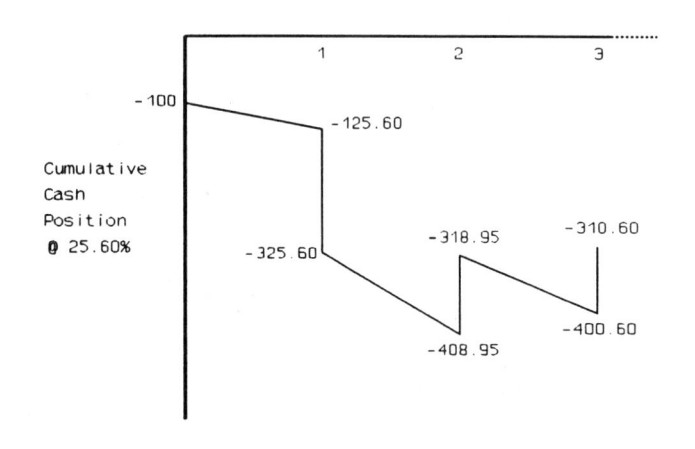

CHAPTER 3 PROBLEM SOLUTIONS

3-11 Solution: Continued

B) Continuous Interest, Discrete Dollar Values (Appendix B)

PW Eq: $0 = -100 - 200(P/F_{r,1}) + 90(P/A_{r,9})(P/F_{r,1}) + 150(P/F_{r,10})$

$i=25\%$ = -100 -200(0.7788)+90(3.1497)(0.7788)+150(0.0821) = -22.68
$i=20\%$ = -100 -200(0.8187)+90(3.7701)(0.8187)+150(0.1353) = 34.35

i = ROR = 20% + (25%-20%)(34.35-0)/(34.35+22.68) = 23.01%

C) Continuous Interest, Continuous Flowing Dollars (Appendix C).
   Year 0 cost flows from year 0 to 1.

```
   --C=100-- --C=200-- --I=90--   .......    --I=90--    --L=150--
 ─────────────────────────────────────────────────────────────────
   0         1         2         3 ....... 10          11         12
```

PW Eq: $0=-100(P/F^*_{r,1})-200(P/F^*_{r,2})+90(P/A^*_{r,9})(P/F_{r,2})+150(P/F^*_{r,12})$

(Note that $P/F_{r,2}$ is a continuous interest, discrete value factor. It is used because $P/A^*_{r,9}$ converts the income stream of 90 to a discrete sum at the beginning of year 3, i.e., the end of year 2.)

$i=25\%$=-100(0.8848)-200(0.6891)+90(3.5784)(0.6065)+150(0.0566)=-22.48
$i=20\%$=-100(0.9064)-200(0.7421)+90(4.1735)(0.6703)+150(0.1004)= 27.77

i = ROR = 20% + (25%-20%)[(27.77-0)/(27.77+22.48)] = 22.76%

D) Continuous Interest, Continuous Flowing Dollars.
   Year 0 cost is a discrete sum at year 0.

```
 C=100  --C=200--  --I=90--    .......    --I=90--    --L=150--
 ─────────────────────────────────────────────────────────────────
   0         1         2 ....... 9          10          11
```

PW Eq: $0 = -100-200(P/F^*_{r,1})+90(P/A^*_{r,9})(P/F_{r,1})+150(P/F^*_{r,11})$

(Note that $P/F_{r,1}$ is a continuous interest, discrete value factor. It is used because $P/A^*_{r,9}$ converts the income stream of 90 to a discrete sum at the beginning of year 2, i.e., the end of year 1.)

$i=25\%$ = -100-200(0.8848)+90(3.5784)(0.7788)+150(0.0726) = -15.25
$i=20\%$ = -100-200(0.9064)+90(4.1735)(0.8187)+150(0.1227) = 44.64

i = ROR = 20% + (25%-20%)(44.64-0)/(44.64+15.25) = 23.73%

3-12 Solution: All Values in Thousands of Dollars

```
              C=240
              OC= 20       OC=40        OC=50        OC=30
Purchase     ─────────────────────────────────────────────── L=100
              0            1            2            3

              OC=10        OC=20        OC=20        OC=10
              OC=60        OC=120       OC=120       OC=60
Lease        ─────────────────────────────────────────────── L=0
              0            1            2            3
```

PW Cost Purchase = $260 + 40(P/F_{15,1}) + 50(P/F_{15,2})$

$\qquad\qquad\qquad + (30-100)(P/F_{15,3}) = 286.6$

PW Cost Lease = $70 + 140(P/F_{15,1}) + 140(P/F_{15,2}) + 70(P/F_{15,3})$

$\qquad\qquad = 343.6$

Select Purchasing with the smaller present worth cost.

```
Purchase   C=190     Savings=100   Savings=90   Savings=40
- Lease    ─────────────────────────────────────────────── L=100
            0           1             2            3
```

Incremental NPV = $-190 + 100(P/F_{15,1}) + 90(P/F_{15,2}) + 140(P/F_{15,3})$

$\qquad\qquad = +57.0 > 0$, accept purchase

Incremental ROR = 31.4% is the "i" value that makes incremental NPV=0.

Incremental PVR = 57.0 / 190 = 0.30 > 0, accept purchase.

CHAPTER 3 PROBLEM SOLUTIONS

3-13 Solution:

```
           -         OC=120,000 ................................ OC=120,000
Purchase  ─────────────────────────────────────────────────────────────────
           0            1 ......................................... 5

                                       C= 10,000
          C=40,000   OC=100,000 .......  OC=100,000  OC=100,000  OC=100,000
Produce   ─────────────────────────────────────────────────────────────────
           0            1 ................. 3           4           5

                                       C=10,000
Increm.C=40,000   OC=-20,000  -20,000   -20,000       -20,000     -20,000
Produce   ─────────────────────────────────────────────────────────────────
-Purch.    0          1         2         3             4           5
```

Negative incremental operating costs give positive savings
each year = 20,000 = ($0.04/lb)(500,000 lb)

A) ROR, NPV, and PVR Analysis:

$40,000 + 10,000(P/F_{i,3}) = 20,000(P/A_{i,5})$

Re-arranging:

$40,000 = 20,000(P/A_{i,5}) - 10,000(P/F_{i,3})$

i=30% = 20,000(2.436) - 10,000(0.4552) = 44,168 > 40,000 so i > 30%

i=40% = 20,000(2.035) - 10,000(0.3644) = 37,056

$i = 30\% + 10\% \left(\dfrac{44,168 - 40,000}{44,168 - 37,056} \right)$ = 35.87% > 30% so satisfactory.

$$NPV = 20,000(P/A_{30,5})^{2.436} - 10,000(P/F_{30,3})^{.4552} - 40,000 = +4,168$$

Positive NPV shows more than enough savings to cover costs at 30% ROR.

PVR = 4,168/40,000 = 0.1042 > 0 so accept internal production.

B) PW Cost Analysis:

PW Cost of Purchase = $120,000(P/A_{30,5})^{2.436}$ = $292,320

PW Cost Internal Production:
= $40,000 + 100,000(P/A_{30,5})^{2.436} + 10,000(P/F_{30,3})^{.4552}$

= $288,152 which is < $292,320 therefore select internal production.

3-14 Solution:

```
Stock      C=30        Div=2 .... Div=2   Div=4 ..... Div=4   Stock Sale
Investment ─────────────────────────────────────────────────   Value, F₁=93
           0           1 ....... 5       6 ......... 10
```

PW Eq: $0 = -30 + 2(P/A_{i,5}) + 4(P/A_{i,5})(P/F_{i,5}) + 93(P/F_{i,10})$

By trial and error, i = ROR = 17.75%

```
Dividend    -          C=2 ...... C=2     C=4 ...... C=4
Reinvest.   ─────────────────────────────────────────────   F₂=40.71
@ i=8%/yr   0          1 ........ 5       6 ........ 10
                    5.867      1.469         5.867
```

where $F_2 = 2(F/A_{8\%,5})(F/P_{8\%,5}) + 4(F/A_{8\%,5}) = 40.71$

Reinvestment i = ROR = 8.0%

```
           C=30        - ............................. -
TOTAL      ─────────────────────────────────────────────   F₁+F₂=133.71
           0           1 ............................. 10
```

PW Eq: $0 = -30 + 133.71(P/F_{i,10})$

By trial and error, i = Growth ROR = 16.12%

3-15 Solution:

```
     C=250,000   I=100,000 ........... I=100,000
A)   ───────────────────────────────────────────── L=150,000   ROR_A=36.1%
     0           1 .................. 5
```

```
                                      C=150,000
      -           C=100,000 ......... C=100,000   F=2,000,000  ROR_B=45.8%
B)   ─────────────────────────────────────────────────────────
     0           1 .................. 5            6
```

```
     C=250,000    - .................. -           F=2,000,000
A+B) ─────────────────────────────────────────────────────────
     0           1 .................. 5            6
```

PW Eq: $250{,}000 = 2{,}000{,}000(P/F_{i,6})$

therefore $P/F_{i,6} = 0.125$, or by interpolation i = 41.73% = Growth ROR

CHAPTER 3 PROBLEM SOLUTIONS

3-16 Solution:

Value=$100,000

```
Payments  X     X     X ................. X     Balloon=$25,000
          ─────────────────────────────────
          0     1     2 ................. 29         30 months
```

PW Eq: $100{,}000 = X + X(P/A_{1,29}) + 25{,}000(P/F_{1,30})$

with $(P/A_{1,29}) = 25.066$ and $(P/F_{1,30}) = .7419$

$$X = \frac{100{,}000 - 25{,}000(0.7419)}{1 + 25.066} = \$3{,}124.86 \text{ or } \$3{,}125$$

Payment	Month	Interest	Unpaid Principal
1	0	-	96,875
2	1	969	94,719
3	2	947	92,541 prin. owed during 3rd month
4	3	925	90,341

An alternative calculation of remaining unpaid mortgage principal after the fourth payment equals the present worth at end-of-month 3 remaining payments to be made with calculations at the mortgage interest rate:

$= \$3{,}124.86(P/A_{1,26}) + \$25{,}000(P/F_{1,27}) = \$90{,}341$

with $(P/A_{1,26}) = 22.795$ and $(P/F_{1,27}) = .7644$

3-17 Solution:

Period $i = 8\%/4 = 2\%$; $A = 50{,}000(A/P_{2,80}) = \$1{,}258$ per quarter

with $(A/P_{2,80}) = .02516$

```
-1,000
50,000   A     A ................. A
         ──────────────────────────────
  0      1     2 ................ 80 quarters
```

$50{,}000 - 1{,}000 = (50{,}000(A/P_{2,80}))(P/A_{i,80})$

$49{,}000 = 1{,}258(P/A_{i,80})$

$38.951 = P/A_{i,80}$

@ $i=2\%$ $P/A_{2,80} = 39.745$

@ $i=3\%$ $P/A_{3,80} = 30.201$

$i = 2\% + 1\%\left(\frac{39.745-38.951}{39.745-30.201}\right) = 2\% + 1\%\left(\frac{0.794}{9.544}\right) = 2.083\%$ per quarter

Nominal Annual Rate = 8.332%

3-18 Solution: All Values in Millions of Dollars

A)
```
            C=2.0
            I=1.8        I=1.8                          I=1.8
  C=1.0     OC=0.7       OC=0.7  .....................  OC=0.7
  ─────────────────────────────────────────────────────────────
    0          1           2  .........................  10
```

B)
```
                         I=2.0                          I=2.0
  C=1.0     C=0.9        OC=0.9  .....................  OC=0.9
  ─────────────────────────────────────────────────────────────
    0          1           2  .........................  10
```

Incremental:
B-A)
```
   C=0       C=0         I=0  ........................  I=0
  ─────────────────────────────────────────────────────────────
    0          1           2  .........................  10
```

ROR Analysis:

ROR_A PW Eq: $1.0 = 1.1(P/A_{i,10}) - 2.0(P/F_{i,1})$ $\underline{i = 45.1\%}$

ROR_B PW Eq: $1.0 = [1.1(P/A_{i,9}) - 0.9](P/F_{i,1})$ $\underline{i = 45.1\%}$

ROR_{B-A} PW Eq: $0 = 0$

There are no economic differences between alternatives A and B.

NPV Analysis:

$$NPV_A = 1.1\overset{5.019}{(P/A_{15,10})} - 2.0\overset{.8696}{(P/F_{15,1})} - 1.0 = \underline{\$2.782}$$

$$NPV_B = [1.1\overset{4.772}{(P/A_{15,9})} - 0.9]\overset{.8696}{(P/F_{15,1})} - 1.0 = \underline{\$2.782}$$

$NPV_{B-A} = 0$, so A and B are economically equivalent.

PVR Analysis:

PVR_A Denominator $= 1.0 + [2.0-(1.8-0.7)]\overset{.8696}{(P/F_{15,1})} = 1.783$

$$PVR_A = \frac{2.782}{1.783} = 1.56 > 0$$

PVR_B Denominator $= 1.0 + 0.9\overset{.8696}{(P/F_{15,1})} = 1.783$

$$PVR_B = \frac{2.782}{1.783} = 1.56 > 0$$

Note that if you do not net the year 1 costs and revenues for "A" before calculating the present worth cost denominator for PVR_A, you do not get the equivalence of A and B shown with both ROR and NPV.

Incorrect $PVR_A = \dfrac{2.782}{1 + 2(P/F_{15,1})} = 1.01$

CHAPTER 3 PROBLEM SOLUTIONS

3-19 Solution: All Values in Thousands of Dollars

```
        --- Sunk ---
A)  C=100      C=200        -        I=120     I=120 ............. I=120
   ─────────────────────────────────────────────────────────────────────
     -2          -1          0         1         2 ................. 12

                                -       C=350     I=150 ........ I=150
B)                           ──────────────────────────────────────────
                                0         1         2 .......... 10
```

$$\text{Yr 0 NPV}_A = 120(P/A_{20,12}^{4.439}) = \$532.7$$

$$\text{Yr 0 NPV}_B = [-350 + 150(P/A_{20,9}^{4.031})](P/F_{20,1}^{.8333}) = \$212.2$$

Cumulative NPV = 532.7 + 212.2 = **744.9** = Max. Value of Company @ i*=20%

3-20 Solution: All Values in Thousands of Dollars

Before-tax Cash Flows, NPV, ROR and PVR Calculations

Year	0	1	2	3	4	5
Revenues		1,612.0	1,378.0	910.0	655.2	487.9
-Royalties		-225.7	-192.9	-127.4	-91.7	-68.3
-Operating Cost		-175.0	-193.0	-212.0	-233.0	-256.0
-Research & Dev.	-750.0	-250.0				
-Equipment		-670.0				
-Patent Rights	-100.0					
Before-Tax CF	-850.0	291.3	992.1	570.6	330.5	163.6

NPV @ 15% = $-850 + 291.3(P/F_{15,1})^{.8696} + 992.1(P/F_{15,2})^{.7561} + 570.6(P/F_{15,3})^{.6575}$

$+ 330.5(P/F_{15,4})^{.5718} + 163.6(P/F_{15,5})^{.4972} = +798.9 > 0$, so satisfactory

ROR Analysis:

PW Eq: $0 = -850 + 291.3(P/F_{i,1}) + 992.1(P/F_{i,2}) + 570.6(P/F_{i,3})$

$+ 330.5(P/F_{i,4}) + 163.6(P/F_{i,5})$

NPV @ 50% = +41
NPV @ 70% = -168   ROR = i = 50% + 20%(41/209) = 53.9% > i*=15%
53.9% is the "i" value that makes the NPV equation equal to zero.

PVR = 798.9/850 = 0.94 > 0
B/C Ratio = PVR + 1 = 1.94 > 1.0 so satisfactory

Before-Tax Breakeven Price Analysis

Year	0	1	2	3	4	5
Revenues		62X	53X	35X	24X	17X
-Royalties		-8.68X	-7.42X	-4.90X	-3.36X	-2.38X
-Operating Cost		-175.0	-193.0	-212.0	-233.0	-256.0
-Research & Dev.	-750.0	-250.0				
-Equipment Cost		-670.0				
-Patent Rights	-100.0					
Before-Tax CF	-850.0	53.32X	45.58X	30.10X	20.64X	14.62X
		-1,095	-193	-212	-233	-256

PW Eq: $0 = -850 + (53.32X-1,095)(P/F_{15\%,1})^{.8696} + (45.58X-193)(P/F_{15\%,2})^{.7561}$

$+ (30.10X-212)(P/F_{15\%,3})^{.6575} + (20.64X-233)(P/F_{15\%,4})^{.5718}$

$+ (14.62X-256)(P/F_{15\%,5})^{.4972}$

0 = -2,348.0 + 119.69X,   Breakeven Price, X = $19.62 per unit

CHAPTER 3 PROBLEM SOLUTIONS

3-21 Solution: All Values in Thousands of Dollars

Before-tax Cash Flows, NPV, ROR and PVR Calculations

Year	0	1	2	3	4	5
Revenues		1,612.0	1,378.0	910.0	655.2	487.9
-Royalties		-225.7	-192.9	-127.4	-91.7	-68.3
-Operating Cost		-175.0	-193.0	-212.0	-233.0	-256.0
-Intangible	-750.0	-250.0				
-Tangible		-670.0				
-Min Rghts Acq.	-100.0					
Before-Tax CF	-850.0	291.3	992.1	570.6	330.5	163.6

$$NPV = -850.0 + 291.3(P/F_{15,1})^{.8696} + 992.1(P/F_{15,2})^{.7561} + 570.6(P/F_{15,3})^{.6575}$$

$$+ 330.5(P/F_{15,4})^{.5718} + 163.6(P/F_{15,5})^{.4972} = +798.9 > 0, \text{ so satisfactory}$$

ROR Analysis:
PW Eq: $0 = -850 + 291.3(P/F_{i,1}) + 992.1(P/F_{i,2}) + 570.6(P/F_{i,3})$

$+ 330.5(P/F_{i,4}) + 163.6(P/F_{i,5})$

NPV @ 50% = +41
NPV @ 70% = -168   ROR = i = 50% + 20%(41/209) = 53.9% > i*=15%
53.9% is the "i" value that makes the NPV equation equal to zero.

PVR = 798.9/850 = 0.94 > 0
B/C Ratio = PVR + 1 = 1.94 > 1.0, so satisfactory

Before-Tax Breakeven Price Analysis

Year	0	1	2	3	4	5
Revenues		62X	53X	35X	24X	17X
-Royalties		-8.68X	-7.42X	-4.9X	-3.36X	-2.38X
-Operating Cost		-175.0	-193.0	-212.0	-233.0	-256.0
-Intangible	-750.0	-250.0				
-Tangible		-670.0				
-Min Rghts Acq.	-100.0					
Before-Tax CF	-850.0	53.32X	45.58X	30.10X	20.64X	14.62X
		-1,095	-193	-212	-233	-256

PW Eq: $0 = -850 + (53.32X-1,095)(P/F_{15,1})^{.8696} + (45.58X-193)(P/F_{15,2})^{.7561}$

$+ (30.10X-212)(P/F_{15,3})^{.6575} + (20.64X-233)(P/F_{15,4})^{.5718}$

$+ (14.62X-256)(P/F_{15,5})^{.4972}$

0 = -2,348.0 + 119.69X,   Breakeven Price, X = $19.62 per bbl

3-22 Solution: All Values in Thousands of Dollars

Before-tax Cash Flows, NPV, ROR and PVR Calculations

Year	0	1	2	3	4	5
Revenues		1,612.0	1,378.0	910.0	655.2	487.9
-Royalties		-225.7	-192.9	-127.4	-91.7	-68.3
-Operating Cost		-175.0	-193.0	-212.0	-233.0	-256.0
-Mine Develop	-750.0	-250.0				
-Mine Equipment		-670.0				
-Min Rghts Acq.	-100.0					
Before-Tax CF	-850.0	291.3	992.1	570.6	330.5	163.6

$$\text{NPV} = -850.0 + 291.3(P/F_{15,1})^{.8696} + 992.1(P/F_{15,2})^{.7561} + 570.6(P/F_{15,3})^{.6575}$$

$$+ 330.5(P/F_{15,4})^{.5718} + 163.6(P/F_{15,5})^{.4972} = +798.9 > 0, \text{ so satisfactory}$$

ROR Analysis:
PW Eq: $0 = -850 + 291.3(P/F_{i,1}) + 992.1(P/F_{i,2}) + 570.6(P/F_{i,3})$

$+ 330.5(P/F_{i,4}) + 163.6(P/F_{i,5})$

NPV @ 50% = +41
NPV @ 70% = -168   ROR = i = 50% + 20%(41/209) = 53.9% > i*=15%
53.9% is the "i" value that makes the NPV equation equal to zero.

PVR = 798.9/850 = 0.94 > 0
B/C Ratio = PVR + 1 = 1.94 > 1.0, so satisfactory

Before-Tax Breakeven Price Analysis

Year	0	1	2	3	4	5
Revenues		62X	53X	35X	24X	17X
-Royalties		-8.68X	-7.42X	-4.9X	-3.36X	-3.38X
-Operating Cost		-175.0	-193.0	-212.0	-233.0	-256.0
-Mine Develop	-750.0	-250.0				
-Mine Equipment		-670.0				
-Min Rghts Acq.	-100.0					
Before-Tax CF	-850.0	53.32X	45.58X	30.10X	20.64X	14.62X
		-1,095	-193	-212	-233	-256

PW Eq: $0 = -850 + (53.32X-1,095)(P/F_{15,1})^{.8696} + (45.58X-193)(P/F_{15,2})^{.7561}$

$+ (30.10X-212)(P/F_{15,3})^{.6575} + (20.64X-233)(P/F_{15,4})^{.5718}$

$+ (14.62X-256)(P/F_{15,5})^{.4972}$

0 = -2,348.0 + 119.69X,   Breakeven Price, X = $19.62 per ton

CHAPTER 3 PROBLEM SOLUTIONS

3-23 Solution:

```
              C=25,000
 C=0   OC=4,500  OC=5,500  OC=2,500  OC=3,000  OC=3,500  OC=4,000
A)─────────────────────────────────────────────────────────────── Salv=7,000
 0       1         2         3         4         5         6
```

$$PW_A = 4{,}500(P/F_{20,1})^{.8333} + (25{,}000+5{,}500)(P/F_{20,2})^{.6944} - 7{,}000(P/F_{20,6})^{.3349}$$

$$+ [2{,}500+500(A/G_{20,4})^{1.274}](P/A_{20,4})^{2.589}(P/F_{20,2})^{.6944} = \underline{\$28{,}224}$$

$$AC_A = (28{,}224)(A/P_{20,6})^{.30071} = \underline{\$8{,}487}$$


```
 C=21,000  OC=2,000  OC=2,500  OC=3,000  OC=3,500  OC=4,000  OC=4,500
B)─────────────────────────────────────────────────────────────── Salv=4,000
 0         1         2         3         4         5         6
```

$$PW_B = 21{,}000 + [2{,}000+500(A/G_{20,6})^{1.979}](P/A_{20,6})^{3.326} - 4{,}000(P/F_{20,6})^{.3349}$$

$$= \underline{\$29{,}603}$$

$$AC_B = (29{,}603)(A/P_{20,6})^{.30071} = \underline{\$8{,}902}$$

Incremental Analysis:

```
                        C=-25,000
 C=21,000  OC=-2,500    OC=-3,000   C=500    C=500    C=500    C=500
B-A)──────────────────────────────────────────────────────────────── L=-3,000
 0           1            2           3        4        5        6
```

$$\text{Incremental NPV} = -21{,}000 + 2{,}500(P/F_{20,1})^{.8333} + 28{,}000(P/F_{20,2})^{.6944}$$

$$- 500(P/A_{20,4})^{2.589}(P/F_{20,2})^{.6944} - 3{,}000(P/F_{20,6})^{.3349}$$

$$= -1{,}377 \quad \text{so reject B and select A}$$

3-24 Solution:

The specified discount rates on Treasury Bills are annual rates, so half of 15% or 7.5% is the interest on this six month T-Bill. The interest is paid within 10 days of the T-Bill purchase date, so assume the purchase cost and interest occur at the same time.

```
Int=$750  }
  C=$10,000 } Net C=$9,250                    Terminal Value=$10,000
——————————————————————————————————————————————————————————————————
0                                             1  six month period
```

PW Eq: $9{,}250 = 10{,}000(P/F_{i,1})$

i = 6 month period interest rate = 8.1%
So, nominal annual rate of return = 16.2% compounded semi-annually.

3-25 Solution:

```
                C=4
    C=1.5       C=5           I=4 ............. I=4
                                                      L=6
————————————————————————————————————————————————————————
    0           1             2 ................ 9
```

PW Eq: $0 = -1.5 - 9(P/F_{i,1}) + 4(P/A_{i,8})(P/F_{i,1}) + 6(P/F_{i,9})$

at i=40%, right side = +0.52
at i=30%, right side = +2.64, by interpolation, i = ROR = <u>35.4%</u>

For Growth ROR:
```
Reinvest      -       -       C=4 ............. C=4
Income                                                C=6    F=60.91
@ i*=15%      0       1       2 ................ 9
```

where $F = 4(F/A_{i*=15\%,8}) + 6 = 60.91$
                    13.727

```
              C=1.5   C=4
Initial               C=5      - ................ -
+ Reinvest                                             F=60.91
              0       1        2 ................ 9
```

Yr 0 PW Eq: $0 = -1.5 - 9.0(P/F_{i,1}) + 60.91(P/F_{i,9})$

i = 20% = -1.5 - 9.0(0.8333) + 60.91(0.1938) = 2.805
i = 25% = -1.5 - 9.0(8000) + 60.91(0.1342) = -0.526

i = Growth ROR = 20% + (25%-20%)[(2.805-0)/(2.805+0.526)] = 24.2%

                  .8696   4.487   .8696   .2843
NPV = -1.5 - 9.0(P/F_{15,1}) + 4.0(P/A_{15,8})(P/F_{15,1}) + 6(P/F_{15,9}) = +7.99

Calculating NPV from the values used to determine growth ROR gives the same NPV result. Reinvestment of revenues at the minimum ROR is implicitly built into all net value calculations.

NPV = $-1.5 - 9.0(P/F_{15,1}) + 60.91(P/F_{15,9}) = +7.99$

PVR = $7.99 / [1.5 + 9.0(P/F_{15,1})] = 0.86$

CHAPTER 3 PROBLEM SOLUTIONS

3-26 Solution: All Values in Millions of Dollars

```
C=?      C=1.5    C=2.0    I=1.0    I=1.0 ........ I=1.0
─────────────────────────────────────────────────────────── L=3.0
0        1        2        3        4 ........... 10
```

On a before-tax basis, NPV represents the additional cost that could be incurred at year 0 to receive a 15% rate of return. In this problem, NPV equals the maximum year 0 development cost that can be incurred and still have the project return 15% on invested capital.

$$\text{NPV} = -1.5(P/F_{15\%,1})^{.8696} - 2.0(P/F_{15\%,2})^{.7561} + 1.0(P/A_{15\%,8})^{4.487}(P/F_{15\%,2})^{.7561}$$
$$+ 3.0(P/F_{15\%,10})^{.2472} = +1.32$$

Changing minimum ROR to 10%:

$$\text{NPV} = -1.5(P/F_{10\%,1})^{.9091} - 2.0(P/F_{10\%,2})^{.8264} + 1.0(P/A_{10\%,8})^{5.335}(P/F_{10\%,2})^{.8264}$$
$$+ 3.0(P/F_{10\%,10})^{.3855} = +2.56$$

At the lower discount rate of 10% the project NPV increased by more than $1.2 million, nearly doubling the original value. Lower discount rates always lead to increased value from positive revenue streams.

3-27 Solution: Property Acquisition Cost Evaluation

```
C=X      -        -        C_Dev=2.5 I=1.5  I=1.3 ...grad/yr=-0.2 ...
─────────────────────────────────────────────────────────── L=0
0        1        2        3         4      5 ................ 11
```

In a before-tax analysis, the year 0 breakeven property acquisition cost, X, equals the year 0 NPV for property.

Yr 0 NPV Eq:

$$X = -2.5(P/F_{20,3})^{.5787} + [1.5-0.2(A/G_{20,8})^{2.576}](P/A_{20,8})^{3.837}(P/F_{20,3})^{.5787}$$

X = **$0.74** to breakeven with a 20% ROR.

This represents the maximum price a buyer could pay to develop the property 3 years later to get a 20% ROR. The owner should make the same analysis. The minimum sales price for an owner who uses the same analysis numbers would be $.740 million. Any amount over that price would make selling economically better than developing, from the owner viewpoint.

3-28 Solution:

Year	0	1	2	3	4
Intangible Drilling	$250,000				
Tangible Completion	$100,000				
Lease Cost	$0				
Production, bbls/yr		17,500	9,000	6,500	3,000
Selling Price, $/bbl		$20.00	$20.00	$21.00	$22.05
Operating Cost, $/bbl		$4.00	$4.00	$4.00	$4.00
Royalties (12.5% Gross, $/bbl)		$2.50	$2.50	$2.625	$2.756

Before-Tax Cash Flows Calculations:

Year	0	1	2	3	4
Gross Revenue		350,000	180,000	136,500	66,150
-Royalties		-43,750	-22,500	-17,063	-8,269
Net Revenue Interest		306,250	157,500	119,438	57,881
-Operating Expenses		-70,000	-36,000	-26,000	-12,000
-Capital Costs	-350,000				
Before-Tax CF	-350,000	236,250	121,500	93,438	45,881

$$\text{NPV @12\%} = -350{,}000 + 236{,}250(P/F_{12,1})^{.8929} + 121{,}500(P/F_{12,2})^{.7972}$$

$$+ 93{,}438(P/F_{12,3})^{.7118} + 45{,}881(P/F_{12,4})^{.6355} = \underline{\$53{,}473}$$

PVR = 53,473 / 350,000 = <u>0.15</u>

PW Eq: $0 = -350{,}000 + 236{,}250(P/F_{i,1}) + 121{,}500(P/F_{i,2})$

$\qquad + 93{,}438(P/F_{i,3}) + 45{,}881(P/F_{i,4})$

PW @ 25% = -16,607
PW @ 20% = 7,438
i = ROR = 20% + (25%-20%)(7,438-0)/(7,438+16,607) = <u>21.55%</u>

Two other analyses not required are Growth ROR and Breakeven analysis:

Growth ROR Calculation:

$$F = 236{,}250(F/P_{12,3})^{1.4049} + 121{,}500(F/P_{12,2})^{1.2544} + 93{,}438(F/P_{12,1})^{1.1200} + 45{,}881 = 634{,}849$$

PW Eq: $0 = -350{,}000 + 634{,}849(P/F_{i,4})$; GROR = i = 16.05%

Breakeven Uniform Price per Barrel: Let X = price/barrel each year. Due to royalties, only 87.5% of production is available to generate revenues to pay off the initial investment, and give a 12.0% ROR.

$$0 = -350{,}000 + (15{,}313X-70{,}000)(P/F_{12,1})^{.8929} + (7{,}875X-36{,}000)(P/F_{12,2})^{.7972}$$

$$+ (5{,}688X-26{,}000)(P/F_{12,3})^{.7118} + (2{,}625X-12{,}000)(P/F_{12,4})^{.6355}$$

25,667X = 467,335; X = $18.21/bbl

CHAPTER 3 PROBLEM SOLUTIONS

3-29 Solution:

5.0% Carried Interest, Backing in for a 25.0% Working Interest, and a 21.875% Net Revenue Interest.

Year	0	1	2	3	4
Intangible Drilling	$250,000				
Tangible Completion	$100,000				
Lease Cost	$0				
Production, bbls/yr		17,500	9,000	6,500	3,000
Selling Price, $/bbl		$20.00	$20.00	$21.00	$22.05
Operating Cost, $/bbl		$4.00	$4.00	$4.00	$4.00
Royalties (12.5% Gross, $/bbl)		$2.50	$2.50	$2.63	$2.76

Payout Calculation Using Production:

When the cumulative value of net revenue (defined here as production times the selling price less royalties and cash operating costs) gives revenue equal to the total dollars invested, the project is at payout. In this case, we know we've spent $350,000, and the price in years 1 and 2 is constant at $20.00 per barrel. Due to the two royalties, the producer only gets 82.5% of each barrel to pay off the investment. Hence, payout in production is calcuated as follows:

Yr 1 Payout Basis $350,000 - [17,500x($20.00(0.825)-$4.00)] = $131,250
Yr 2 Payout Basis $131,250 - [9,000x($20.00(0.825)-$4.00)] = $ 18,750
Yr 3 Payout: $ 18,750 = (X bbl)($21.00(0.825)-$4.00)   X = 1,407 bbl

So, in year 3, 1,407 barrels would be subject to the over-riding royalty interest of 5.0%, after which (the reversion point), 5,093 barrels would be subject to the 25.0% working interest, and a 21.875% net revenue interest (25.0% adjusted for 12.5% royalty).

Year	0	1	2	3	4
Carried Interest Rev. (5%)		17,500	9,000	1,477	–
+N.R.I.*(25% After Reversion)		0	0	23,396	14,470
Total Net Revenue		17,500	9,000	24,873	14,470
-Operating Exp. (25% A.R.**)		0	0	-5,093	-3,000
Before-Tax CF	0	17,500	9,000	19,780	11,470

* N.R.I. = Net Revenue Interest;   ** A.R. = After Reversion

$$\text{NPV @ 12\%} = 17,500(P/F_{12,1})^{.8929} + 9,000(P/F_{12,2})^{.7972}$$
$$+ 19,780(P/F_{12,3})^{.7118} + 11,470(P/F_{12,4})^{.6355} = \$44,169$$

PVR and ROR are infinite (undefined) due to zero investment.

3-30 Solution: All Dollar Values in Thousands

$$\text{Period Interest Rate} = \frac{\text{Nominal Rate of 12.0\%}}{\text{12 Monthly Compounding Periods}}$$

$$= 1\% \text{ per month}$$

Purchase Compressor:

```
Install Cost=   75
    Acq.Cost=1,000       -            -       Cost=225      -       Salv=300
                    _____
Years               0            1            2            3            4            5
Months              0           12           24           36           48           60
```

Using period interest rate, i:

$$\text{PW Cost Purchase} = 1,075 + 225(P/F_{1,36})^{.6989} - 300(P/F_{1,60})^{.5504} = \underline{\$1,067.13}$$

Using effective rate, E, where $E = [(1.01)^{12} - 1] = 0.1268$ or 12.68%:

Annual Period
$$\text{PWC Purchase} = 1,075 + 225(P/F_{12.68,3})^{.6989} - 300(P/F_{12.68,5})^{.5504} = \underline{\$1,067.13}$$

$$\text{Equivalent Monthly Cost (1-60)} = 1,067.13(A/P_{1,60})^{.02224} = \underline{\$23.73}$$

Lease Compressor:

```
Install Cost= 75
Lease Pmt.  = 24        24           24                              24
              _____
Months        0 ..... 12 ..... 24 ................. 59
```

Using a period interest rate, i:

$$\text{PW Cost Leasing} = 99 + 24(P/A_{1,59})^{44.4046} = \underline{\$1,164.71}$$

$$\text{Equivalent Monthly Cost (1-60)} = 1,164.71(A/P_{1,60})^{.02224} = \underline{\$25.90}$$

Purchasing gives the smallest PW Cost and Equivalent Monthly Cost (at 1% monthly), therefore the economic decision is to purchase the compressor.

Equivalent Annual Analysis for Leasing:

```
75+6(24)=219  12(24)=288  12(24)=288  12(24)=288  12(24)=288  6(24)=144
             _____
Year   0            1           2           3           4           5
```

Using effective annual rate: $i = (1+0.01)^{12} - 1 = 0.1268$ or 12.68%

Annual Period
$$\text{PW Cost Lease} = 219 + 288(P/A_{12.68,4})^{2.99436} + 144(P/F_{12.68,5})^{0.5505} = \underline{\$1,160.64}$$

CHAPTER 3 PROBLEM SOLUTIONS

3-31 Solution:

A) 10 Year Bond Analysis

```
Value=?    I=$800 ................ I=$800   Maturity Value
─────────────────────────────────────────── = $10,000
  0          1 ................... 10 yr
```

at 8% interest, P = Value = $10,000

at 6% interest, P = 800(P/A$_{6,10}$) + 10,000(P/F$_{6,10}$) = $11,472
$7.360\phantom{(P/A_{6,10}) + 10,000(}$.5584

at 10% interest, P = 800(P/A$_{10,10}$) + 10,000(P/F$_{10,10}$) = $8,770
$6.144\phantom{(P/A_{10,10}) + 10,000(}$.3855

B) 30 Year Bond Analysis

```
Value=?    I=$800 ......................... I=$800   Maturity Value
──────────────────────────────────────────────────── = $10,000
  0          1 ............................ 30 yr
```

at 8% interest, P = Value = $10,000

at 6% interest, P = 800(P/A$_{6,30}$) + 10,000(P/F$_{6,30}$) = $12,753
$13.765\phantom{(P/A_{6,30}) + 10,000(}$.1741

at 10% interest, P = 800(P/A$_{10,30}$) + 10,000(P/F$_{10,30}$) = $8,115
$9.427\phantom{(P/A_{10,30}) + 10,000(}$.05731

C) 30 Year Zero Coupon Bond

```
Value=?       -                              -       Maturity Value
──────────────────────────────────────────────────── = $10,000
  0          1 ............................ 30 yr
```

at 8% interest, P = Value = 10,000(P/F$_{8,30}$) = $994
.099377

at 6% interest, P = Value = 10,000(P/F$_{6,30}$) = $1,741
.17411

at 10% interest P = Value = 10,000(P/F$_{10,30}$) = $573
.05731

CHAPTER 4 PROBLEM SOLUTIONS

4-1 Solution: All values in thousands of dollars

```
       C=300     I=450     I=450 ................ I=450
A) ────────────────────────────────────────────────────
       0         1         2 .................... 10

       C=900     I=550     I=550 ................ I=550
B) ────────────────────────────────────────────────────
       0         1         2 .................... 10

                 I=750
       C=1,200   C=800     I=850 ................ I=850
C) ────────────────────────────────────────────────────
       0         1         2 .................... 10
```

ROR Analysis:

"A" PW Eq: $0 = -300 + 450(P/A_{i,10})$, $i = ROR_A = 150\% > i^* = 15\%$, ok

"B" PW Eq: $0 = -900 + 550(P/A_{i,10})$, $i = ROR_B = 60.6\% > i^* = 15\%$, ok

"C" PW Eq: $0 = -1,200 - 50(P/F_{i,1}) + 850(P/A_{i,9})(P/F_{i,1})$,

$\qquad\qquad i = ROR_C = 45.7\% > i^* = 15\%$, ok

```
       C=600     I=100     I=100 ................ I=100
B-A) ──────────────────────────────────────────────────
       0         1         2 .................... 10
```

"B-A" PW Eq: $0 = -600 + 100(P/A_{i,10})$,

$\qquad i = ROR_{B-A} = 10.5\% < 15\%$, so reject B

```
       C=900     C=500     I=400 ................ I=400
C-A) ──────────────────────────────────────────────────
       0         1         2 .................... 10
```

"C-A" PW Eq: $0 = -900 - 500(P/F_{i,1}) + 400(P/A_{i,9})(P/F_{i,1})$,

$\qquad i = ROR_{C-A} = 20.5\% > i^* = 15\%$, so select C.

Alternative "C" is the economic choice for $i^* = 15\%$

NPV Analysis:

$NPV_A = -300 + 450(P/A_{15,10}) = +1,958$
$NPV_B = -900 + 550(P/A_{15,10}) = +1,860$
$NPV_C = -1,200 - 50(P/F_{15,1}) + 850(P/A_{15,9})(P/F_{15,1}) = +2,283$

Select maximum alternative "C", since $NPV_{B-A} = -98$ and $NPV_{C-A} = +325$

Alternative "C" is the economic choice for $i^*=15\%$ since NPV_{C-A} and NPV_{C-B} are both positive. As always, the largest total investment NPV is the economic choice.

CHAPTER 4 PROBLEM SOLUTIONS

4-1 Solution: Continued

PVR Analysis:

$PVR_A = 1,958/300 = 6.5 > 0$, so satisfactory
$PVR_B = 1,860/900 = 2.1 > 0$, so satisfactory
$PVR_C = 2,283/[1,200+50(P/F_{15,1})] = 1.8 > 0$, so satisfactory

$PVR_{B-A} = (1,860-1,958)/600 = -0.2 < 0$, unsatisfactory, select A over B
$PVR_{C-A} = (2,283-1,958)/(900 + 500(P/F_{15,1})) = +0.2 > 0$ select C over A

NPV Analysis for $i^* = 25\%$:

$NPV_A = -300 + 450(P/A_{25,10}) = +1,307$ Select Maximum
$NPV_B = -900 + 550(P/A_{25,10}) = +1,064$
$NPV_C = -1,200 - 50(P/F_{25,1}) + 850(P/A_{25,9})(P/F_{25,1}) = 1,115$

The economic choice switches to alternative "A" for $i^* = 25\%$. Comparing the incremental ROR results to $i^* = 25\%$ verifies the NPV result.

4-2 Solution: All Values in Thousands of Dollars

```
    C= 80      I=290            I=290
    C=200      OC=160  ......   OC=160      C=360
    |_____|_____|_____|
    0          1      .........  5          6
```

Net Present Value:

$NPV = -280 + 130(P/A_{i,5}) - 360(P/F_{i,6})$

i	NPV
0%	+10.0
5%	+14.2
10%	+ 9.6
15%	+0.1% Dual i = 15%,
20%	-11.8 the other dual "i" is negative

Since NPV @ 20% is -$11.8, reject the project for $i^* = 20\%$

PW Cost Modified ROR Analysis:

$$280 + 360(P/F_{20,6})^{0.3349} = 130(P/A_{i,5})$$

$400.56 = 130(P/A_{i,5})$

i = PW Cost Modified ROR = 18.6% < $i^* = 20\%$ so reject.

Since NPV equals zero for $i^* = 15\%$, a 15% minimum ROR is the breakeven minimum ROR that makes the project economics equivalent to investing elsewhere.

4-3 Solution:

Insulation Thickness(in.)	Total Savings Due to Insulation	NPV Analysis Eq.	NPV	
0	$ 0	(3.326)	0	
1	600	$600(P/A_{20,6})-1,200$ =	+$795.60	
2	800	$800(\ "\ )-1,800$ =	+ 860.80*	Select
3	900	$900(\ "\ )-2,500$ =	+ 493.40	Largest
4	1,000	$1,000(\ "\ )-3,500$ =	− 174.00	NPV

Alternate Solution: Minimize Total PW Cost

Insulation	PW Cost Calculation	PW Cost	
0	$1,400(P/A_{20,6})$ =	$4,656.40	
1	$800(\ "\ )+1,200$ =	3,860.80	
2	$600(\ "\ )+1,800$ =	3,795.60*	Select Min. PW Cost
3	$500(\ "\ )+2,500$ =	4,163.30	
4	$400(\ "\ )+3,500$ =	4,830.40	

4-4 Solution: All Values in Thousands of Dollars

This is an income-cost-income analysis situation and involves the Dual ROR problem, as does the cost-income-cost problem.

```
                C=50    C=50    C=50   C=1,450
        I=450   I=450   I=450   I=450   I=450   I=450            I=450
  -     OC=310  OC=310  OC=310  OC=310  OC=310  OC=310  .....   OC=310
  ─────────────────────────────────────────────────────────────────────── L=300
  0       1       2       3       4       5       6 ........ 10
```

$NPV = 140(P/F_{i,1}) + 90(P/A_{i,3})(P/F_{i,1}) - 1,310(P/F_{i,5})$

$\quad + 140(P/A_{i,5})(P/F_{i,5}) + 300(P/F_{i,10})$

i	NPV	
0	+100.0	
5	−0.6	4.95%
10	−37.5	
15	−43.4	These are the project dual "i" values
20	−35.0	(NOT valid for ROR economic decision making)
30	−5.8	
40	21.9	32.90%
50	42.5	

Although the Dual "i" values are not valid for ROR economic decision-making, the NPV results that were the basis for determining the dual "i" values are valid for economic decision making.

NPV @ i^* = 5% is similar to zero indicating breakeven economics
NPV @ i^* = 15% is negative indicating unsatisfactory economics
NPV @ i^* = 50% is positive indicating satisfactory economics

Increasing the minimum ROR to 50% from 15% improves the economics because of the strong rate of reinvestment meaning (as opposed to rate of return meaning) associated with i^* in this income-cost-income analysis.

CHAPTER 4 PROBLEM SOLUTIONS

4-4 Solution: Continued - PW Cost Modified ROR Analysis

$i^* = 5\%$, Modified Year 0 PW Cost = $1,310(P/F_{5,5}) = 1,026$

PW Eq: $1,026 = 140(P/F_{i,1}) + 90(P/A_{i,3})(P/F_{i,1}) + 140(P/A_{i,5})(P/F_{i,5})$
$\qquad + 300(P/F_{i,10})$

i = PW Cost Modified ROR = 5.0% = i^* of 5%, so breakeven economics

$i^* = 15\%$, Modified Yr 0 PW Cost = $1,310(P/F_{15,5})^{.49718} = 651.3$

PW Eq: $651.3 = 140(P/F_{i,1}) + 90(P/A_{i,3})(P/F_{i,1}) + 140(P/A_{i,5})(P/F_{i,5})$
$\qquad + 300(P/F_{i,10})$

i = PW Cost Modified ROR = 13.5% < i^* = 15% so unsatisfactory

$i^* = 50\%$, Modified Yr 0 PW Cost = $1,310(P/F_{50,5})^{.13169} = 172.5$

PW Eq: $172.5 = 140(P/F_{i,1}) + 90(P/A_{i,3})(P/F_{i,1}) + 140(P/A_{i,5})(P/F_{i,5})$
$\qquad + 300(P/F_{i,10})$

i = PW Cost Modified ROR = 63.3% > i^* = 50% so satisfactory.

PW Cost Modified ROR analysis and NPV analysis give the same economic conclusion for the different minimum rates of return.

4-5 Solution:

A) $NPV_1 = 80,000(P/A_{40,6})^{2.168} - 150,000 = +\$23,440$ Select largest NPV
$NPV_2 = 115,000(\quad " \quad) - 230,000 = +\$19,320$
$NPV_2 - NPV_1 = -4,120$, so select NPV_1

B) To determine breakeven service (evaluation life), n, set $NPV_1 = NPV_2$ for unknown life, n:

$80,000(P/A_{40,n}) - 150,000 = 115,000(P/A_{40,n}) - 230,000$

$P/A_{40,n} = 2.286$, therefore Breakeven n = 7.34 years.

For evaluation life, n, less than 7.34 years, change 1 is best
For evaluation life, n, greater than 7.34 years, change 2 is best

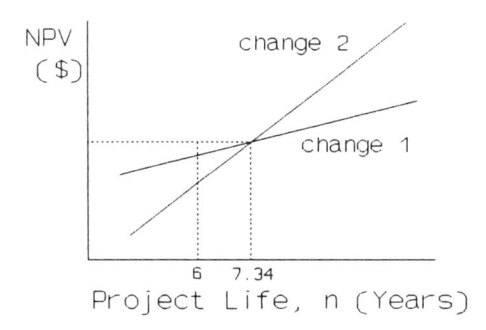

4-6 Solution: All Values in Dollars

A)
```
         C=100   C=200    I=110   C=230   I=110 ........ I=110
                 I=110            I=110
         ─────────────────────────────────────────────────────
          0       1        2       3       4 ............ 8
```

$NPV_A = 110(P/A_{15,8}) - 230(P/F_{15,3}) - 200(P/F_{15,1}) - 100 = +\$68.4$

$PVR_A = 68.4 / [100 + (200-110)(P/F_{15,1})] = +0.38$

The year 3 cost of 230 does not affect the PVR_A denominator because it is offset by the combination of year 2 and 3 income as follows: $[(-230+110)(P/F_{15,1}) + 110] = +5.65$ which is year 2 net income, not a net cost, resulting from the year 2 and 3 incomes and cost.

B)
```
         C=100   C=200    I=20    C=180   I=110 ........ I=110
                 I=110            I=110
         ─────────────────────────────────────────────────────
          0       1        2       3       4 ............ 8
```

$NPV_B = 110(P/A_{15,5})(P/F_{15,3}) - 70(P/F_{15,3}) + 20(P/F_{15,2}) - 90(P/F_{15,1})$
$\quad\quad - 100 = +\$33.3$

$PVR_B = 33.3/\{100+(200-110)(P/F_{15,1})+[(180-110)(P/F_{15,1})-20](P/F_{15,2})\}$

$\quad\quad = 33.3/209.2 = +0.16$

Project "A" with PVR of +0.38 ranks first, project "B" with PVR of +0.16 ranks second.

4-7 Solution:

Writing Annual Worth equations for projects A & B gives:

Project A ROR = 40%, Project B ROR = 40%

a) Incremental Analysis gives:

```
                         L=+150,000              C=100,000
C=50,000   I=+20,000 ... I=+20,000   C=40,000    C= 40,000
─────────────────────────────────────────────────────────
  0           1 ............ 3         4           5
```

PW Eq: $50,000 = 20,00(P/A_{i,3}) + 150,000(P/F_{i,3}) - 40,000(P/F_{i,4})$
$\quad\quad\quad - 140,000(P/F_{i,5})$

Two values of i exist that make right side of equation = 50,000:

i = 12%, and i = 40%

No decision can be made from dual "i" values, except to establish the range of i* values for which the incremental NPV in this problem will be positive.

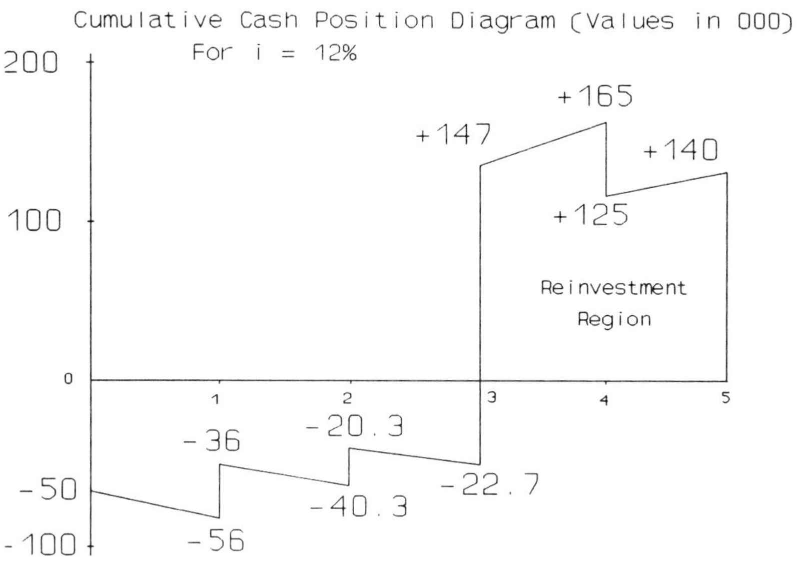
Cumulative Cash Position Diagram (Values in 000)
For i = 12%
200
100
0
-50
-100
1
2
3
4
5
+165
+147
+140
+125
Reinvestment
Region
-36
-20.3
-40.3
-22.7
-56

b) NPV Analysis:

$$NPV_A = 40{,}000\overset{2.991}{(P/A_{20,5})} + 100{,}000\overset{.4019}{(P/F_{20,5})} - 100{,}000 = +59{,}830$$

$$NPV_B = 60{,}000\overset{2.106}{(P/A_{20,3})} + 150{,}000\overset{.5787}{(P/F_{20,3})} - 150{,}000 = +63{,}165 \quad \text{Select}$$

c) Incremental Growth ROR Analysis B-A:

	0	1	2	3	4	5	
B-A)	C=50,000	I=20,000	I=20,000	L=150,000 I=20,000	C=40,000	C=140,000	
Reinvest Income @ 20%	-	C=20,000	C=20,000	C=150,000 C=20,000	-	-	F=$320,832

$$\text{where } F = [20{,}000\overset{3.640}{(F/A_{20,3})}+150{,}000]\overset{1.440}{(F/P_{20,2})} = \$320{,}832$$

	0	1	2	3	4	5	
B-A) + Reinvest	C=50,000	-	-	-	C=40,000	-	Net F=180,832

$$\text{PW Eq: } 0 = -50{,}000 - 40{,}000(P/F_{i,4}) + 180{,}832(P/F_{i,5})$$

By trial and error, i = Incremental Growth ROR = 21.5% > i*=20%, so satisfactory, select B.

4-7 Solution: Continued

d) PWC Modified Incremental ROR Analysis (Time Line Values in 000):

$$\text{Mod. } C = 50 + 40(P/F_{20,4}) + 140(P/F_{20,5}) \quad I=20 \quad I=20 \quad I=170 \quad - \quad -$$

| 0 | 1 | 2 | 3 | 4 | 5 |

PW Eq: Modified Cost = $125{,}560 = 20{,}000(P/A_{i,2}) + 170{,}000(P/F_{i,3})$

By trial and error, i = PW Cost Modified ROR = 21.2% > i* = 20%

e) reduce i* to 10% from 20%:

$$NPV_A = -100 + 40\overset{3.791}{(P/A_{10,5})} + 100\overset{0.6209}{(P/F_{10,5})} = +\$113.7 \quad \text{Select Maximum}$$

$$NPV_B = -150 + 60\overset{2.487}{(P/A_{10,3})} + 150\overset{0.7513}{(P/F_{10,3})} = +\$111.9$$

4-8 Solution: All Values in Dollars

$$I=1{,}000 \quad I=1{,}000 \quad I=1{,}000 \quad C=9{,}000 \quad I=1{,}000 \ldots\ldots I=1{,}000$$

| 0 | 1 | 2 | 3 | 4 .... 10 |

A) $NPV = 1{,}000 + 1{,}000\overset{1.528}{(P/A_{20,2})} - 9{,}000\overset{0.5787}{(P/F_{20,3})}$

$$+ 1{,}000\overset{3.605}{(P/A_{20,7})}\overset{0.5787}{(P/F_{20,3})}$$

$$= -\$595, \text{ so reject}$$

B) PW Cost Modified ROR Analysis:

Bring the year 3 cost back to year 0 at the minimum ROR:

$$9{,}000\overset{0.5787}{(P/F_{20,3})} = 1{,}000 + 1{,}000(P/A_{i,2}) + 1{,}000(P/A_{i,7})(P/F_{i,3})$$

i = PW Cost Modified ROR = 15.9% < i* of 20%, reject

4-9 Solution:

A) C=100   Net I=40 .... Net I=40

| 0 | 1 .... 5 |

B) C=150   Net I=55 .... Net I=55

| 0 | 1 .... 5 |

NPV Analysis @ i* = 20%:

$$NPV_A = -100 + 40\overset{2.991}{(P/A_{20,5})} = +\$19.6 \quad \text{Select A, Maximum}$$

$$NPV_B = -150 + 55(P/A_{20,5}) = +\$14.5$$

CHAPTER 4 PROBLEM SOLUTIONS

4-9 Solution: Continued

ROR Analysis:

"A" PW Eq: $0 = -100 + 40(P/A_{i,5})$, so $i = ROR_A = 28.6\% > i^* = 20\%$, ok

"B" PW Eq: $0 = -150 + 55(P/A_{i,5})$, so $i = ROR_B = 24.3\% > i^* = 20\%$, ok

```
B-A)   C=50           Net I=15 .............. Net I=15
      ─────────────────────────────────────────────────
       0              1 .................... 5
```

"B-A" PW Eq: $0 = -50 + 15(P/A_{i,5})$, so $i = ROR_{B-A} = 15.2\% < i^* = 20\%$

Therefore, reject B, select A.

PVR Analysis:

$PVR_A = 19.6/100 = 0.196 > 0$, satisfactory

$PVR_B = 14.5/150 = 0.097 > 0$, satisfactory

$PVR_{B-A} = (14.5-19.6)/(150-100) = -0.10 < 0$, unsatisfactory, select A

Change the Minimum ROR to 12% from 20% over all 5 years:

The total investment and incremental investment ROR results are the same, but comparing them to $i^*=12\%$ gives a different economic conclusion, select B.

$NPV_A = -100 + 40(P/A_{12,5}) = +\$44.4$

$NPV_B = -150 + 55(P/A_{12,5}) = +\$48.3$ Select B, Maximum, Consistent With ROR Analysis

Change the Min. ROR to 12% in years 1 & 2, and 20% for years 3, 4 & 5:

$$NPV_A = -100 + 40(P/A_{20,3})\overset{2.106}{}(P/F_{12,2})\overset{0.7972}{} + 40(P/A_{12,2})\overset{1.690}{} = +\$34.75$$

$$NPV_B = -150 + 55(P/A_{20,3})(P/F_{12,2}) + 55(P/A_{12,2}) = +\$35.28$$

Results are effectively breakeven since the NPV results are approximately equal. The slight advantage is to B with the bigger NPV.

4-10 Solution:

```
         -         I=450       I=450  ............ I=450
A)     ─────────────────────────────────────────────────
         0           1           2    .............. 10


      C=800        I=700       I=700  ............ I=700
B)     ─────────────────────────────────────────────────
         0           1           2    .............. 10


                   I=850
     C=1,300      C=900       I=1,050 ........ I=1,050
C)     ─────────────────────────────────────────────────
         0           1           2    .............. 10
```

Net Present Value @ i*=15%:

A) $450(P/A_{15,10})$ = +$2,259
    where $(P/A_{15,10}) = 5.019$

B) $700(P/A_{15,10})$ − 800 = +$2,713
    where $(P/A_{15,10}) = 5.019$

C) $[1,050(P/A_{15,9}) - 50](P/F_{15,1}) - 1,300$ = +$3,014   (economic choice)
    where $(P/A_{15,9}) = 4.772$, $(P/F_{15,1}) = 0.8696$

Since NPV_{C-B} and NPV_{C-A} are positive, "C" with maximum NPV is the economic choice. The mutually exclusive alternative with maximum NPV on total investment always turns out to be the economic choice from incremental NPV analysis.

Present Value Ratio @ i*=15%:

A) 2,259 / 0 = ∞ > 0, so ok
B) 2,713 / 800 = +3.39 > 0, so ok
C) 3,014 / (1,300+50(P/F$_{15,1}$)) = 3,014/1,344 = +2.24 > 0, so ok

B-A) (2,713−2,259)/(800−0)=+0.57 > 0, (Alt.B ok, next compare C to B)
C-B) (3,014−2,713)/(500+652.2) = +0.26 > 0, (C is the economic choice)

Since B was preferred to A, there is no real value in comparing C to A. Comparing the next level of incremental investment (C-B), it is determined that C is preferred to B since the incremental C-B PVR is positive. This result tells us that the additional dollars invested in C over B will be earning a present worth profit of $0.55 per present worth dollar invested. This exceeds the PVR of 0 obtained by investing elsewhere at the minimum rate of return and verifies that alternative C will provide the maximum return possible from available investment dollars.

CHAPTER 4 PROBLEM SOLUTIONS

4-10 Solution: Continued

Rate of Return Analysis for $i^*=15.0\%$:

ROR_A: $0 = 450(P/A_{i,10})$ $i = \infty\% > i^* = 15\%$

ROR_B: $800 = 700(P/A_{i,10})$ $i = 87.34\% > i^* = 15\%$

ROR_C: $1,300 = 1,050(P/A_{i,9})(P/F_{i,1}) - 50(P/F_{i,1})$

$i = 50.9\% > i^* = 15\%$

ROR_{B-A}: $800 = 250(P/A_{i,10})$

$i = 28.8\% > 15\%$, Accept B over A

ROR_{C-B}: $500 = \{350(P/A_{i,9}) - 750\}(P/F_{i,1})$

$i = 21.25\% > i^* = 15\%$, "C" is the economic choice.

Changing the Minimum Rate of Return to $i^*=25\%$:

A) $450(P/A_{25,10}^{3.571}) = +\$1,607$

B) $700(P/A_{25,10}^{3.571}) - 800 = +\$1,700$ ("B" is now the economic choice.)

C) $[1,050(P/A_{25,9}^{3.463}) - 50](P/F_{25,1}^{0.800}) - 1,300 = +\$1,569$

For rate of return analysis, the only incremental alternative generating an incremental rate of return in excess of the new 25.0% minimum rate is (B-A) which indicates selecting alternative "B" is the economic choice, consistent with the NPV results. Incremental C-B is shown below to verify that "B" is preferred to "C". PVR would select "B" also.

ROR_{C-B} $500 = \{350(P/A_{i,9}) - 750\}(P/F_{i,1})$

$i = 21.25\% < i^* = 25\%$, Accept B

Change the minimum rate of return to 25 percent for year 1 and 2, then back to 15 percent for years 3 through 10:

With ROR analysis, we can't tell if $ROR_{C-B} = 21.25\%$ is satisfactory or not. Therefore, we have to go to another evaluation technique such as net present value.

$NPV_A = 450(P/A_{15,8})(P/F_{25,2}) + 450(P/A_{25,2}) = +1,940$

$NPV_B = 700(P/A_{15,8})(P/F_{25,2}) + 700(P/A_{25,2}) - 800 = +2,218$

$NPV_C = 1,050(P/A_{15,8})(P/F_{25,2}) + 1,050(P/A_{25,2}) - 50(P/F_{25,1}) - 1,300$

$= +2,347$ Maximum, so select C.

4-10 Solution: Continued

Changing the minimum ROR with time gives the economic choice of selecting project "C". This is not the same result achieved by changing the minimum ROR to 25% over the entire evaluation life. The minimum ROR is a very significant evaluation parameter and must represent other opportunities for investing capital both now and in the future over the evaluation life of projects. If the minimum ROR is projected to change with time, that change must be built into evaluation calculations as illustrated to achieve valid economic analysis results.

4-11 Solution: Values in Millions of Dollars

```
A)    C=32        I=12        I=12 ................. I=12
      ─────────────────────────────────────────────────────
       0           1           2 ..................... 5

B)    C=38        I=13.5      I=13.5 ............... I=13.5
      ─────────────────────────────────────────────────────
       0           1           2 ..................... 5

B-A)  C=6         I=1.5       I=1.5 ................ I=1.5
      ─────────────────────────────────────────────────────
       0           1           2 ..................... 5
```

ROR_A: $0 = -32 + 12(P/A_{i,5})$; $32/12 = (P/A_{i,5}) = 2.667$

$i = 25\% + 5\%[(2.689-2.667)/(2.689-2.436)] = 25.43\% > i^*=15\%$, so OK

ROR_B: $0 = -38 + 13.5(P/A_{i,5})$; $38/13.5 = (P/A_{i,5}) = 2.815$

$i = 20\% + 5\%[(2.991-2.815)/(2.991-2.689)] = 22.91\% > i^*=15\%$, so OK

ROR_{B-A}: $0 = -6 + 1.5(P/A_{i,5})$; $6/1.5 = (P/A_{i,5}) = 4.000$

$i = 7\% + 1\%[(4.100-4.000)/(4.000-3.993)] = \underline{7.93\%} < i^*=15\%$, reject B.

$NPV_A = -32 + 12(P/A_{15,5})^{3.352} = \underline{+8.22}$, select A with largest NPV.

$NPV_B = -38 + 13.5(P/A_{15,5}) = +7.25$

$NPV_{B-A} = -6 + 1.5(P/A_{15,5})^{3.352} = \underline{-0.97} < 0$, reject B.

CHAPTER 4 PROBLEM SOLUTIONS

4-12 Solution:

A)
```
    C=240      I=50 ........................ I=50
    ─────────────────────────────────────────────── Salvage=240
    0          1 ........................... 5
```

Using Text Eq 3-2, AW Eq: $(240 - 240)(A/P_{i,5}) + 240(i) = 50$

$i = ROR_A = 50/240 = 21\% > i^* = 10\%$, satisfactory

B)
```
    C=240      I=98.5 ...................... I=98.5
    ─────────────────────────────────────────────── Salvage=0
    0          1 ........................... 5
```

PW Eq: $240 = 98.5(P/A_{i,5})$

By trial and error, $i = ROR_B = 30\% > i^* = 10\%$, satisfactory

Incremental Analysis:

A-B)
```
    C=0        I=-48.5 ..................... I=-48.5
    ─────────────────────────────────────────────── Salv=+240
    0          1 ........................... 5
```

AW Eq: $48.5 = 240(A/F_{i,5})$

$i = ROR = -0.5\% < i^* = 10\%$ so reject A, select B

$NPV_A = 50(P/A_{10,5}) + 240(P/F_{10,5}) - 240 = +\$98.57$

$NPV_B = 98.5(P/A_{10,5}) - 240 = +\$133.41$, Select B

4-13 Solution:

$NPV_A = 90,000\underset{3.326}{(P/A_{20,6})} - 200,000 = +99,340$

$NPV_B = 300,000\underset{2.106}{(P/A_{20,3})} - 500,000 = +131,800$

$NPV_C = 120,000\underset{2.991}{(P/A_{20,5})} + 100,000\underset{.4019}{(P/F_{20,5})} - 300,000 = +99,110$

Maximum Cumulative NPV from $500,000 = NPV_A + NPV_C = \$198,450$

$PVR_A = 0.497$, 1st Choice

$PVR_B = 0.264$, 3rd Choice

$PVR_C = 0.330$, 2nd Choice

4-13 Solution: Continued

Growth ROR Analysis using a 6 year evaluation life:

A) $[90,000(F/A_{20,6})^{9.930}]P/F_{i,6} = 200,000$

$893,700(P/F_{i,6}) = 200,000$; $P/F_{i,6} = 0.2238$; i=Growth ROR = 28.5%, <u>1st</u>

B) $[300,000(F/A_{20,3})^{3.640}(F/P_{20,3})^{1.728}]P/F_{i,6} = 500,000$

$1,886,976(P/F_{i,6}) = 500,000$; $P/F_{i,6} = 0.2650$; i=Growth ROR = 24.8%

C) $[120,000(F/A_{20,5})^{7.442}+100,000](F/P_{20,1})^{1.200}P/F_{i,6} = 300,000$

$1,191,648(P/F_{i,6}) = 300,000$; $P/F_{i,6} = 0.25175$; i=Growth ROR=25.9%, <u>2nd</u>

4-14 Solution: All Values in Thousands of Dollars

```
     C=20        I=12 .................................. I=12
A)   ─────────────────────────────────────────────────────── L=20
      0           1 .................................... 12

     C=28        I=14 .................................. I=14
B)   ─────────────────────────────────────────────────────── L=28
      0           1 .................................... 12
```

ROR Analysis:

"A" PW Eq: $0 = -20 + 12(P/A_{i,12}) + 20(P/F_{i,12})$, i=ROR$_A$=60% > i*=15% satisfactory

"B" PW Eq: $0 = -28 + 14(P/A_{i,12}) + 28(P/F_{i,12})$, i=ROR$_B$=50% > i*=15% satisfactory

```
       C=8         I=2 ................................... I=2
B-A)   ─────────────────────────────────────────────────────── L=8
        0           1 .................................... 12
```

"B-A" PW Eq: $0 = -8 + 2(P/A_{i,12}) + 8(P/F_{i,12})$

i = ROR$_{B-A}$ = 25% > i* = 15%, satisfactory, select B

NPV Analysis:

$NPV_A = -20 + 12(P/A_{15,12})^{6.194} + 20(P/F_{15,12})^{.2567} = +48.79 > 0$, acceptable

$NPV_B = -28 + 14(P/A_{15,12}) + 28(P/F_{15,12}) = +53.13 > 0$, select B

Note incremental NPV$_{B-A}$ is positive: 53.13-48.79 = 4.34, indicates select B.

CHAPTER 4 PROBLEM SOLUTIONS

4-14 Solution: Continued

PVR Analysis:

$PVR_A = 48.79/20 = 2.44 > 0$, satisfactory

$PVR_B = 53.13/28 = 1.90 > 0$, satisfactory

$PVR_{B-A} = (53.13-48.79)/(28-20) = 0.54 > 0$, satisfactory, select B

Change the minimum ROR to 30% from 15%:

$NPV_A = -20 + 12(P/A_{30,12})^{3.190} + 20(P/F_{30,12})^{.0429} = +19.1 > 0$, select A

$NPV_B = -28 + 14(P/A_{30,12}) + 28(P/F_{30,12}) = +17.8 > 0$

Note incremental NPV_{B-A} is negative: $17.8-19.1 = -1.3$, indicates Select A, ROR and PVR give the same conclusion.

4-15 Solution: Values in Thousands of Dollars

$NPV_A = 150(P/A_{20,5})^{2.991} + 50(P/F_{20,5})^{0.4019} - 160 = +308.75$

$NPV_B = 275(P/A_{20,4})^{2.589} + 70(P/F_{20,4})^{0.4823} - 320 = +425.74$

$NPV_C = 500(P/A_{20,3})^{2.106} + 100(P/F_{20,3})^{0.5787} - 480 = +630.87$

If A, B, and C are mutually exclusive, select C with the largest NPV. If A, B, and C are non-mutually exclusive and the budget is $480,000, select A+B to maximize cumulative NPV. Note this does not involve selecting C, even though it has the largest NPV.

$PVR_A = \frac{308}{160} = 1.93$; $PVR_B = \frac{425}{320} = 1.33$; $PVR_C = \frac{630}{480} = 1.31$

If A, B, and C are mutually exclusive, incremental PVR analysis must be made. The project with the largest PVR is not necessarily the choice.

$PVR_{B-A} = \frac{425-308}{320-160} = +0.73 > 0$, satisfactory, Select B

$PVR_{C-B} = \frac{630-425}{480-320} = +1.28 > 0$, satisfactory, Select C

C is selected even though it has the smallest PVR on total investment if the alternatives are mutually exclusive.

If the alternatives are non-mutually exclusive, select the projects in order of decreasing PVR: "A" first, "B" second, "C" third. Growth ROR analysis of A, B, and C would rank the projects the same as PVR. To make ROR analysis of mutually exclusive alternatives A, B, and C, incremental ROR analysis must be made:

4-15 Solution: Continued

```
        C=160      I=150 ........................ I=150      I=150
A)    ─────────────────────────────────────────────────────────── L=50
        0          1 ............................ 4          5
```

PW Eq: $0 = -160 + 150(P/A_{i,5}) + 50(P/F_{i,5})$, $i = ROR_A = 91\%$ by trial and error

```
        C=320      I=275 ........................ I=275
B)    ─────────────────────────────────────────────────── L=70
        0          1 ............................ 4
```

PW Eq: $0 = -320 + 275(P/A_{i,4}) + 70(P/F_{i,4})$, $i = ROR_B = 79\%$ by trial and error

```
        C=160      I=125 ........................ I=125+70   C=200
B-A)  ───────────────────────────────────────────────────────────
        0          1 ............................ 4          5
```

PW Cost Modified ROR: $160 + 200(P/F_{20,5})^{.4019} = 125(P/A_{i,4}) + 70(P/F_{i,4})$

i = PW Modifed Incremental ROR = 42.4% > i*=20%, Select B

Incremental C-B analysis would also give an acceptable C-B ROR indicating accept C, which is the mutually exclusive alternative choice consistent with NPV and PVR analysis.

4-16 Solution:

```
                   C=170      C=120
        C=120      I= 90      I=90       I= 90      I=90 ................. I=90
A)    ──────────────────────────────────────────────────────────────────────────
        0          1          2          3          4 .................... 10
```

```
                                         C= 80
                              C=150      I=100      I=100 ..... I=100
B)    ─────────────────────────────────────────────────────────────────
        0          1          2          3          4 .......... 8
```

```
                                         C=300
                   C=200      I=100      I=100      I=150 ............. I=150
C)    ─────────────────────────────────────────────────────────────────────────
        0          1          2          3          4 ................ 9
```

To properly compare net values on a present, annual or future basis it is necessary to have all net values at the same point in time (year 0 is chosen in this analysis) or spread uniformly over the same evaluation periods for net annual value analysis. Remember the key underlying assumption to both of these analyses is that money can always be invested elsewhere at the minimum rate of return, i*, (15.0% in this problem).

CHAPTER 4 PROBLEM SOLUTIONS

4-16 Solution: Continued

$$NPV_A = -120 - 170(P/F_{15,1})^{0.8696} - 120(P/F_{15,3})^{0.6575} + 90(P/A_{15,10})^{5.019} = +\$105$$

$$NPV_B = -150(P/F_{15,2})^{0.7561} + 20(P/F_{15,3})^{0.6575} + 100(P/A_{15,5})^{3.352}(P/F_{15,3})^{0.6575} = +\$120$$

$$NPV_C = -200(P/F_{15,1})^{0.8696} + 100(P/F_{15,2})^{0.7561} - 200(P/F_{15,3})^{0.6575}$$
$$+ 150(P/A_{15,6})^{3.784}(P/F_{15,3})^{0.6575} = +\$143$$

A) If the alternatives are mutually exclusive, select the largest NPV which is alternative C. Alternative C has a positive incremental NPV compared to both alternatives A and B which is why it is the economic choice. The maximum NPV alternative always has positive incremental NPV compared to the other investment alternatives. Net values calculated at any point in time give the same economic conclusion. Do not compare net values calculated at different points in time.

B) If the alternatives are non-mutually exclusive, use PVR to rank the alternatives. NPV is *not* a valid ranking technique for non-mutually exclusive alternatives. Year 0 PVR results are calculated here, but PVR results calculated at any year will be the same.

$PVR_A = 105 / (120 + 80(P/F_{15,1})) = 105 / 189.6 = +0.55$ (rank third)

$PVR_B = 120 / (150(P/F_{15,2})) = 120 / 113 = +1.06$ (rank first)

$PVR_C = 143 / \{200 + [(300-100)(P/F_{15,1})-100](P/F_{15,1})\}(P/F_{15,1})$

$\quad = 143 / 230 = +0.62$ (rank second)

The differences in starting dates of projects A, B and C merit further discussion, considering whether the projects are mutually exclusive or non-mutually exclusive.

First, if the projects are mutually exclusive alternatives, selecting project C with maximum NPV means starting the project a year from now at year 1 rather than at year 0. Using a minimum discount rate of 15% in the analysis means we should keep our money invested elsewhere at 15% between year 0 and year 1 and then invest in project C at year 1 to maximize value generated by available investment dollars.

4-16 Solution: Continued

Second, if the projects are non-mutually exclusive and budget dollars are limited so that we can only do one or two projects, B is our first choice and C is our second choice. This requires keeping our budget dollars invested elsewhere at our minimum discount rate of 15% until the start of project B at year 2 and the start of project C at year 1. If due to capital rationing we estimate that we will only have enough money to do one project, investing in project B starting at year 2 is our choice to maximize value to be generated from available investment dollars. If enough capital is available to do two projects, B is our first choice and C is the second choice. We would forgo investing in A at year 0 to invest in C at year 1 and B at year 2.

Third, whether the projects are mutually exclusive or non-mutually exclusive, you might consider that investing today in project A at year 0 will give more than a 15% ROR (the project A ROR is 25.5%), so the minimum ROR should be 25.5% rather than 15%. That logic is only partially valid. Remember that the minimum discount rate represents other opportunities for investing capital in the future over the life of projects as well as now. Although 25.5% represents the ROR on other opportunities for investing capital now at year 0, over years 1 through 10 a 15% discount rate may be considered to be more representative of other investment opportunities. This is a case where we should change the minimum ROR over time from 25.5% between year 0 and year 1 to 15% from year 1 to year 10. In this case, that does not change our mutually exclusive or non-mutually exclusive choices. Most companies in practice do not change the discount rate with time, so it is not emphasized here.

Fourth, in industry practice companies with significant budgets each year often will only evaluate and rank projects to be started in that budget year, considering that projects to be started in later years will be measured against other projects in future budget years. However, a small company or individual with limited budget dollars may need to look at future and present investment opportunities simultaneously now, because once investment dollars are spent, there may not be another similar investment dollar budget to spend next year or thereafter. It may be better to set aside money today to invest in projects like B and C a year or two from today to make optimum use of available investment capital.

CHAPTER 4 PROBLEM SOLUTIONS

4-17 Solution: Values in Thousands

A) Current:

Production	2,000 tons	2,000 tons
Profit	$20/ton	$20/ton
Revenue	$40,000	$40,000

```
0          1 ................................ 7
```

ROR_A: infinite, so ok

NPV_A @ 15% = 40,000(P/A$_{15\%,7}$) = $166,416 > 0, so ok
(4.1604)

B) Improved:

Production	2,500 tons ...	2,500 tons	1,500 tons	–
Profit	$20/ton	$20/ton	$20/ton	–
Revenue	$50,000	$50,000	$30,000	–
Cost C=$11,000	–	–	–	–

```
0          1 ........... 5         6         7
```

ROR_B PW Eq: 0 = -11,000 + 50,000(P/A$_{i,5}$) + 30,000(P/F$_{i,6}$)

ROR_B, i = 454% > i*=15%, so ok

NPV_B @ 15% = $169,578 > 0, so ok

C) Incremental Improved-Current:

```
C=$11,000   I=$10,000        I=$10,000   C=$10,000   C=$40,000

0           1 ........... 5             6           7
```

PW Eq: 0 = -11,000 + 10,000(P/A$_{i,5}$) - 10,000(P/F$_{i,6}$) - 40,000(P/F$_{i,7}$)

Dual "i" values are 8.93% and 78.85%. Neither of these results are valid for evaluation purposes because of the combination rate of return and rate of reinvestment meaning included in each. They do however establish the range over which our incremental net present value will be positive. Remember, net present value is only valid in this situation when your minimum rate of return reflects the other opportunities that exist for the use of capital. The use of a financial cost of capital measure here for a discount rate results in a meaningless net present value. (In general, this is true unless financial cost of capital equals opportunity cost of capital due to assumed unlimited financing.)

Use Modified PW Eq:

0 = -11,000 - 10,000(P/F$_{15,6}$) - 40,000(P/F$_{15,7}$) + 10,000(P/A$_{i,5}$)
             (0.4323)   (0.3759)

0 = -30,359 + 10,000(P/A$_{i,5}$)

@15% NPV = 3,162.6   Incremental NPV is positive, accept improvement.
@20% NPV = -452.8

ROR = 15%+5%[(3,163-0)/(3,163+453)] = **19.37%** > 15.0% Min ROR, accept improvement.

4-18 Solution: Values in Thousands of Units or Dollars

A) Existing Haul Road

Year	0	1-5	6	7
Production (Tons)		2,000	2,000	2,000
Production (oz)		153	153	153
Revenue ($350/oz gold)x(oz)		53,550	53,550	53,550
-Oper. Costs ($190/oz)x(oz)		29,070	29,070	29,070
Net Revenue		24,480	24,480	24,480
-Capital Costs	-	-	-	-
Cash Flow	0	24,480	24,480	24,480

PW Eq: $0 = 24{,}480(P/A_{i,7})$; ROR is infinite (no costs)

$$NPV = 24{,}480 \underset{4.1604}{(P/A_{15,7})} = \$101{,}847, \text{ accept "existing haul road"}$$
since maximum NPV

B) Proposed Haul Road:

Year	0	1-5	6	7
Production (Tons)		2,500	1,500	0
Production (oz)		191.25	114.75	0
Revenue		66,937.50	40,162.50	0
-Operating Costs		-36,337.50	-21,802.50	0
Net Revenue		30,600	18,360	0
-Capital Costs	-11,000	-	-	-
Cash Flow	-11,000	30,600	18,360	0

PW Eq: $0 = -11{,}000 + 30{,}600(P/A_{i,5}) + 18{,}360(P/F_{i,6})$; ROR = 278%

$$NPV = -11{,}000 + 30{,}600\underset{3.3522}{(P/A_{15,5})} + 18{,}360\underset{.4323}{(P/F_{15,6})} = \$99{,}514 \text{ (reject)}$$
since minimum NPV

C) Incremental Proposed-Existing:

Year	0	1-5	6	7
Proposed Cash Flow	-11,000	30,600	18,360	0
-Existing Cash Flow	0	24,480	24,480	24,480
Incremental Cash Flow	-11,000	6,120	-6,120	-24,480

Incremental ROR leads to dual rates, unless cash flows are modified:

$$\text{Mod. Yr 0 Cost: } -11{,}000 - 6{,}120\underset{.4323}{(P/F_{15,6})} - 24{,}480\underset{.3759}{(P/F_{15,7})} = -22{,}848$$

Mod. PW Eq = $-22{,}848 + 6{,}120(P/A_{i,5})$

ROR = 10.6% < i*=15%, so reject haul road improvement.

CHAPTER 5 PROBLEM SOLUTIONS

5-1 Solution: All Values in Millions of Dollars

```
                Rev=200         Rev=200
    C=400       OC=100          OC=100
                                                L=0
    ─────────────────────────────────────────────
    0           1               5, 10 or 15 yr(s).
```

PW Eq: $0 = -400 + (200-100)(P/A_{i,n})$ where n = 5, 10, or 15

Project Life	Cost=400	Cost=600	Cost=800
5 yr ROR=	7.9%	-5.8%	-13.9%
10 yr ROR=	21.4%	10.5%	4.3%
15 yr ROR=	24.0%	14.5%	9.1%

5-2 Solution: Analysis of GDP (All Values in Trillions of Dollars)

Escalated (Current or Nominal) Dollars:
```
$4.54                                    $4.90
─────────────────────────────────────────────
1987                                     1988
```

Current (nominal) dollar % gain = $[(4.90-4.54)/4.54](100) = 7.95\%$

Constant (Real) Dollars, 4% inflation:
```
$4.54                          $4.90(P/F_{4,1}) = 4.71
─────────────────────────────────────────────
1987                           1988
```

Constant (real) dollar % gain: $[(4.71-4.54)/4.54](100) = 3.79\%$

5-3 Solution:

A) Escalated Dollar Analysis (Values in Thousands of Dollars)

```
                                I=200(F/P_{10,2})=242.0
C_0=50    C_1=150(F/P_{15,1})=172.5    OC=100(F/P_{15,2})=132.2
                                                Net=109.8
─────────────────────────────────────────────────────────
0              1                        2
```

```
I=200(F/P_{10,3})=266.2   I=200(F/P_{10,4})=292.8   I=200(F/P_{10,5})=322.2
OC=100(F/P_{15,3})=152.1  OC=100(F/P_{15,4})=174.9  OC=100(F/P_{15,5})=201.1
     Net=114.1                 Net=117.9                 Net=121.1
─────────────────────────────────────────────────────────
     3                         4                         5
```

PW Eq: $0 = -50 - 172.5(P/F_{i,1}) + 109.8(P/F_{i,2}) + 114.1(P/F_{i,3})$
$+ 117.9(P/F_{i,4}) + 121.1(P/F_{i,5})$

ROR = i = 32.29% from programmed calculator.

5-3 Solution: Continued

B) Constant Dollar Analysis of Case A

Net Escalated Dollar Time Diagram From Case A:

C_0=50	C_1=172.5	Net_2=109.8	Net_3=114.1	Net_4=117.9	Net_5=121.1
0	1	2	3	4	5

Constant Dollar Equivalent Time Diagram for Inflation of 10% per Year:

	156.82		90.74		85.72	
C_0=50	C_1=172.5$(P/F_{10,1})$		109.8$(P/F_{10,2})$		114.1$(P/F_{10,3})$	....
0	1		2		3	....

PW Eq: $0 = -50 - 156.82(P/F_{i',1}) + 90.74(P/F_{i',2}) + 85.72(P/F_{i',3})$

$\qquad + 80.53(P/F_{i',4}) + 75.19(P/F_{i',5})$

i' = Constant Dollar ROR = 20.26%

An alternate solution would be to utilize Equation 5-1 as follows:
$1+i = (1+f)(1+i')$ and $i=32.29\%$ from Case A and $f=10\%$ as given, so the constant dollar ROR = $i' = (1.3229)/(1.10) - 1 = 0.2026$ or 20.26%.

C) Escalated Dollar Analysis Using the Washout Assumption

The "washout" assumption is: the dollar (not percent) escalation of operating costs is offset by the same dollar escalation of revenue, so profit margins remain constant at what they would be today.

C_0=50	C_1=172.5	Net_2=100.0	Net_3=100.0	Net_4=100.0	Net_5=100.0
0	1	2	3	4	5

PW Eq: $0 = -50 - 172.5(P/F_{i,1}) + 100(P/A_{i,4})(P/F_{i,1})$

i = Escalated Dollar ROR = 25.25%

5-4 Solution: Escalated and Constant Dollar Selling Price

Price = $100/Unit   Escalated $ Price = ?

```
              Year    0           1           2           3
Escalation Rates  |-- 6.0% ---|-- 8.0% ---|-- 10.0% --|
```

Yr 3 Escalated Dollar Price = $100(F/P_{6,1})(F/P_{8,1})(F/P_{10,1}) = \$125.93$

Constant $ Price = ?

```
              Year    0           1           2           3
Inflation Rates   |-- 5.0% ---|-- 9.0% ---|-- 12.0% --|
```

Yr 3 Constant $ Price = $(\$125.93)(P/F_{12,1})(P/F_{9,1})(P/F_{5,1}) = \$98.24$

CHAPTER 5 PROBLEM SOLUTIONS

5-5 Solution:

```
C=$100,000                          Esc. $ Sale Price = X
_____
0                   1                   2
                                    Const. $ Sale Price = X(P/F_{10,2})
```

Constant $ PW Eq: $\$100{,}000 = X(P/F_{10,2})(P/F_{25,2})$

$X = \$100{,}000 / [(0.82645)(0.6400)] = \$189{,}062$

$1+i = (1+f)(1+i')$ where $f = 0.10$ and $i' = 0.25$

Escalated $ Growth Rate $= i = (1+f)(1+i') - 1$
$= (1.10)(1.25) - 1 = 0.375$ or 37.5%

To prove the equivalence of the 37.5% escalated dollar Growth Rate:

Escalated $ PW Eq: $\$100{,}000 = \$189{,}062(P/F_{37.5,2})$ so proof is complete

5-6 Solution: Breakeven Selling Price (All Values in Thousands)

	Year 1	Year 2
Escalated $ Sales	$X(F/P_{10,1})=1.1X$	$X(F/P_{10,2})=1.21X$
Escalated $ OC	$50(F/P_{15,1})=57.50$	$50(F/P_{15,2})=66.13$
Escalated Profit	$1.1X - 57.50$	$1.21X - 66.13$
Constant $ Profit	$(1.1X - 57.50)(P/F_{12,1})$	$(1.21X - 66.13)(P/F_{12,2})$

<u>Constant Dollar PW Eq</u>: Constant $ minimum ROR = $i^{*\prime} = 15\%$

$$100 = (1.1X-57.50)\underset{0.8929}{(P/F_{12,1})}\underset{0.8696}{(P/F_{15,1})}$$
$$+ (1.21X - 66.13)\underset{0.7972}{(P/F_{12,2})}\underset{0.7561}{(P/F_{15,2})}$$

$X = \$116.55$/unit in today's dollar value.

<u>Escalated Dollar PW Eq</u>:

$1+i^* = (1+f)(1+i^{*\prime})$, where $f=12\%$, $i^{*\prime}=15\%$,

$i^* = 28.8\%$

$100 = (1.1X - 57.50)(P/F_{28.8,1}) + (1.21X - 66.13)(P/F_{28.8,2})$

$X = \$116.55$/unit in today's dollar value.

Escalated $ year 1 sales price $= 116.55(F/P_{10,1}) = \$128.21$/unit

Escalated $ year 2 sales price $= 116.55(F/P_{10,2}) = \$141.03$/unit

5-7 Solution: (Today's Dollar Time Diagram in Thousands of Dollars)

```
                              Rev=150    Rev=150    Rev=150
  C_Acq=?        -     C=200  OC=50      OC=50      OC=50
  |_____|_____|_____|_____|_____|_____ L=0
  0             1      2      3          4          5
```

                                    2.283   0.7561   0.7561
Case 1) $C_{Acq} = NPV_{time\,0} = 100(P/A_{15\%,3})(P/F_{15\%,2}) - 200(P/F_{15\%,2}) = +21.4$

Case 2) For constant dollar NPV analysis we must use a constant dollar minimum rate of return obtained from equation 5-1:

Eq. 5-1: $1+i = (1+f)(1+i')$ or rearranged, $i' = [(1+i)/(1+f)] - 1$
Constant $ Minimum ROR $i^{*'} = [(1.15)/(1.07)] - 1 = 0.07477$ or 7.477%

$C_{Acq} = NPV_{time\,0} = 100(P/A_{7.47\%,3})(P/F_{7.47\%,2}) - 200(P/F_{7.47\%,2}) = +52.1$

The above Case 2 solution assumes that the escalation rate for costs and revenues equals the rate of inflation, as is illustrated below:

Escalated Dollar Time Diagram:

```
                                                  1.2250
                        1.1449                     Rev=150(F/P_7,3)=183.76
  C_acq=?        -      C=200(F/P_7,2)=228.98      OC= 50(F/P_7,3)= 61.25
                                                                  Net=122.51
  |_____|_____|_____|_____
  0             1      2                           3
```

```
                        1.3108                     1.4025
                        Rev=150(F/P_7,4)=196.62    Rev=150(F/P_7,5)=210.38
                        OC= 50(F/P_7,4)= 65.54     OC= 50(F/P_7,5)= 70.12
                                      Net=131.08                 Net=140.26
  _____|_____|_____
                       4                           5
```

                              .7561   .6575   .5718
Escalated $ NPV = $-228.98(P/F_{15,2}) + 122.51(P/F_{15,3}) + 131.08(P/F_{15,4})$

                        .4972
                  $+140.26(P/F_{15,5}) = +52.1$

Constant Dollar Time Diagram:

```
                                                  .81630
                        .87344                     Rev=183.76(P/F_7,3)=150
  C_acq=?        -      C=228.98(P/F_7,2)=200      OC= 61.25(P/F_7,3)= 50
                                                                  Net=100
  |_____|_____|_____|_____
  0             1      2                           3
```

```
                        .76289                     .71299
                        Rev=196.62(P/F_7,4)=150    Rev=210.38(P/F_7,5)=150
                        OC= 65.54(P/F_7,4)= 50     OC= 70.12(P/F_7,5)= 50
                                      Net=100                     Net=100
  _____|_____|_____
                       4                           5
```

CHAPTER 5 PROBLEM SOLUTIONS

5-7 Solution: Case 2 Continued

From Text Eq 5-1, $1+i = (1+f)(1+i')$

so Constant \$ Minimum ROR Equivalent to 15% Escalated \$ Minimum ROR

$= i*' = [(1+i*)/(1+f)]-1 = [(1+0.15)/(1+0.07)]-1 = 0.07477$ or 7.477%

Constant \$ NPV $= -200(P/F_{7.477,2})^{.86570} + 100(P/F_{7.477,3})^{.80548} + 100(P/F_{7.477,4})^{.74944}$

$+ 100(P/F_{7.477,5})^{.69730} = +52.1$

Case 3)

```
                        1.254                    1.331
                   200(F/P_12,2)          (150-50)(F/P_10,3)
  C_Acq       -      C=250.8                Net R=133.1
  ─────────────────────────────────────────────────────────
     0        1         2                       3
```

```
                                 1.464                    1.611
                          (150-50)(F/P_10,4)       (150-50)(F/P_10,5)
                             Net R=146.4              Net R=161.1
                        ─────────────────────────────────────────────
                                   4                        5
```

$C_{Acq} = NPV_{time\ 0} = 133.1(P/F_{15,3})^{0.6575} + 146.4(P/F_{15,4})^{0.5718}$

$+ 161.1(P/F_{15,5})^{0.4972} - 250.8(P/F_{15,2})^{0.7561}$

$= +\$61.69$

Case 4) Constant Dollar Diagram:

```
              C'=250.8X    Net R'=133.1X   Net R'=146.4X   Net R'=161.1X
  C_Acq   -   (P/F_7,2)     (P/F_7,3)        (P/F_7,4)       (P/F_7,5)
  ──────────────────────────────────────────────────────────────────────
     0    1      2              3                4               5
```

Constant Dollar NPV must be made using $i*' = 7.477\%$:

$C_{Acq} = NPV_{time\ 0} = 133.1\overbrace{(P/F_{7,3})(P/F_{7.477,3})}^{P/F_{15,3}} + 146.4\overbrace{(P/F_{7,4})(P/F_{7.477,4})}^{P/F_{15,4}}$

$+ 161.1\overbrace{(P/F_{7,5})(P/F_{7.477,5})}^{P/F_{15,5}} - 250.8\overbrace{(P/F_{7,2})(P/F_{7.477,2})}^{P/F_{15,2}}$

$= +\$61.69$, Identical to the Case 3 escalated dollar results, since the equations are identical.

5-7 Solution: Continued

Case 5)

```
               200(F/P₁₂,₂)
                  ⌣
C_Acq      -    C=250.8      Net R=100    Net R=100    Net R=100
─────────────────────────────────────────────────────────────────
    0           1                2            3             4            5
```

$$C_{Acq} = NPV_{time0} = 100(P/A_{15,3})\overset{2.283}{}(P/F_{15,2})\overset{0.7561}{} - 250.8(P/F_{15,2})\overset{0.7561}{} = -\$17.0$$

5-8 Solution: Breakeven Sales Price Analysis, Values in Thousands of Dollars

```
              R=5X     R=5X(F/P₁₀,₁)=5.5X   R=5X(F/P₁₀,₁)(F/P₆,₁)=5.83X
C=100         OC=8     OC=8(F/P₁₅,₁)=9.2    OC=8(F/P₁₅,₁)(F/P₈,₁)=9.94
─────────────────────────────────────────────────────────────────
  0            1              2                      3
```

Constant $ PW Eq for i*' = 12%:

$$0 = -100 + (5X-8)(P/F_{7,1})(P/F_{12,1}) + (5.5X-9.2)(P/F_{7,2})(P/F_{12,2})$$
$$+ (5.83X-9.94)(P/F_{7,3})(P/F_{12,3})$$

To work in escalated dollars, calculate i* equivalent to i*':

$(1+i) = (1+f)(1+i')$ so i* = 19.84%, is equivalent to i*' = 12%
for inflation of 7% per year.

Escalated $ PW Eq for equivalent i* = 19.84%:

$$0 = -100 + (5X-8)(P/F_{19.84,1})\overset{0.83445}{} + (5.5X-9.2)(P/F_{19.84,2})\overset{0.69630}{}$$
$$+ (5.83X-9.94)(P/F_{19.84,3})\overset{0.58102}{}$$

Either the constant dollar or escalated dollar present worth equation simplifies as follows:

$0 = -100 + 11.389X - 18.8569;\quad 118.8569 = 11.389X$

Escalated Dollar Selling Price X = $10.44 per unit in year 1.

X(1.1) = $11.48 per unit in year 2

X(1.1)(1.06) = $12.17 per unit in year 3.

CHAPTER 5 PROBLEM SOLUTIONS

5-9 Solution: Reclamation Cost, Escrow Fund Analysis
All Values in Thousands

Let X equal the annual reclamation costs in years 27 through 56, therefore:

$$1,000 = X(P/A_{5\%,30})(P/F_{5\%,26})$$
$$\;\;\;\;\;\;15.372\;\;\;\;\;\;0.2812$$

$$1,000 = X(4.3226), \text{ therefore } X = \$231.34$$

Since the problem statement indicated that the escrowed dollars today are to be invested in 9.0% U.S. Treasury Bonds, we need to discount the future reclamation costs at the 9.0% rate in order to determine the dollars to be invested today.

$$231.34(P/A_{9\%,30})(P/F_{9\%,26}) = \$252.89$$
$$10.274\;\;\;\;\;\;0.1064$$

$252,890 is the total amount of 9.0% bonds to be purchased today, to cover anticipated reclamation costs over 30 years, beginning 27 years from today.

CHAPTER 6 PROBLEM SOLUTIONS

6-1 Solution:

a) Expected Value = $(1/38)(\$35)-(37/38)(\$1) = -\$0.0526$
b) EV = $(2/38)(\$17)-(36/38)(\$1) = -\$0.0526$
c) EV = $(4/38)(\$8)-(34/38)(\$1) = -\$0.0526$
d) EV = $(18/38)(\$1)-(20/38)(\$1) = -\$0.0526$

6-2 Solution:

Expected Cost = $0.10(5,000)+0.30(8,000)+0.40(10,000)+0.20(14,000)$
              = $500 + 2,400 + 4,000 + 2,800$
              = $\$9,700$

6-3 Solution:

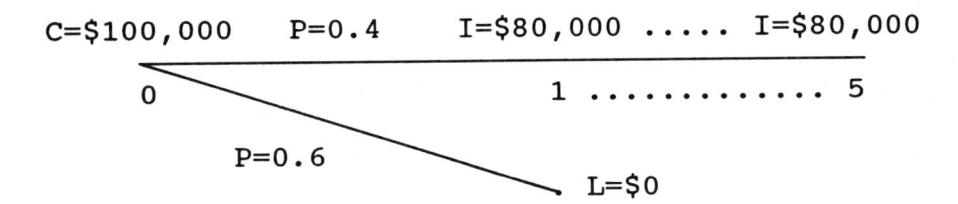

```
C=$100,000   P=0.4    I=$80,000 ..... I=$80,000
     |_____|_____|
     0                1 ........... 5
              P=0.6
                       L=$0
```

Expected NPV = $\$80,000(P/A_{20,5})(0.4) - \$100,000 = -\$4,288$, reject

(2.991)

Alternative Solution:

Expected NPV = $[\$80,000(P/A_{20,5}) - \$100,000](0.4) - \$100,000(0.6)$

= $-\$4,288$, reject

Expected ROR is the "i" value that makes Expected NPV = 0

Expected PW Eq: $0 = \$80,000(P/A_{i,5})(0.4) - \$100,000$

By trial and error, i = Expected ROR = 18.3% < i^* of 20%, reject

6-4 Solution:
There are 8 possible combinations of winning and losing teams for 3 games. The bettor wins on only 1 of these outcomes.

EV = $(1/8)(\$25-\$5)-(7/8)(\$5) = -\$1.875$

Over the long run, for many repeated bets of this type the bettor would lose an average of $1.875 for each $5 bet placed.

CHAPTER 6 PROBLEM SOLUTIONS

6-5 Solution: All Values in Thousands of Dollars

Expected cash flow year 1 = 0.4(25) + 0.6(18) = 20.80
"   "   "   " 2 = 0.5(30) + 0.5(20) = 25.00
"   "   "   " 3 = 0.7(35) + 0.3(25) = 32.00

$$\text{ENPV} = 20.80(P/F_{15,1})^{0.8696} + 25.00(P/F_{15,2})^{0.7561} + 32.00(P/F_{15,3})^{0.6575} - 50 = +8.03$$

6-6 Solution: Breakeven Research Cost Analysis (All Values in Dollars)

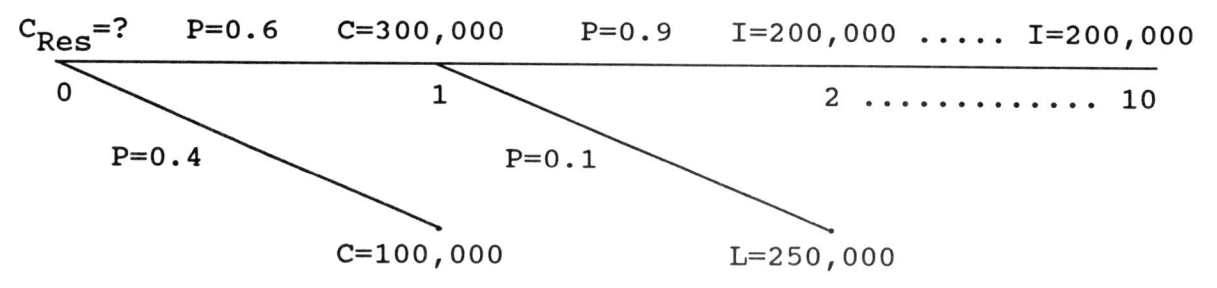

```
C_Res=?   P=0.6    C=300,000   P=0.9   I=200,000 ..... I=200,000
────────────────────────────────────────────────────────────────
0                    1                    2 ............ 10
     P=0.4                P=0.1
         C=100,000            L=250,000
```

$$\text{ENPV} = 200{,}000(P/A_{25,9})^{3.463}(0.9)(P/F_{25,1})(0.6) - 300{,}000(P/F_{25,1})^{0.8000}(0.6)$$

$$+ 250{,}000(P/F_{25,2})^{0.6400}(0.1)(0.6) - 100{,}000(P/F_{25,1})^{0.8000}(0.4)$$

= +$132,800 = maximum acceptable time zero research cost.

Alternate Time Diagram (Risk-Adjusted Net Cost and Net Income):

This approach builds all risk into the cash flows before applying time value of money considerations as follows:

```
           C=300,000(.6)  I=200,000(.9)(.6)
           C=100,000(.4)  L=250,000(.1)(.6)   I=200,000(.9)(.6) ......
C_Res=?   Net C=220,000   Net I=123,000      Net I=108,000 ... Net I=108,000
─────────────────────────────────────────────────────────────────────────
0              1                2                  3 ............ 10
```

$$\text{ENPV} = [108{,}000(P/A_{25,8})(P/F_{25,2}) + 123{,}000(P/F_{25,2}) - 220(P/F_{25,1})]$$

= +$132,800 = maximum acceptable time zero research cost.

Neglecting risk of failure gives the following risk free NPV:

The risk-free analysis is based on assuming 100% certainty that the project will be successful and follow the top branch of the time diagram (decision tree) through year 10.

$$\text{NPV} = [200{,}000(P/A_{25,9})^{3.463} - 300{,}000](P/F_{25,1})^{0.8000} = \$314{,}080$$

= $314,080 is the risk free maximum time zero research cost

6-7 Solution: Expected Net Present Value

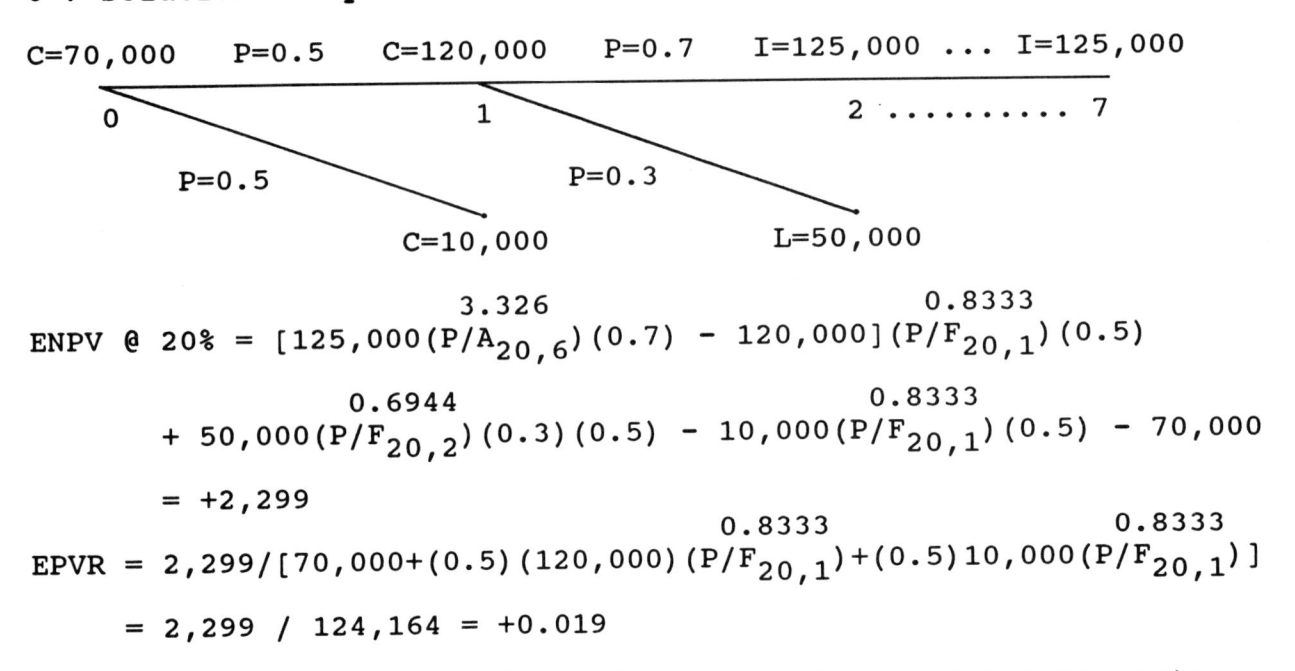

```
C=70,000    P=0.5   C=120,000    P=0.7   I=125,000 ... I=125,000
─────────────────────────────────────────────────────────────────
    0                   1                    2 ......... 7
            P=0.5               P=0.3
                    C=10,000            L=50,000
```

$$\text{ENPV @ 20\%} = [125{,}000(P/A_{20,6})\overset{3.326}{}(0.7) - 120{,}000](P/F_{20,1})\overset{0.8333}{}(0.5)$$

$$+ 50{,}000(P/F_{20,2})\overset{0.6944}{}(0.3)(0.5) - 10{,}000(P/F_{20,1})\overset{0.8333}{}(0.5) - 70{,}000$$

$$= +2{,}299$$

$$\text{EPVR} = 2{,}299/[70{,}000 + (0.5)(120{,}000)(P/F_{20,1})\overset{0.8333}{} + (0.5)10{,}000(P/F_{20,1})\overset{0.8333}{}]$$

$$= 2{,}299 / 124{,}164 = +0.019$$

Alternate Time Diagram (Risk-Adjusted Net Cost and Net Income):

This approach builds all risk into the cash flows before applying time value of money considerations as follows:

```
             C=120,000(.5)    I=125,000(.7)(.5)
             C=10,000(.5)     I=50,000(.3)(.5)   I=125,000(.7)(.5) ...
C=70,000     Net C=65,000     Net I=51,250       Net I=43,750 ... Net I=43,750
─────────────────────────────────────────────────────────────────────────────
   0              1                 2                  3 ............ 7
```

$$\text{ENPV} = -70{,}000 - 65{,}000(P/F_{20,1}) + 51{,}250(P/F_{20,2})$$

$$+ 43{,}750(P/A_{20,5})(P/F_{20,2}) = +2{,}299$$

Risk Free Analysis:

The risk free analysis is based on assuming 100% certainty that the project will be successful and follow the top branch of the time diagram (decision tree) through year 7.

$$\text{Risk Free NPV @ 20\%} = [125{,}000(P/A_{20,6})\overset{3.326}{} - 120{,}000](P/F_{20,1})\overset{0.8333}{} - 70{,}000$$

$$= +176{,}448$$

Risk Free Rate of Return = 50.7% (by financial calculator)

CHAPTER 6 PROBLEM SOLUTIONS

6-8 Solution: All Values in Thousands of Dollars

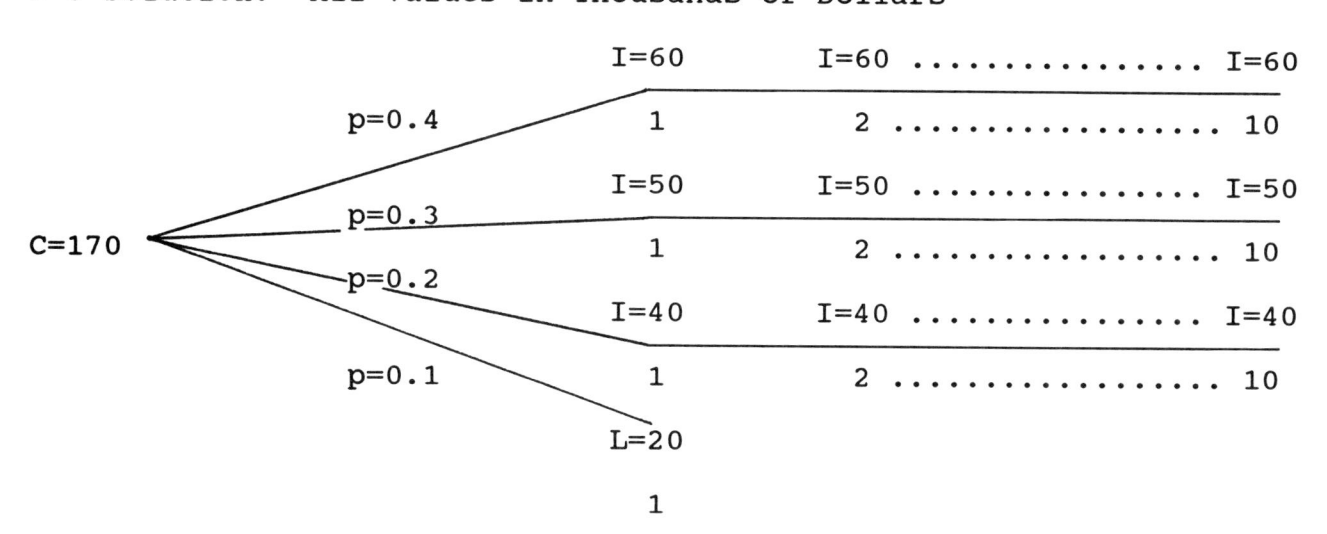

```
                        I=60      I=60 ............ I=60
              p=0.4  ─────────────────────────────────
                        1         2   ............. 10
                        I=50      I=50 ............ I=50
              p=0.3  ─────────────────────────────────
C=170                   1         2   ............. 10
              p=0.2     I=40      I=40 ............ I=40
                     ─────────────────────────────────
                        1         2   ............. 10
              p=0.1
                        L=20
                        1
```

$$\text{ENPV} = 60(P/A_{20,10})(0.4) + 50(P/A_{20,10})(0.3) + 40(P/A_{20,10})(0.20)$$

$$+ 20(P/F_{20,1})(0.1) - 170$$

$$= [60(0.4) + 50(0.3) + 40(0.2)](P/A_{20,10}) + 20(P/F_{20,1})(0.1) - 170$$

$$\overset{4.192}{} \overset{0.8333}{}$$

$$= [24+15+8](P/A_{20,10}) + 20(P/F_{20,1})(0.1) - 170$$

$$= \underline{+28.69} > 0, \text{ so satisfactory.}$$

Expected ROR is the i value that makes the ENPV Equation = 0.
By trial and error, EROR = <u>24.9%</u> > i* = 20%, so satisfactory.

6-9 Solution: All Values in Millions of Dollars

Sell Now for $1.0 = NPV_{Sell}$, or Develop for Following Cash Flows:

```
   CF=-1.5    P=0.6    1.0     1.8     1.2     0.8     0.4
   ──────────────────────────────────────────────────────
      0                 1       2       3       4       5
             P=0.4
                        0
```

$$\overset{0.8333}{} \overset{0.6944}{} \overset{0.5787}{}$$
$$\text{ENPV}_{\text{Develop}} = -1.5 + [1.0(P/F_{20,1}) + 1.8(P/F_{20,2}) + 1.2(P/F_{20,3})$$

$$\overset{0.4823}{} \overset{0.4019}{}$$
$$+ (0.8)(P/F_{20,4}) + (0.4)(P/F_{20,5})](0.6)$$

$$= +\$0.49 < \text{NPV}_{\text{Sell}} = +\$1.0 \quad \text{Therefore, select sell.}$$

68 Economic Evaluation and Investment Decision Methods

6-10 Solution: Mutually Exclusive Alternatives, All Values in Millions of Dollars

```
          C=20
   C=10   R= 6    R=12    R=12    R=12           R=12
A) ─────────────────────────────────────────────────────
    0      1       2       3       4   ......    10
```

```
                          C=30
    -      -     C=15    R= 9    R=18    R=18    R=18    R=18
B) ──────────────────────────────────────────────────────────
    0      1      2       3       4   ......    10      11      12
```

```
   C=10   C=14   R=27    R=33    C= 6    C= 6    C=18    C=18
A-B) ────────────────────────────────────────────────────────
    0      1      2       3       4   ......    10      11      12
```

Case A 100% Probability of Success Solutions:

$$\text{NPV}_A \ @ \ 20\% = -10 - 14(P/F_{20,1})^{.8333} + 12(P/A_{20,9})^{4.031}(P/F_{20,1})^{.8333} = +18.64$$

$$\text{NPV}_B \ @ \ 20\% = [(18(P/A_{20,9})^{4.031} - 21)(P/F_{20,1})^{.8333} - 15](P/F_{20,2})^{.6944} = +19.42, \text{Select B}$$

For mutually exclusive alternatives, select largest NPV which is alternative B. This is verified using incremental analysis.

$\text{NPV}_A - \text{NPV}_B = 18.64 - 19.42 = -0.78$, so reject A and select B.

$\text{PVR}_A = 18.64 \ / \ [10 + 14(P/F_{20,1})] = +0.86$

$\text{PVR}_B = 19.42 \ / \ [15(P/F_{20,2}) + 21(P/F_{20,3})] = +0.86$

$\text{PVR}_{A-B} = (18.64-19.42) \ / \ [10 + 14(P/F_{20,1})] = -0.04$, reject A, select B

Case B Expected Value Analysis:

$$\text{ENPV}_A \ @ \ 20\% = -10 + [-14(P/F_{20,1})^{.8333} + 12(P/A_{20,9})^{4.031}(P/F_{20,1})^{.8333}](0.6) = +7.18$$

$$\text{ENPV}_B \ @ \ 20\% = [(18(P/A_{20,9})^{4.031} - 21)(P/F_{20,1})^{.8333}(0.8) - 15](P/F_{20,2})^{.6944} = +13.4$$

$\text{EPVR}_A = 7.18 \ / \ [10 + 14(P/F_{20,1})(0.6)] = +0.42$

$\text{EPVR}_B = 13.45 \ / \ [15(P/F_{20,2}) + 21(P/F_{20,3})(0.8)] = +0.67$

$\text{EPVR}_{A-B} = (7.18-13.45) \ / \ [10 + 14(P/F_{20,1})(0.6)] = -0.37$, Select B

CHAPTER 6 PROBLEM SOLUTIONS

6-11 Solution: Breakeven Sales Price Analysis, Values in Thousands of Dollars

```
                    R=5X       R=5.5X=5X(F/P_10,1)     R=5.83X=5X(F/P_10,1)(F/P_6,1)
C=100    P=0.7      OC=8       OC=9.2=8(F/P_15,1)      OC=9.94=8(F/P_15,1)(F/P_8,1)
─────────────────────────────────────────────────────────────────────────────
0           1                    2                           3
    P=0.3
         ╲  CF=$0
```

Constant $ PW Eq:

$0 = -100 + [(5X-8)(P/F_{7,1})(P/F_{12,1}) + (5.5X-9.2)(P/F_{7,2})(P/F_{12,2})$
$\quad + (5.83X-9.94)(P/F_{7,3})(P/F_{12,3})](0.70)$

To work in escalated dollars, calculate i* that is equivalent to i*' of 12.0% as follows:

$(1+i) = (1+f)(1+i')$ so i* = 19.84%, is equivalent to i*' = 12%
for inflation of 7% per year.

Escalated $ PW Eq:

$$0 = -100 + [(5X-8)\overset{.83445}{(P/F_{19.84,1})} + (5.5X-9.2)\overset{.69630}{(P/F_{19.84,2})}$$
$$+ (5.83X-9.94)\overset{.58102}{(P/F_{19.84,3})}](0.70)$$

For either approach the constant dollar or escalated dollar present worth equation simplifies to the following:

$0 = -100 + [11.389X - 18.8569](0.70)$

$113.19 = 7.9723X$

Escalated Dollar Selling Price X = $14.20 per unit in year 1.

X(1.1) = $15.62 per unit in year 2.

X(1.1)(1.06) = $16.56 per unit in year 3.

CHAPTER 7 PROBLEM SOLUTIONS

7-1 Solution: Modified ACRS and Straight Line Depreciation Using the Half-Year Convention (All Dollar Values in Thousands).

Period	200% DB Switching to St Line		Straight Line Depreciation	
Yr 1	(2,000)(2/7)(.5)	= 285.7	2,000(1/7)(.5)	= 142.9
Yr 2	(2,000-285.7)(2/7)	= 489.8	2,000(1/7)	= 285.7
Yr 3	(1,714.3-489.8)(2/7)	= 349.9	2,000(1/7)	= 285.7
Yr 4	(1,224.5-349.9)(2/7)	= 249.9	2,000(1/7)	= 285.7
Yr 5	(874.6-249.9)(1/3.5)	= 178.5*	2,000(1/7)	= 285.7
Yr 6	(624.7)(1/3.5)	= 178.5	2,000(1/7)	= 285.7
Yr 7	(624.7)(1/3.5)	= 178.5	2,000(1/7)	= 285.7
Yr 8	(624.7)(1/3.5)(.5)	= 89.2	2,000(1/7)(.5)	= 142.9

Total Cumulative Depreciation $2,000.0 $2,000.0

* Switch in the year you get equal or more depreciation with straight line than you would get by continuing with 200% double declining balance.

Alternatively, you could also calculate the depreciation using modified ACRS rates from Table 7-3 on page 295 of the text. Some roundoff error does exist due to the number of decimals carried in the table.

Using Table 7-3

Period	Modified ACRS Depreciation	
Yr 1	2,000(0.1429)	= 285.8
Yr 2	2,000(0.2449)	= 489.8
Yr 3	2,000(0.1749)	= 349.8
Yr 4	2,000(0.1249)	= 249.8
Yr 5	2,000(0.0893)	= 178.6
Yr 6	2,000(0.0892)	= 178.4
Yr 7	2,000(0.0893)	= 178.6
Yr 8	2,000(0.0446)	= 89.2

Total Cumulative Deprec. $2,000.0

7-2 Solution: Units of Production Depreciation in Thousands of Dollars

Period	Modified ACRS Depreciation	
Yr 1	(100)(30/120)	= 25.0
Yr 2	(100)(30/120)	= 25.0
Yr 3	(100)(20/120)	= 16.7
Yr 4	(100)(10/120)	= 8.3
Yr 5	(100)(10/120)	= 8.3
Yr 6	(100)(10/120)	= 8.3
Yr 7	(100)(10/120)	= 8.3

Total Cumulative Deprec.   100.0 Within Roundoff

CHAPTER 7 PROBLEM SOLUTIONS

7-3 Solution: Modified ACRS and Straight Line Depreciation Using the Mid-Quarter Convention With Dollar Amounts in Thousands.

Modified ACRS Depreciation

Yr	Light Trucks, Purchased, 1st Qtr		R&D Equipment Purchased, 4th Qtr	
1	(100.0)(2/5)(10.5/12)	= 35.0	(500.0)(2/5)(1.5/12)	= 25.0
2	(100.0-35.0)(2/5)	= 26.0	(500.0-25.0)(2/5)	= 190.0
3	(65.0-26.0)(2/5)	= 15.6	(475.0-190.0)(2/5)	= 114.0
4	(39.0-15.6)(1/2.125)	= 11.0*	(285.0-114.0)(2/5)	= 68.4
5	(39.0-15.6)(1/2.125)	= 11.0	(171.0-68.4)(1/1.875)	= 54.7
6	(23.5)(1/2.125)(1.5/12)	= 1.4	(102.6)(1/1.875)(10.5/12)	= 47.9

Total Cumulative Deprec. $100.0 $500.0

* Switch in the year you get equal or more depreciation with straight line than you would by continuing with 200% double declining balance.

Straight Line Depreciation

Yr	Light Trucks, Purchased, 1st Qtr		R&D Equipment Purchased, 4th Qtr	
1	(100.0)(1/5)(10.5/12)	= 17.5	(500.0)(1/5)(1.5/12)	= 12.5
2	(100.0)(1/5)	= 20.0	(500.0)(1/5)	= 100.0
3	(100.0)(1/5)	= 20.0	(500.0)(1/5)	= 100.0
4	(100.0)(1/5)	= 20.0	(500.0)(1/5)	= 100.0
5	(100.0)(1/5)	= 20.0	(500.0)(1/5)	= 100.0
6	(100.0)(1/5)(1.5/12)	= 2.5	(500.0)(1/5)(10.5/12)	= 87.5

Total Cumulative Deprec. $100.0 $500.0

7-4 Solution: Depreciable Residential Rental Real Property

Straight Line Depreciation

Year	1	$800,000(1/27.5)(9.5/12)	= $23,030.3
Year	2-27	$800,000(1/27.5)	= $29,090.9
Year	28*	$800,000(1/27.5)(8.5/12)	= $20,606.1

Cumulative Depreciation $800,000.0   Within Roundoff

* The Ratio of 8.5/12 in year 28 occurs because in the first year we generated 9.5 out of 12 months depreciation which left 2.5 months to be depreciated, plus there was half a year on the 27.5 year rate remaining, therefore, 2.5 months + 6 months = 8.5 months.

7-5 Solution: Petroleum Property Evaluation - Project Cash Flows

Year	0	1
Min Rts Acq Cost	500,000	
Intangible (IDC)	1,334,000	
Tangible Equip.	1,050,000	
Production (Bbls)		200,000
Selling Price ($/Bbl)		18.00
Operating Cost		200,000

Independent Producer (less than 1,000 Bbl/day average production)

Year	Time 0	1	Time 0 (Integrated)	1
Production		200,000		200,000
Gross Revenue		3,600,000		3,600,000
-Royalties (16%)		-576,000		-576,000
Net Revenue		3,024,000		3,024,000
-Operating Costs		-200,000		-200,000
-IDC	-1,334,000		-933,800	
-Depreciation		-150,000		-150,000
-Amortization			-80,040	-80,040
Taxable Before Depln	-1,334,000	2,674,000	-1,013,840	2,593,960
-100% Limit		2,674,000		n/a
-Percentage Depletion		-453,600		n/a
-Cost Depletion		100,000		-100,000
-Loss Forward		-1,334,000		-1,013,840
Taxable Income	-1,334,000	886,400	-1,013,840	1,480,120
-Tax Due @ 40%		-354,560		-592,048
Net Income	-1,334,000	531,840	-1,013,840	888,072
+Depreciation		150,000		150,000
+Depletion Taken		453,600		100,000
+Amortization			80,040	80,040
+Loss Forward		1,334,000		1,013,840
-Capital Costs	-1,550,000		-1,950,200	
Cash Flow	-2,884,000	2,469,440	-2,884,000	2,231,952

Depreciation ($1,050,000)(0.1429) = $150,000

Petroleum 100% Percentage Depletion Limit = $2,674,000(1.0) = $2,674,000
Percentage Depletion = 0.15($3,024,000) = $453,600 (Independent Only)
Cost Depletion = ($500,000)(200,000/1,000,000) = $100,000

If no other income exists, losses (negative taxable income) must be carried forward and used against project income in later years. This loss forward deduction is a non-cash deduction similar to depreciation, depletion and amortization so it is added back to net income in determining project cash flow.

Capital Costs Independent Producer - $500,000 Mineral Rights Acq and the Tangible Completion cost of $1,050,000. For the Integrated Producer, capital costs include 30% of amortized IDCs ($1,334,000)(.3) = $400,200.

CHAPTER 7 PROBLEM SOLUTIONS

7-6 Solution: Mineral Property Cash Flow Calculations, Corporate Mineral Investor

Year	0	1
Min Rts Acq Cost	500,000	
Development	1,334,000	
Mining Equipment	1,050,000	
Production (Tons Ore)		200,000
Selling Price ($/Ton)		18.00
Operating Cost		200,000

Year	Time 0	1
Production		200,000
Gross Revenue		3,600,000
-Royalties (16%)		-576,000
Net Revenue		3,024,000
-Operating Costs		-200,000
-Development	-933,800	
-Depreciation		-150,000
-Amortization	-80,040	-80,040
Taxable Before Depln	-1,013,840	2,593,960
-50% Limit		1,296,980
-Percentage Depletion		-453,600
-Cost Depletion		100,000
-Loss Forward		-1,013,840
Taxable Income	-1,013,840	1,126,520
-Tax Due @ 40%		-450,608
Net Income	-1,013,840	675,912
+Depreciation		150,000
+Amortization	80,040	80,040
+Depletion Taken		453,600
+Loss Forward		1,013,840
-Capital Costs	-1,950,200	
Cash Flow	-2,884,000	2,373,392

Depreciation ($1,050,000)(0.1429) = $150,000

Mining 50% Percentage Depletion Limit = 2,593,960(0.5) = $1,296,980
Percentage Depletion = 0.15(3,024,000) = $453,600
Cost Depletion = (500,000)(200,000/1,000,000) = $100,000

If no other income exists, losses (negative taxable income) must be carried forward and used against project income in later years. This loss forward deduction is a non-cash deduction similar to depreciation, depletion and amortization so it is added back to net income in determining project cash flow.

Capital Costs = $500,000 Mineral Rights Acquisition, the Mine Equipment cost of $1,050,000 and 30% of Development that is amortized ($1,334,000)(0.3) = $400,200 over sixty months.

7-7 Solution: Gold Property, Individual Investor
All Values in Thousands of Dollars

Development Cost	500					
Acquisition Cost	600					
Mining Equipment Cost	1,000					
Revenues		2,400	2,700	3,000	3,300	3,600
Operating Costs		900	1,000	1,100	1,200	1,300
Year	0	1	2	3	4	5

Cash Flow Calculations

Year	0	1	2	3	4	5
Net Revenue		2,400	2,700	3,000	3,300	3,600
−Operating Costs		−900	−1,000	−1,100	−1,200	−1,300
−Depreciation		−143	−245	−175	−125	−89
−Depreciation Writeoff						−223
−Development	−500					
Taxable Before Depln	−500	1,357	1,455	1,725	1,975	1,988
−50% Limit		678	727	862	987	994
−Percentage Depln (15%)		−360	−405	−450	−495	−540
−Cost Depletion		120	60			
−Loss Forward		−500				
Taxable Income	−500	497	1,050	1,275	1,480	1,448
−Tax @ 40%		−199	−420	−510	−592	−579
Net Income	−500	298	630	765	888	869
+Depreciation		143	245	175	125	89
+Deprec Writeoff						223
+Depletion Taken		360	405	450	495	540
+Loss Forward		500				
−Capital Costs	−1,600					
Cash Flow	−2,100	1,301	1,280	1,390	1,508	1,721

Depreciation was taken on the $1,000,000 equipment cost using Table 7-3 and rounding off the decimal places:
  Yr 1   1,000(0.1429) = 143
  Yr 2   1,000(0.2449) = 245 etc.
Cost depletion calculations follow:
  Yr 1   (600)(20/100)   = 120
  Yr 2   (600−360)(20/80) = 60
  Yr 3   (240−405) < 0, stop cost depletion calculations
Capital Costs include the $1,000,000 equipment and the $600,000 mineral rights acquisition cost.

DCFROR Calculation:

PW Eq: $= 0 = -2,100 + 1,301(P/F_{i,1}) + 1,280(P/F_{i,2}) + 1,390(P/F_{i,3})$

$+ 1,508(P/F_{i,4}) + 1,721(P/F_{i,5})$

$i = 58.2\%$

7-7 Solution: Gold Property, Corporate Investor
All Values in Thousands of Dollars

Development Cost	500					
Acquisition Cost	600					
Mining Equipment Cost	1,000					
Revenues		2,400	2,700	3,000	3,300	3,600
Operating Costs		900	1,000	1,100	1,200	1,300

Year	0	1	2	3	4	5
Net Revenue		2,400	2,700	3,000	3,300	3,600
-Operating Costs		-900	-1,000	-1,100	-1,200	-1,300
-Depreciation		-143	-245	-175	-125	-89
-Depreciation Writeoff						-223
-Development	-350					
-Amortization	-30	-30	-30	-30	-30	
Taxable Before Depln	-380	1,327	1,425	1,695	1,945	1,988
-50% Limit		664	713	848	973	994
-Percentage Depln (15%)		-360	-405	-450	-495	-540
-Cost Depletion		120	60			
-Loss Forward		-380				
Taxable Income	-380	587	1,020	1,245	1,450	1,448
-Tax @ 40%		-235	-408	-498	-580	-579
Net Income	-380	352	612	747	870	869
+Depreciation		143	245	175	125	89
+Depreciation Writeoff						223
+Depletion Taken		360	405	450	495	540
+Amortization	30	30	30	30	30	
+Loss Forward		380				
-Capital Costs	-1,750					
Cash Flow	-2,100	1,265	1,292	1,402	1,520	1,721

Depreciation was taken on the $1,000,000 equipment cost using Table 7-3 and rounding off the decimal places:
  Yr 1   1,000(0.1429) = 143
  Yr 2   1,000(0.2449) = 245   etc...
Amortization: 500(0.30) = 150(12/60) = 30 per year
Cost depletion calculations follow:
  Yr 1   (600)(20/100)   = 120
  Yr 2   (600-360)(20/80) = 60
  Yr 3   (240-405) < 0, stop cost depletion calculations
Capital Costs include the $1,000,000 equipment, $600,000 mineral rights acquisition cost and 30% of development ($500,000)(0.3) = $150,000.

DCFROR Calculation:
PW Eq: = 0 = -2,100 + 1,265(P/F$_{i,1}$) + 1,292(P/F$_{i,2}$) + 1,402(P/F$_{i,3}$)

   + 1,520(P/F$_{i,4}$) + 1,721(P/F$_{i,5}$)

  i = 57.7% by trial and error

7-8 Solution: Processing Project
Values in Thousands of Dollars & Gallons

Patent Cost	2,000			
Equipment Cost	3,000			
Res. & Dev. Cost	1,500			
Revenues		5,000	5,500	6,000
Operating Costs		3,000	3,300	3,600
Production (gallons)		500	500	500

Cash Flow Calculations

Year	0	1	2	3
Gross Revenue		5,000	5,500	6,000
−Royalties		−500	−550	−600
−Operating Cost		−3,000	−3,300	−3,600
−Development	−1,500			
−Depreciation*		−429	−735	−525
−Amortization	−200	−400	−400	−400
−Loss Forward		−1,700	−1,029	−513
Taxable Income	−1,700	−1,029	−513	362
−Tax Due @ 40%	0	0	0	−145
Net Income	−1,700	−1,029	−513	217
+Depreciation		429	735	525
+Amortization	200	400	400	400
+Write Off				
+Loss Forward		1,700	1,029	513
−Capital Costs**	−5,000			
Cash Flow	−6,500	1,500	1,650	1,655

*Depreciation Calculated Using Table 7-3:

    Yr 1: 3,000(0.1429) = 429
    Yr 2: 3,000(0.2449) = 735   No writeoff was asked for in the problem
    Yr 3: 3,000(0.1749) = 525   so it is neglected in year 3 cash flows.

**Capital Cost Includes $2,000 Mineral Rights Acquisition, and $3,000 Depreciable Equipment.

CHAPTER 7 PROBLEM SOLUTIONS

7-9 Solution: Mining Project, Values in Thousands of Dollars & Tons
Case A, Corporation

Acquisition Cost	2,000			
Equipment Cost	3,000			
Development Cost	1,500			
Revenues		5,000	5,500	6,000
Operating Costs		3,000	3,300	3,600
Total Reserves(tons)	5,000			
Production (tons)		500	500	500

Cash Flow Calculations

Year	0	1	2	3
Gross Revenue		5,000	5,500	6,000
-Royalties		-500	-550	-600
Net Revenue		4,500	4,950	5,400
-Operating Cost		-3,000	-3,300	-3,600
-Development	-1,050			
-Depreciation*		-429	-735	-525
-Amortization**	-45	-90	-90	-90
Before Depletion	-1,095	981	825	1,185
-50% Limit		-491	-413	-593
-Percent Depln(15%)		675	742	810
-Cost Depletion***		200	168	137
-Loss Forward		-1,095	-605	-193
Taxable Income	-1,095	-605	-193	399
-Tax Due @ 40%	0	0	0	-160
Net Income	-1,095	-605	-193	239
+Depreciation		429	735	525
+Depletion Taken		491	413	593
+Amortization	45	90	90	90
+Loss Forward		1,095	605	193
-Capital Costs****	-5,450			
Cash Flow	-6,500	1,500	1,650	1,640

*Depreciation Calculated Using Table 7-3 in Text:
Yr 1   3,000(0.1429) = 429
Yr 2   3,000(0.2449) = 735   No writeoff was asked for in the problem
Yr 3   3,000(0.1749) = 525   so it is neglected in year 3 cash flows.

**Amortization Calculations on   ***Cost Depletion Calculations:
30% of Mine Develop=0.3(1,500):
Yr 1   450(6/60) = 45   Yr 1 (2,000)(500/5,000)   = 200
Yr 2   450(12/60) = 90   Yr 2 (2,000-491)(500/4,500) = 168
Yr 3   450(12/60) = 90   Yr 3 (1,509-413)(500/4,000) = 137

****Capital Cost Includes $2,000 Mineral Rights Acquisition,
$3,000 Depreciable Equipment, and 30% of Development Cost $450.

7-9 Solution: Mining Project, Values in Thousands of Dollars & Tons
Case B, Individual

Acquisition Cost	2,000			
Equipment Cost	3,000			
Development Cost	1,500			
Revenues		5,000	5,500	6,000
Operating Costs		3,000	3,300	3,600
Total Reserves (tons)	5,000			
Production (tons)		500	500	500

Cash Flow Calculations

Year	0	1	2	3
Gross Revenue		5,000	5,500	6,000
−Royalties		−500	−550	−600
Net Revenue		4,500	4,950	5,400
−Operating Cost		−3,000	−3,300	−3,600
−Development	−1,500			
−Depreciation*		−429	−735	−525
Before Depletion	−1,500	1,071	915	1,275
−50% Limit		−536	−458	−638
−Percent Depln (15%)		675	742	810
−Cost Depletion**		200	163	126
−Loss Forward		↗−1,500	↗−964	↗−507
Taxable Income	−1,500	−964	−507	131
−Tax Due @ 40%	0	0	0	−52
Net Income	−1,500	−964	−507	79
+Depreciation		429	735	525
+Depletion Taken		536	458	638
+Loss Forward		1,500	964	507
−Capital Costs***	−5,000			
Cash Flow	−6,500	1,500	1,650	1,749

*Depreciation Calculated Using Table 7-3:

    Yr 1   3,000(0.1429) = 429
    Yr 2   3,000(0.2449) = 735   No writeoff was asked for in the problem
    Yr 3   3,000(0.1749) = 525   so it is neglected in year 3 cash flows.

**Cost Depletion Calculations Follow:

    Yr 1   (2,000)(500/5,000)   = 200
    Yr 2   (2,000−536)(500/4,500)   = 163
    Yr 3   (1,454−458)(500/4,000)   = 126

***Capital Cost Includes $2,000 Mineral Rights Acquisition, and $3,000 Depreciable Equipment.

CHAPTER 7 PROBLEM SOLUTIONS

7-10 Solution: Petroleum Project in Thousands of Dollars & Barrels
Case A, Integrated Producer

Acquisition Cost	2,000			
Equipment Cost	3,000			
IDC	1,500			
Revenues		5,000	5,500	6,000
Operating Costs		3,000	3,300	3,600
Total Reserves(Bbl)	5,000			
Production (Bbl)		500	500	500

Cash Flow Calculations:

Year	0	1	2	3
Gross Revenue		5,000	5,500	6,000
-Royalties		-500	-550	-600
-Operating Cost		-3,000	-3,300	-3,600
-IDC	-1,050			
-Depreciation*		-429	-735	-525
-Amortization**	-45	-90	-90	-90
-Cost Depletion***		-200	-200	-200
-Loss Forward		-1,095	-314	
Taxable Income	-1,095	-314	312	985
-Tax Due @ 40%	0	0	-125	-394
Net Income	-1,095	-314	187	591
+Depreciation		429	735	525
+Cost Depletion		200	200	200
+Amortization	45	90	90	90
+Loss Forward		1,095	314	
-Capital Costs****	-5,450			
Cash Flow	-6,500	1,500	1,525	1,406

*Depreciation Calculated Using Table 7-3 in Text:
 Yr 1   3,000(0.1429) = 429
 Yr 2   3,000(0.2449) = 735   No writeoff was asked for in the problem
 Yr 3   3,000(0.1749) = 525   so it is neglected in year 3 cash flows.

**Amortization Calculations on   ***Cost Depletion Calculations:
   30% of IDC = 0.3(1500):
   Yr 1   450(6/60) = 45   Yr 1 (2,000)(500/5,000)   = 200
   Yr 2   450(12/60) = 90   Yr 2 (2,000-200)(500/4,500)   = 200
   Yr 3   450(12/60) = 90   Yr 3 (1,800-200)(500/4,000)   = 200

****Capital Cost Includes $2,000 Mineral Rights Acquisition,
    $3,000 Depreciable Equipment, and 30% of IDC or $450.

7-10 Solution: Petroleum Project in Thousands of Dollars & Barrels
Case B, Independent Producer < 1000 Bbl/day

Acquisition Cost	2,000			
Equipment Cost	3,000			
IDC	1,500			
Revenues		5,000	5,500	6,000
Operating Costs		3,000	3,300	3,600
Total Reserves(Bbl)	5,000			
Production (Bbl)		500	500	500

Cash Flow Calculations:

Year	0	1	2	3
Gross Revenue		5,000	5,500	6,000
-Royalties		-500	-550	-600
Net Revenue		4,500	4,950	5,400
-Operating Cost		-3,000	-3,300	-3,600
-IDC	-1,500			
-Depreciation*		-429	-735	-525
Before Depletion	-1,500	1,071	915	1,275
100% Limit		1,071	915	1,275
Percent Depln(15%)		-675	-743	-810
Cost Depletion**		200	147	73
-Loss Forward		-1,500	-1,104	-931
Taxable Income	-1,500	-1,104	-931	-466
-Tax Due @ 40%	0	0	0	186
Net Income	-1,500	-1,104	-931	-280
+Depreciation		429	735	525
+Depletion Taken		675	743	810
+Loss Forward		1,500	1,104	931
-Capital Costs***	-5,000			
Cash Flow	-6,500	1,500	1,650	1,986

*Depreciation Calculated Using Table 7-3 in Text:

Yr 1   3,000(0.1429) = 429
Yr 2   3,000(0.2449) = 735   No writeoff was asked for in the problem
Yr 3   3,000(0.1749) = 525   so it is neglected in year 3 cash flows.

**Cost Depletion Calculations:

Yr 1   (2,000)(500/5,000)   = 200
Yr 2   (2,000-675)(500/4,500)   = 147
Yr 3   (1,325-743)(500/4,000)   = 73

***Capital Cost Includes $2,000 Mineral Rights Acquisition, and $3,000 Depreciable Equipment.

CHAPTER 7 PROBLEM SOLUTIONS

7-10 Solution: Petroleum Project in Thousands of Dollars & Barrels
Case C, Independent Producer > 1000 Bbl/day

Acquisition Cost	2,000			
Equipment Cost	3,000			
IDC	1,500			
Revenues		5,000	5,500	6,000
Operating Costs		3,000	3,300	3,600
Total Reserves (Bbl)	5,000			
Production (Bbl)		500	500	500

Cash Flow Calculations:

Year	0	1	2	3
Gross Revenue		5,000	5,500	6,000
−Royalties		−500	−550	−600
Net Revenue		4,500	4,950	5,400
−Operating Cost		−3,000	−3,300	−3,600
−IDC	−1,500			
−Depreciation*		−429	−735	−525
−Cost Depletion**		−200	−200	−200
−Loss Forward		−1,500 ↗	−629 ↗	
Taxable Income	−1,500	−629	87	1,075
−Tax Due @ 40%	0	0	−35	−430
Net Income	−1,500	−629	52	645
+Depreciation		429	735	525
+Cost Depletion		200	200	200
+Loss Forward		1,500	629	
−Capital Costs***	−5,000			
Cash Flow	−6,500	1,500	1,615	1,370

*Depreciation Calculated Using Table 7-3 in Text:

Yr 1   3,000(0.1429) = 429
Yr 2   3,000(0.2449) = 735   No writeoff was asked for in the problem
Yr 3   3,000(0.1749) = 525   so it is neglected in year 3 cash flows.

**Cost Depletion Calculations:

Yr 1   (2,000)(500/5,000)   = 200
Yr 2   (2,000−200)(500/4,500)   = 200
Yr 3   (1,800−200)(500/4,000)   = 200

***Capital Cost Includes $2,000 Min Rights Acquisition, and $3,000 Depreciable Equipment.

7-11 Solution: Petroleum Project in Thousands of Dollars & Barrels
Case A, Integrated

Acquisition Cost	200					
Intangible Drilling	500					
Tangible Completion	400					
Revenues		700	600	500	400	300
Operating Costs		50	50	50	50	50
Reserves	200					
Production (bbl)		30	27	24	21	18

Year	0	1	2	3	4	5
Gross Revenue		700	600	500	400	300
-Royalties		-105	-90	-75	-60	-45
Net Revenue		595	510	425	340	255
-Operating Costs		-50	-50	-50	-50	-50
-Intangible	-350					
-Depreciation		-57	-98	-70	-50	-36
-Depr. Writeoff						-89
-Amortization	-15	-30	-30	-30	-30	-15
-Cost Depletion		-30	-27	-24	-21	-18
-Depln Writeoff						-80
-Loss Forward		-365				
Taxable Income	-365	63	305	251	189	-33
-Tax @ 40%		-25	-122	-100	-76	13
Net Income	-365	38	183	151	113	-20
+Depreciation		57	98	70	50	36
+Cost Depletion		30	27	24	21	18
+Writeoffs						169
+Amortization	15	30	30	30	30	15
+Loss Forward		365				
-Capital Costs*	-750					
Cash Flow	-1,100	520	338	275	214	218

Depreciation Calculations:
Yr 1: 400(0.1429) = 57
Yr 2: 400(0.2449) = 98
Yr 3: 400(0.1749) = 70
Yr 4: 400(0.1249) = 50
Yr 5: 400(0.0893) = 36
Writeoff: 400-311 = 89

Cost Depletion Calculations:
Yr 1: (200)(30/200)   = 30
Yr 2: (200-30)(27/170)   = 27
Yr 3: (170-27)(24/143)   = 24
Yr 4: (143-24)(21/119)   = 21
Yr 5: (119-21)(18/98)   = 18
Writeoff: 200-120   = 80

Amortization (30% of IDC):
Yr 0: 500(0.3)(6/60) = 15
Yr 1-4: 500(0.3)(12/60) = 30
Yr 5: 500(0.3)(6/60) = 15

*Capital Cost Includes
$200 Mineral Rights Acquisition,
$400 Tangible Depreciable Equipment,
and 30% of the $500 IDC ($150).

PW Eq: $0 = -1{,}100 + 520(P/F_{i,1}) + 338(P/F_{i,2}) + 275(P/F_{i,3}) + 214(P/F_{i,4}) + 218(P/F_{i,5})$

DCFROR = 15.9% (by financial calculator)

CHAPTER 7 PROBLEM SOLUTIONS

7-11 Solution: Petroleum Project in Thousands of Dollars & Barrels
Case B, Independent < 1,000 Bbl/day

Acquisition Cost	200						
Intangible Drilling	500						
Tangible Completion	400	700	600	500	300	300	
Revenues		50	50	50	50	50	
Operating Costs							
Reserves	200						
Production		30	27	24	21	18	

Year	0	1	2	3	4	5	Salv
Gross Revenue		700	600	500	400	300	
-Royalties		-105	-90	-75	-60	-45	
Net Revenue		595	510	425	340	255	
-Operating Costs		-50	-50	-50	-50	-50	
-Intangible	-500						
-Depreciation		-57	-98	-70	-50	-36	
-Depr. Writeoff							-89
Before Depln	-500	488	362	305	240	169	-89
-100% Limit		488	362	305	240	169	
-Percentage Depln		-89	-77	-64	-51	-38	
-Cost Depletion		30	18	6			
-Loss Forward		↗-500	↗-101				
Taxable Income	-500	-101	184	241	189	131	-89
-Tax @ 40%			-74	-97	-76	-52	36
Net Income	-500	-101	110	145	113	79	-53
+Depreciation		57	98	70	50	36	
+Writeoff							89
+Depletion Taken		89	77	64	51	38	
+Loss Forward		500	101				
-Capital Costs*	-600						
Cash Flow	-1,100	545	386	278	214	153	36

Depreciation Calculations:
Yr 1: 400(0.1429) = 57
Yr 2: 400(0.2449) = 98
Yr 3: 400(0.1749) = 70
Yr 4: 400(0.1249) = 50
Yr 5: 400(0.0893) = 36
Writeoff: 400-311 = 89

Cost Depletion Calculations:
Yr 1: (200)(30/200)   = 30
Yr 2: (200-89)(27/170)   = 18
Yr 3: (111-77)(24/143)   = 6
Yr 4: (34-64)(21/119) < 0

*Capital Cost Includes $200 Mineral Rights Acquisition, and $400 Tangible Depreciable Equipment.

PW Eq: $0 = -1,100 + 545(P/F_{i,1}) + 386(P/F_{i,2}) + 278(P/F_{i,3})$
$\qquad + 214(P/F_{i,4}) + 189(P/F_{i,5})$

DCFROR = 18.1%   (by financial calculator)

7-11 Solution: Petroleum Project in Thousands of Dollars & Barrels
Case C, Independent > 1,000 Bbl/day

Acquisition Cost	200					
Intangible Drilling	500					
Tangible Completion	400					
Revenues		700	600	500	300	300
Operating Costs		50	50	50	50	50
Reserves	200					
Production		30	27	24	21	18

Year	0	1	2	3	4	5
Gross Revenue		700	600	500	400	300
-Royalties		105	90	75	60	45
Net Revenue		595	510	425	340	255
-Operating Costs		-50	-50	-50	-50	-50
-IDC	-500					
-Depreciation		-57	-98	-70	-50	-36
-Depr. Writeoff						-89
-Cost Depletion		-30	-27	-24	-21	-18
-Depln Writeoff						-80
-Loss Forward		-500	-42			
Taxable Income	-500	-42	293	281	219	-18
-Tax Due @ 40%			-100	-96	-74	7
Net Income	-500	-42	193	185	145	-11
+Depreciation		57	98	70	50	36
+Cost Depletion		30	27	24	21	18
+Writeoffs						169
+Loss Forward		500	42			
-Capital Costs*	-600					
Cash Flow	-1,100	545	360	279	216	212

Depreciation Calculations:
Yr 1: 400(0.1429) = 57
Yr 2: 400(0.2449) = 98
Yr 3: 400(0.1749) = 70
Yr 4: 400(0.1249) = 50
Yr 5: 400(0.0893) = 36
Writeoff: 400-311 = 89

Cost Depletion Calculations:
Yr 1: (200)(30/200) = 30
Yr 2: (200-30)(27/170) = 27
Yr 3: (170-27)(24/143) = 24
Yr 4: (143-24)(21/119) = 21
Yr 5: (119-21)(18/98) = 18
Writeoff: 200-120 = 80

*Capital Cost Includes $200 Mineral Rights Acquisition, and $400 Tangible Depreciable Equipment.

PW Eq: $0 = -1,100 + 545(P/F_{i,1}) + 360(P/F_{i,2}) + 279(P/F_{i,3}) + 216(P/F_{i,4}) + 212(P/F_{i,5})$

DCFROR = 17.7%   (by financial calculator)

CHAPTER 7 PROBLEM SOLUTIONS

7-12 Solution: General Process Facility Evaluation
All Values in Thousands of Dollars

Patent Acquisition	600					
Research & Exper.	500					
Equipment	1,000					
Revenues		2,000 escalating 10% per yr ...				
Operating Costs		1,000 escalating 10% per yr ...				

Year	0	1	2	3	4	5	Salvage
Revenue		2,000	2,200	2,420	2,662	2,928	
-Operating Costs		-1,000	-1,100	-1,210	-1,331	-1,464	
-Research & Exper.	-500						
-Depreciation		-200	-320	-192	-115	-115	-58
-Amortization	-60	-120	-120	-120	-120	-60	
-Loss Forward		-560					
Taxable Income	-560	120	660	898	1,096	1,289	-58
-Tax Due @ 40%		-48	-264	-359	-438	-516	23
Net Income	-560	72	396	539	657	773	-35
+Depreciation		200	320	192	115	115	58
+Amortization	60	120	120	120	120	60	
+Loss Forward		560					
-Capital Costs	-1,600						
Cash Flow	-2,100	952	836	851	893	949	23
						972	

Revenue Calculations:
Yr 2 = 2,000(1.1) = 2,200
Yr 3 = 2,200(1.1) = 2,420 etc...

Operating Costs:
Yr 2 = 1,000(1.1) = 1,100
Yr 3 = 1,100(1.1) = 1,210 etc...

Research and Experimentation are expensed in the full amount in the year incurred. The problem statement assumes the patent had a remaining life of 5 years upon which amortization has been based. Assuming the patent cost was incurred in the middle of the tax year gives the following amortization:

Year 0 = (600)(6 months / 60 months) = 60
Year 1-4 = (600)(12 months / 60 months) = 120
Year 5 = (600)(6 months / 60 months) = 60

Depreciation of Equipment (Using MACRS Table 7-3, pg 295 in text):

Year 1 = 1,000(0.2000) = 200
Year 2 = 1,000(0.3200) = 320
Year 3 = 1,000(0.1920) = 192 etc...

DCFROR Analysis:

PW Eq: $0 = -2,100 + 952(P/F_{i,1}) + 836(P/F_{i,2}) + 851(P/F_{i,3})$
$+ 893(P/F_{i,4}) + 972(P/F_{i,5})$

i = DCFROR = 32.2% by trial and error.

CHAPTER 8 PROBLEM SOLUTIONS

8-1 Solution: All Values in Dollars

Case A) Straight Line ACRS Depreciation, Half-Year Convention

```
Equipment Cost      20,000
Working Capital      2,000
Salvage (Including WC Return)                         14,000
Revenue                         35,000    35,000    35,000
Operating Costs                 25,000    25,000    25,000
```

Year	0	1	2	3

Depreciation Calculations (St Line, 5 Year With Half Year Convention)

```
Yr 1    20,000(1/5)(0.5) = 2,000,    Remaining Book Value = 18,000
Yr 2    20,000(1/5)      = 4,000,    Remaining Book Value = 14,000
Yr 3    20,000(1/5)      = 4,000,    Remaining Book Value = 10,000
```

Yr 3 Working Capital Book Value Equals Initial Cost of 2,000

Cash Flow Calculations

Year	0	1	2	3
Revenue		35,000	35,000	49,000*
-Operating Costs		-25,000	-25,000	-25,000
-Depreciation		-2,000	-4,000	-4,000
-Deprec Writeoff				-10,000
-Work Cap Writeoff				-2,000
Taxable Income		8,000	6,000	8,000
Tax @ 40%		-3,200	-2,400	-3,200
Net Income		4,800	3,600	4,800
+Depreciation		2,000	4,000	4,000
+Deprec Writeoff				10,000
+Work Cap Writeoff				2,000
-Capital Costs	-22,000**			
Cash Flow	-22,000	6,800	7,600	20,800

*Year 3 Revenue Includes Sale Value of 14,000

**Capital Costs include $20,000 for business equipment plus $2,000 for working capital.

PW Eq: $-22,000 + 6,800(P/F_{i,1}) + 7,600(P/F_{i,2}) + 20,800(P/F_{i,3})$

i = DCFROR = 22.3% by trial and error

CHAPTER 8 PROBLEM SOLUTIONS

8-1 Solution: Continued - All Values in Dollars

Case B) Modified ACRS Depreciation 5 Year Life, Half Year Convention

```
Equipment Cost      20,000
Working Capital      2,000
Salvage (Including WC Return)                           14,000
Revenue                         35,000   35,000   35,000
Operating Costs                 25,000   25,000   25,000
```

Year	0	1	2	3

MACRS Depreciation, 5 Year Life With Half Year Convention

```
Yr 1   20,000(0.200) = 4,000,   Remaining Book Value = 16,000
Yr 2   20,000(0.320) = 6,400,   Remaining Book Value =  9,600
Yr 3   20,000(0.192) = 3,840,   Remaining Book Value =  5,760
```

Yr 3 Working Capital Book Value Equals Initial Cost, or 2,000

Cash Flow Calculations

Year	0	1	2	3
Revenue		35,000	35,000	49,000*
-Operating Costs		-25,000	-25,000	-25,000
-Depreciation		-4,000	-6,400	-3,840
-Deprec Writeoff				-5,760
-Work Cap Writeoff				-2,000
Taxable Income		6,000	3,600	12,400
Tax @ 40%		-2,400	-1,440	-4,960
Net Income		3,600	2,160	7,440
+Depreciation		4,000	6,400	3,840
+Deprec Writeoff				5,760
+Work Cap Writeoff				2,000
-Capital Costs	-22,000**			
Cash Flow	-22,000	7,600	8,560	19,040

*Year 3 Revenue Includes Sale Value of 14,000

**Capital Costs include $20,000 for business equipment plus $2,000 for working capital.

PW Eq: $-22,000 + 7,600(P/F_{i,1}) + 8,560(P/F_{i,2}) + 19,040(P/F_{i,3})$

i = DCFROR = 23.2% by trial and error

8-2 Solution: All Values in Dollars

Case A) Expense R&D as an Operating Cost Against Other Income

```
Working Capital      50,000
Research & Exper    100,000 (Expense at year 0)
Working Capital Return Revenue              50,000
Sales Revenue                      500,000  500,000
Operating Costs                    400,000  400,000
```

| Year | 0 | 1-4 | 5 |

Cash Flow Calculations

Year	0	1-4	5
Sales/Year		500,000	550,000*
-Oper. Costs		-400,000	-400,000
-R&D as O.C.	-100,000		
-WC Writeoff			-50,000
Taxable Income	-100,000	100,000	100,000
Tax @ 40%	40,000	-40,000	-40,000
Net Income	-60,000	60,000	60,000
+WC Writeoff			50,000
-Capital Costs	-50,000		
Cash Flow	-110,000	60,000	110,000

*Year 5 Revenue includes working capital return.

A) PW Eq: $0 = -110{,}000 + 60{,}000(P/A_{i,4}) + 110{,}000(P/F_{i,5})$

i = DCFROR = 50.4%

CHAPTER 8 PROBLEM SOLUTIONS

8-2 Solution: Continued - All Values in Dollars

Case B) Expense R&D as an Operating Cost and Carry Forward to Use Against Project Income (Stand Alone)

```
Working Capital        50,000
Research & Exper      100,000
Working Capital Return Revenue                  50,000
Sales Revenue                    500,000       500,000
Operating Costs                  400,000       400,000
```

Year	0	1-4	5

Cash Flow Calculations

Year	0	1	2-4	5
Sales/Year		500,000	500,000	550,000*
-Op. Costs		-400,000	-400,000	-400,000
-R&D as O.C.	-100,000			
-WC Writeoff				-50,000
-Loss Forward		-100,000		
Taxable Income	-100,000	0	100,000	100,000
Tax @ 40%	0	0	-40,000	-40,000
Net Income	-100,000	0	60,000	60,000
+WC Writeoff				50,000
+Loss Forward		100,000		
-Capital Costs	-50,000			
Cash Flow	-150,000	100,000	60,000	110,000

*Year 5 Revenue includes working capital return.

B) PW Eq: $0 = -150{,}000 + 100{,}000(P/F_{i,1}) + 60{,}000(P/A_{i,3})(P/F_{i,1}) + 110{,}000(P/F_{i,5})$

$i = \text{DCFROR} = 44.1\%$

8-2 Solution: Case C) Capitalize R&D and Deduct by Amortization

Working Capital 50,000
Research & Exper 100,000
Working Capital Return Revenue   50,000
Sales Revenue   500,000 500,000
Operating Costs   400,000 400,000

Cash Flow Calculations:

	Year 0	Year 1-4	Year 5
Sales/Year		500,000	550,000*
-Oper. Costs		-400,000	-400,000
-Amortization		-20,000	-20,000
-WC Writeoff			-50,000
Taxable Income		80,000	80,000
Tax @ 40%		-32,000	-32,000
Net Income		48,000	48,000
+Amortization		20,000	20,000
+WC Writeoff			50,000
-Capital Costs	-150,000		
Cash Flow	-150,000	68,000	118,000

* Year 5 Revenue includes working capital return.

C) PW Eq: $0 = -150,000 + 68,000(P/A_{i,4}) + 118,000(P/F_{i,5})$

$i = \text{DCFROR} = 39.1\%$

Case D) Expense R&D, Deutschemark (DM) Analysis

Case D1): ($0.70 US/DM)(833,330 DM) = $583,333 US revenue per year
Case D2): ($0.50 US/DM)(833,330 DM) = $416,667 US revenue per year

Case D1) Cash Flows:

Year	0	1-4	5
Sales/yr	-	583,333	633,333
-Oper. Costs	-	-400,000	-400,000
-R&D	-100,000	-	-
-WC Writeoff	-	-	-50,000
Taxable Income	-100,000	-183,333	-183,333
-Tax @ 40%	+40,000	-73,333	-73,333
Net Income	-60,000	+110,000	+110,000
+WC Writeoff	-	-	+50,000
-Capital Costs	-50,000	-	-
Cash Flow	-110,000	+110,000	+160,000

Case D1 DCFROR = 98.2%

Case D2) Cash Flows:

Year	0	1-4	5
Sales/yr	-	416,667	466,667
-Oper. Costs	-	-400,000	-400,000
-R&D	-100,000	-	-
-WC Writeoff	-	-	-50,000
Taxable Income	-100,000	16,667	16,667
-Tax @ 40%	+40,000	-6,667	-6,667
Net Income	-60,000	+10,000	+10,000
+WC Writeoff	-	-	+50,000
-Capital Costs	-50,000	-	-
Cash Flow	-110,000	+10,000	+60,000

Case D2 DCFROR = -2.3%

Foreign sales projects are very sensitive to exchange rate variations. Weakened domestic currency always enhances export project economics.

CHAPTER 8 PROBLEM SOLUTIONS

8-3 Solution:

Case A) Stand Alone Economics, Values in Thousands of $

```
Acq. Cost       = 10,000
Working Capital =  2,000
Equipment Cost  = 15,000    I=30,000    I=33,000    I=36,300    I=39,930    I=43,923
Development     = 10,000    OC=12,000   OC=13,200   OC=14,520   OC=15,972   OC=17,569
                        ────────────────────────────────────────────────────────────
                            0           1           2           3           4           5
```

Cash Flow Calculations

Year	Time 0	1	2	3	4	5	Salv
Production		1,000	1,000	1,000	1,000	1,000	
Gross Revenue		30,000	33,000	36,300	39,930	43,923	5,000
-Royalties		-2,400	-2,640	-2,904	-3,194	-3,514	
Net Revenue		27,600	30,360	33,396	36,736	40,409	
-Operating Costs		-12,000	-13,200	-14,520	-15,972	-17,569	
-Development	-7,000						
-Depreciation	-2,143	-3,673	-2,624	-1,874	-1,339	-1,339	-2,008
-Amortization	-600	-600	-600	-600	-600		
-WC Writeoff							-2,000
Before Depletion	-9,743	11,327	13,936	16,402	18,825	21,501	992
50% Limit		5,663	6,968	8,201	9,412	10,751	
Percent Depletion		-2,760	-3,036	-3,340	-3,112*	-3,233	
Cost Depletion		2,000	1,810	1,401	432		
-Loss Forward		-9,743	-1,176				
Taxable Income	-9,743	-1,176	9,724	13,062	15,713	18,268	992
-Tax Due @ 40%	0	0	-3,890	-5,225	-6,285	-7,307	-397
Net Income	-9,743	-1,176	5,834	7,837	9,428	10,961	595
+Depreciation	2,143	3,673	2,624	1,874	1,339	1,339	2,008
+Depletion Taken		2,760	3,036	3,340	3,112	3,233	
+Amortization	600	600	600	600	600		
+Loss Forward		9,743	1,176				
+WC Writeoff							2,000
-Capital Costs	-30,000**						
Cash Flow	-37,000	15,600	13,270	13,651	14,478	15,533	4,603

**Time 0 capital cost includes $15,000 for equip, $2,000 for working capital, $3,000 for 30% of the $10,000 development cost and $10,000 for mineral rights acquisition.

* Cumulative percentage depletion in years 1, 2 and 3 = $9,136 so $864 more depletion equals $10,000 mineral rights acquisition cost. $864/.10 = $8,640 net revenue after royalty is needed for 10% depletion, balance is 8% depletion. 8% depletion revenue = ($36,736-$8,640)(0.08) = $28,096(0.08) =$2,248. Cumulative year 4 percentage depletion = $2,248 + $864 = $3,112.

8-3 Solution:
Case A) Stand Alone Economics - Continued

Depreciation Calculations

Yr 0 15,000(.1429) = 2,143
Yr 1 15,000(.2449) = 3,673
Yr 2 15,000(.1749) = 2,624
Yr 3 15,000(.1249) = 1,874
Yr 4 15,000(.0893) = 1,339
Yr 5 15,000(.0892) = 1,339
Yr 5 Remaining Book Writeoff
      15,000(.1339) = 2,008

Cost Depletion Calculations

Yr 1 10,000(1,000/5,000) = 2,000
Yr 2 (10,000-2,760)(1,000/4,000) = 1,810
Yr 3 (7,240-3,036)(1,000/3,000) = 1,401
Yr 4 (4,204-3,340)(1,000/2,000) = 432
Yr 5 (864-3,112) < 0, stop cost depletion

Amortization of 30% of Development

Yr 0-4   10,000(.30)(12/60) = 600

PW Eq: $0 = -37,000 + 15,600(P/F_{i,1}) + 13,270(P/F_{i,2}) + 13,651(P/F_{i,3})$
        $+ 14,478(P/F_{i,4}) + 20,047(P/F_{i,5})$; $i = DCFROR = 29.4\%$

NPV = $-37,000 + 15,600(P/F_{20,1}) + 13,270(P/F_{20,2}) + 13,651(P/F_{20,3})$
      $+ 14,478(P/F_{20,4}) + 20,047(P/F_{20,5}) = +\$8,154$

Case B, Expense Cash Flows

Year	Time 0	1	2	3	4	5	Salv
Production		1,000	1,000	1,000	1,000	1,000	
Gross Revenue		30,000	33,000	36,300	39,930	43,923	5,000
-Royalties		-2,400	-2,640	-2,904	-3,194	-3,514	
Net Revenue		27,600	30,360	33,396	36,736	40,409	
-Operating Costs		-12,000	-13,200	-14,520	-15,972	-17,569	
-Development	-7,000						
-Depreciation	-2,143	-3,673	-2,624	-1,874	-1,339	-1,339	-2,008
-Amortization	-600	-600	-600	-600	-600		
-Write Off							-2,000
Before Depletion	-9,743	11,327	13,936	16,402	18,825	21,501	992
Percent Depletion		2,760	3,036	3,340	3,112*	3,233	
50% Limit		5,663	6,968	8,201	9,412	10,751	
Cost Depletion		2,000	1,810	1,401	432		
-Depletion Taken		-2,760	-3,036	-3,340	-3,112	-3,233	
Taxable Income	-9,743	8,567	10,900	13,062	15,713	18,268	992
-Tax Due @ 40%	3,897	-3,427	-4,360	-5,225	-6,285	-7,307	-397
Net Income	-5,846	5,140	6,540	7,837	9,428	10,961	595
+Depreciation	2,143	3,673	2,624	1,874	1,339	1,339	2,008
+Depletion		2,760	3,036	3,340	3,112	3,233	
+Amortization	600	600	600	600	600		
+Write Off							2,000
-Capital Costs	-30,000**						
Cash Flow	-33,103	12,173	12,800	13,651	14,478	15,533	4,603

CHAPTER 8 PROBLEM SOLUTIONS

8-3 Solution: Continued

Case B, Expense Cash Flows Continued

**Capital cost includes $15,000 for equipment, $2,000 for working capital, $3,000 which is 30% of the $10,000 development cost and $10,000 for mineral rights acquisition.

* Cumulative percentage depletion in years 1, 2 and 3 = $9,136 so $864 more depletion equals $10,000 mineral rights acquisition cost. $864/0.10 = $8,640 which is the net revenue after royalty needed for 10% depletion, the balance of revenue is 8% depletion. 8% depletion revenue = ($36,736-$8,640)(0.08) = $28,096(0.08) = $2,248. Cumulative year 4 percentage depletion = $2,248 + $864 = $3,112.

$$NPV = -33,103 + 12,173(P/F_{20,1}) + 12,800(P/F_{20,2}) + 13,651(P/F_{20,3})$$
$$+ 14,478(P/F_{20,4}) + 20,136(P/F_{20,5}) = +\$8,904$$

DCFROR = 30.8% is the interest rate that makes NPV = 0

8-4 Solution: Growth Rate of Return Calculations

Cash Flows	-150,000	60,000	70,000	80,000	90,000
Year	0	1	2	3	4

Project DCFROR PW Eq: $150,000 = [60,000 + 10,000(A/G_{i,4})](P/A_{i,4})$

i = DCFROR = 32%

To calculate the project Growth DCFROR, we must account for 40% tax to be paid on 12% treasury bond interest each year, so money grows at 7.2% per year after taxes.

$$\text{PW Eq: } 150,000 = [60,000(F/P_{7.2,3})^{1.2319} + 70,000(F/P_{7.2,2})^{1.1492} + 80,000(F/P_{7.2,1})^{1.072}$$
$$+ 90,000](P/F_{i,4})$$

$$150,000 = 330,118(P/F_{i,4})$$

i = Growth DCFROR = 21.8%

8-5 Solution:

Manufacturing Plant Evaluation, All Values in Thousands of Dollars

```
Working Capital= 20      I=100                I=100
Deprec Equip.  = 180     OC= 40               OC= 40         WC Return = 20
                         ─────────────────────────────        Salvage = 150
                         0    1 ................ 15
```

Project Cash Flow Calculations

Year	0	1	2-7	8	9-15	Salvage Value 15
Revenue		100.00	100.00	100.00	100.00	170.00
-Operating Costs		-40.00	-40.00	-40.00	-40.00	
-Depreciation		-12.86	-25.71	-12.86		
-WC Writeoff						-20.00
Taxable Income		47.14	34.29	47.14	60.00	150.00
-Tax @ 40%		-18.86	-13.71	-18.86	-24.00	-60.00
Net Income		28.29	20.57	28.29	36.00	90.00
+Depreciation		12.86	25.71	12.86		
+Work Cap Ret.						20.00
Capital Costs	-200.00					
Cash Flow	-200.00	41.14	46.29	41.14	36.00	110.00

NPV @ 15% = $-200.00 + 41.14(P/F_{15,1}) + 46.29(P/A_{15,6})(P/F_{15,1})$

$\quad\quad\quad\quad\quad + 41.14(P/F_{15,8}) + 36.00(P/A_{15,7})(P/F_{15,8}) + 110.00(P/F_{15,15})$

$\quad\quad\quad = +\$64.0$

DCFROR = 21.1% is the interest rate that makes NPV equal to zero.

CHAPTER 8 PROBLEM SOLUTIONS

8-6 Solution:

Corporate Mining, Stand Alone Economics - Values in Thousands

Acquisition Cost	$1,000					
Development Cost		$500 (Assume incurred 1st month of tax year)				
Equipment Cost	-	$1,000				
Units Produced	-	-	100	100	150	150

Project Cash Flows

Year	Time 0	1	2	3	4	5	Salvage
Production			100	100	150	150	
Net Revenue			2,000	2,000	3,000	3,000	
-Operating Costs			-800	-800	-1,200	-1,200	
-Development		-350					
-Depreciation			-143	-245	-175	-125	-312
-Amortization		-30	-30	-30	-30	-30	
Before Depletion		-380	1,027	925	1,595	1,645	-312
50% Limit			514	463	798	823	
Percent Depletion			-440	-440	-660	-660	
Cost Depletion			200	140	60		
-Loss Forward			-380				
Taxable Income		-380	207	485	935	985	-312
-Tax Due @ 40%		0	-83	-194	-374	-394	125
Net Income		-380	124	291	561	591	-187
+Depreciation			143	245	175	125	312
+Depletion Taken			440	440	660	660	
+Amortization		30	30	30	30	30	
+Loss Forward			380				
-Capital Costs	-1,000	-1,150					
Cash Flow	-1,000	-1,500	1,117	1,006	1,426	1,406	125
						1,531	

Depreciation Calculations

Yr 2 $1,000(0.1429) = 143$
Yr 3 $1,000(0.2449) = 245$
Yr 4 $1,000(0.1749) = 175$
Yr 5 $1,000(0.1249) = 125$
Depreciable Writeoff = 312

Cost Depletion Calculations

Yr 2 $1,000(100/500) = 200$
Yr 3 $560(100/400) = 140$
Yr 4 $120(150/300) = 60$
Yr 5   Basis < 0, no cost depletion

PW Eq: $0 = -1,000 - 1,500(P/F_{i,1}) + 1,117(P/F_{i,2}) + 1,006(P/F_{i,3})$
$+ 1,426(P/F_{i,4}) + 1,531(P/F_{i,5})$ DCFROR = 27.3%

Net Present Value @ $i^* = 15\% = +\$778$

Present Value Ratio = $778 / [1,000 + 1,500(P/F_{15,1})] = +0.34$

Payback from Start of Project Equals $3 + (377/1,426) = 3.26$ years

8-7 Solution:
Petroleum Property, Independent < 1,000 Bbl/day,
Risk-Free, All Values in Thousands

Acquisition Cost	$100						
Intangible Drilling	$750	$250					
Depreciable Cost		$1,000					
Production			70	56	42	28	14
Year	0	1	2	3	4	5	6

Case A and B) Cash Flows for Expense Against Other Income

Year	0	1	2 (Success)	3	4	5	6	Fail 1
Gross Revenue			1,540	1,331	1,078	776	419	
-Royalties			-216	-186	-151	-109	-59	
Net Revenue			1,324	1,145	927	667	360	
-Oper Costs			-175	-193	-212	-233	-256	-50
-Intangible	-750	-250						
-Depreciation			-143	-245	-175	-125	-89	
-Writeoff							-223	
Before Depln	-750	-250	1,006	707	540	309	-208	-50
-100% Limit			1,006	707	540	309	0	
-% Depln(15%)			-199	-172	-139	-100	54	
-Cost Depln			33	0	0	0	0	-100
Taxable Inc	-750	-250	807	535	401	209	-208	-150
-Tax @ 38%	285	95	-307	-203	-152	-80	79	57
Net Income	-465	-155	500	332	249	130	-129	-93
+Depreciation			143	245	175	125	89	
+Writeoff							223	
+Depletion			199	172	139	100		100
-Cap. Costs	-100	-1,000						
Cash Flow	-565	-1,155	842	749	563	355	183	7

PW Eq: $0 = -565 - 1,155(P/F_{i,1}) + 842(P/F_{i,2}) + 749(P/F_{i,3}) + 563(P/F_{i,4})$
$+ 355(P/F_{i,5}) + 183(P/F_{i,6})$ DCFROR = 18.9%

Net Present Value @ 15% = +$137
Risk Adjust Case A for a 40% Probability of Success after the year 0 expenditures. A $50,000 abandonment cost is incurred in year 1 if the project fails along with a writeoff of the $100,000 acquisition cost. The risk adjusted P.W. equation follows:

$0 = -565 + [-1,155(P/F_{i,1}) + 842(P/F_{i,2}) + 749(P/F_{i,3}) + 563(P/F_{i,4})$
$+ 355(P/F_{i,5}) + 183(P/F_{i,6})](.4) + 7(P/F_{i,1})(.6)$

Expected DCFROR = 1.7%, Expected Net Present Value @ 15% = -$280.7

CHAPTER 8 PROBLEM SOLUTIONS

8-7 Solution: Continued

Case C) Cases A and B from an Integrated Producer Viewpoint With Drill Costs in Month 7 of Year 0 and 1.

Year	0	1	2	3	4	5	6	Fail 1
Gross Revenue			1,540	1,331	1,078	776	419	
-Royalties			-216	-186	-151	-109	-59	
Net Revenue			1,324	1,145	927	667	360	
-Oper Costs			-175	-193	-212	-233	-256	-50
-IDC's	-525	-175						
-Depreciation			-143	-245	-175	-125	-89	
-Writeoff							-223	
-Amortization	-23	-53	-60	-60	-60	-38	-8	-202
-Cost Depln			-33	-27	-20	-13	-7	-100
Taxable Inc	-548	-227	913	620	460	258	-223	-352
-Tax @ 38%	208	86	-347	-236	-175	-98	89	134
Net Income	-339	-141	566	384	285	160	-134	-218
+Depreciation			143	245	175	125	89	
+Writeoff							223	
+Amortization	23	53	60	60	60	38	8	202
+Depletion			33	27	20	13	7	100
-Cap. Costs	-325	-1,075						
Cash Flow	-642	-1,164	802	716	540	336	193	84

PW Eq: $0 = -642 - 1,164(P/F_{i,1}) + 802(P/F_{i,2}) + 716(P/F_{i,3}) + 540(P/F_{i,4})$
$+ 336(P/F_{i,5}) + 193(P/F_{i,6})$

Discounted Cash Flow Rate of Return = 14.5%
Net Present Value @ 15% = -$18

Risk Adjust Case A for a 40% Probability of Success after the year 0 expenditures. A $50,000 abandonment cost is incurred in year 1 if the project fails along with a writeoff of the $100,000 acquisition cost.

Risk Adjusted PW Eq:

$0 = -642 + [-1,164(P/F_{i,1}) + 802(P/F_{i,2}) + 716(P/F_{i,3}) + 540(P/F_{i,4})$
$+ 336(P/F_{i,5}) + 193(P/F_{i,6})](0.4) + 84(P/F_{i,1})(0.6)$

Applying the probabilities to the cash flow streams and combining gives:

$0 = -642 + -415.2(P/F_{i,1}) + 320.8(P/F_{i,2}) + 286.4(P/F_{i,3}) + 216.0(P/F_{i,4})$
$+ 134.4(P/F_{i,5}) + 77.2(P/F_{i,6})$

Expected DCFROR = -0.7%, Expected Net Present Value @ 15% = -$348

8-7 Solution: Continued

(Case D) Independent, Stand Alone Economic Analyses

			————————	Success	————————			Fail
Year	0	1	2	3	4	5	6	1
Gross Revenue			1,540	1,331	1,078	776	419	
-Royalties			-216	-186	-151	-109	-59	
Net Revenue			1,324	1,145	927	667	360	
-Oper Costs			-175	-193	-212	-233	-256	-50
-Intangible	-750	-250						
-Depreciation			-143	-245	-175	-125	-89	
-Writeoff							-223	
Before Depln	-750	-250	1,006	707	540	309	-208	-50
-100% Limit			1,006	707	540	309	0	
-% Depl(15%)			-199	-172	-139	-100	54	
-Cost Depln			33	0	0	0	0	-100
-Loss Forward		-750	-1,000	-193				
Taxable Inc	-750	-1,000	-193	342	401	209	-208	-150
-Tax @ 38%	0	0	0	-130	-152	-79	79	57
Net Income	-750	-1,000	-193	212	249	130	-129	-93
+Depreciation			143	245	175	125	89	
+Writeoff							223	
+Depletion			199	172	139	100		100
+Loss Forward		750	1,000	193				
-Cap. Costs	-100	-1,000						
Cash Flow	-850	-1,250	1,149	822	563	355	183	7

PW Eq: $0 = -850 - 1,250(P/F_{i,1}) + 1,149(P/F_{i,2}) + 822(P/F_{i,3}) + 563(P/F_{i,4})$

$+ 355(P/F_{i,5}) + 183(P/F_{i,6})$ DCFROR = 16.2%

Net Present Value @ 15% = +$50.6

Risk Adjust Case A for a 40% Probability of Success after the year 0 expenditures. A $50,000 abandonment cost is incurred in year 1 if the project fails along with a writeoff of the $100,000 acquisition cost. The risk adjusted P.W. equation follows:

$0 = -850 + [-1,250(P/F_{i,1}) + 1,149(P/F_{i,2}) + 822(P/F_{i,3}) + 563(P/F_{i,4})$

$+ 355(P/F_{i,5}) + 183(P/F_{i,6})](.4) + 7(P/F_{i,1})(.6)$

Applying the probabilities to the cash flow streams and combining gives:

$0 = -850 - 495.8(P/F_{i,1}) + 459.6(P/F_{i,2}) + 328.8(P/F_{i,3}) + 225.2(P/F_{i,4})$

$+ 142.0(P/F_{i,5}) + 73.2(P/F_{i,6})$

Expected DCFROR = -3.1%,   Expected Net Present Value @ 15% = -$487

CHAPTER 8 PROBLEM SOLUTIONS

8-8 Solution:

Case A) 9 Year Evaluation Life, Values in Thousands of Dollars

Year	0	1	2-7	8	9
Revenue		400	400	400	500*
-Operating Costs		-200	-200	-200	-200
-Depreciation		-30	-60	-30	
-Writeoffs					-100
Taxable Income		170	140	170	200
-Tax @ 35%		-59	-49	-59	-70
Net Income		111	91	111	130
+Depreciation		30	60	30	
+Writeoffs					100
-Capital Costs	-520				
Cash Flow	-520	141	151	141	230

* Revenue includes Working Capital Return

PW Eq: $0 = -520 + 141(P/F_{i,1}) + 151(P/A_{i,6})(P/F_{i,1}) + 141(P/F_{i,8})$
$\qquad + 230(P/F_{i,9})$

Discounted Cash Flow Rate of Return = 25.2%
Net Present Value @ 15% = +$210

Case B) 18 Year Evaluation Life, Values in Thousands of Dollars

Year	0	1	2-7	8	9-17	18
Revenue		400	400	400	400	500*
-Operating Costs		-200	-200	-200	-200	-200
-Depreciation		-30	-60	-30		
-Writeoffs						-100
Taxable Income		170	140	170	200	200
-Tax @ 35%		-59	-49	-59	-70	-70
Net Income		111	91	111	130	130
+Depreciation		30	60	30		
+Writeoffs						100
-Capital Costs	-520					
Cash Flow	-520	141	151	141	130	230

* Revenue includes Working Capital Return

PW Eq: $0 = -520 + 141(P/F_{i,1}) + 151(P/A_{i,6})(P/F_{i,1}) + 141(P/F_{i,8})$
$\qquad + 130(P/A_{i,9})(P/F_{i,8}) + 230(P/F_{i,18})$

Discounted Cash Flow Rate of Return = 27.7%
Net Present Value @ 15% = +$366

8-9 Solution:
Processing Facility, Costs ($) and Production (Gal) in Thousands

Year	0	1	2	3	4	5
Production, (Gal)		62	53	35	24	17
Research & Exper.	750	250				
Equipment		670				
Patent Rights	100					
Operating Costs		175	193	212	233	256
Price, ($/Gal)		26.0	26.0	26.0	27.3	28.7

Case 1A, Expense Cash Flows

Year	Time 0	1	2	3	4	5	Salvage
Production		62	53	35	24	17	
Gross Revenue		1,612	1,378	910	655	488	
-Royalties		-226	-193	-127	-92	-68	
Net Revenue		1,386	1,185	783	563	420	
-Operating Costs		-175	-193	-212	-233	-256	
-Research	-750	-250					
-Depreciation		-96	-164	-117	-84	-60	-149
-Amortization	-20	-20	-20	-20	-20		
Taxable Income	-770	846	808	433	227	104	-149
-Tax Due @ 40%	308	-338	-323	-173	-91	-42	60
Net Income	-462	507	485	260	136	62	-89
+Depreciation		96	164	117	84	60	149
+Amortization	20	20	20	20	20		
-Capital Costs	-100	-670					
Cash Flow	-542	-47	669	397	240	122	60
						182	

The year 0 capital cost is the $100 patent rights acquisition cost and the year 1 capital cost is the $670 equipment cost.

PW Eq: $0 = -542 - 47(P/F_{i,1}) + 669(P/F_{i,2}) + 397(P/F_{i,3}) + 240(P/F_{i,4})$
$+ 182(P/F_{i,5})$ i = DCFROR = 40.6% > i^* of 15%, accept

NPV @ 15% = $-542 - 47(P/F_{15,1}) + 669(P/F_{15,2}) + 397(P/F_{15,3}) + 240(P/F_{15,4})$
$+ 182(P/F_{15,5}) = +\$412 > 0$, accept

PVR = $412 / [542 + 47(P/F_{15,1})] = +0.71 > 0$, accept

CHAPTER 8 PROBLEM SOLUTIONS

8-9 Solution: Continued

Case 1B, Stand Alone Cash Flows

Year	Time 0	1	2	3	4	5	Salvage
Production		62	53	35	24	17	
Gross Revenue		1,612	1,378	910	655	488	
-Royalties		-226	-193	-127	-92	-68	
Net Revenue		1,386	1,185	783	563	420	
-Operating Costs		-175	-193	-212	-233	-256	
-Research	-750	-250					
-Depreciation		-96	-164	-117	-84	-60	-149
-Amortization	-20	-20	-20	-20	-20		
-Loss Forward		-770					
Taxable Income	-770	76	808	433	227	104	-149
-Tax Due @ 40%		-30	-323	-173	-91	-42	60
Net Income	-770	45	485	260	136	62	-89
+Depreciation		96	164	117	84	60	149
+Amortization	20	20	20	20	20		
+Loss Forward		770					
-Capital Costs	-100	-670					
Cash Flow	-850	261	669	397	240	122	60

PW Eq: $0 = -850 + 261(P/F_{i,1}) + 669(P/F_{i,2}) + 397(P/F_{i,3}) + 240(P/F_{i,4}) + 182(P/F_{i,5})$, i = DCFROR = 33.9% > i^* of 15%, accept

NPV @ 15% = $-850 + 261(P/F_{15,1}) + 669(P/F_{15,2}) + 397(P/F_{15,3}) + 240(P/F_{15,4}) + 182(P/F_{15,5})$ = +$371 > 0, accept

PVR = 371 / 850 = +0.44 > 0, accept

8-9 Solution: Continued

Case 2, Risk Analysis for Part 1A

Non-Risk Adjusted Cash Flows

Cash Flow	-542	p=0.40	-47	669	397	240	182
Year	0		1	2	3	4	5

p=0.60

-Abandonment Cost	-70
-Patent Bk Value Writeoff	-80
Taxable Income	-150
-Tax @ 40%	60
Net Income	-90
+ Writeoff	80
Failure Cash Flow	-10

Risk Adjusted Cash Flows

Expected Value Cash Flows	-542	-25*	268	159	96	73
Year	0	1	2	3	4	5

* Yr 1 cash flow is determined by combining the two expected cash flows as follows: (-10)(.6) + (-47)(.4) = -25.

Expected Discounted Cash Flow Rate of Return:

PW Eq: $0 = -542 - 25(P/F_{i,1}) + 268(P/F_{i,2}) + 159(P/F_{i,3}) + 96(P/F_{i,4})$
$+ 73(P/F_{i,5})$, i = Expected DCFROR = 1.7% < i^* of 15%, reject

Expected Net Present Value:

ENPV @ 15% = $-542 - 25(P/F_{15,1}) + 268(P/F_{15,2}) + 159(P/F_{15,3})$
$+ 96(P/F_{15,4}) + 73(P/F_{15,5})$ = -$166 < 0, reject

Expected Present Value Ratio:

EPVR = -166 / [542+25(P/F$_{15,1}$)$\overset{.8696}{}$] = -0.29 < 0, reject

CHAPTER 8 PROBLEM SOLUTIONS

8-9 Solution: Continued

Case 3, Breakeven Analysis of the Case 1A Cash Flows

Year	Time 0	1	2	3	4	5	Salvage
Total Production		62	53	35	24	17	
Net Production (86%)		53	46	30	21	15	
Net Revenue		53X	46X	30X	21X	15X	
−Operating Costs		−175	−193	−212	−233	−256	
−Research	−750	−250					
−Depreciation		−96	−164	−117	−84	−60	−149
−Amortization	−20	−20	−20	−20	−20		
Taxable Income	−770	53X−541	46X−377	30X−349	21X−337	15X−316	−149
−Tax Due @ 40%	308	−21X+216	−18X+151	−12X+140	−8X+135	−6X+126	60
Net Income	−462	32X−325	28X−226	18X−209	13X−202	9X−190	−89
+Depreciation		96	164	117	84	60	149
+Amortization	20	20	20	20	20		
−Capital Costs	−100	−670					
Cash Flow	−542	32X−879	28X−42	18X−72	13X−98	9X−130	60

$$0 = -542 + (32X-879)(P/F_{15,1})^{.8696} + (28X-42)(P/F_{15,2})^{.7561} + (18X-72)(P/F_{15,3})^{.6575}$$

$$+ (13X-98)(P/F_{15,4})^{.5718} + (9X-70)(P/F_{15,5})^{.4972}$$

$0 = 72.74X - 1,476.32$, therefore, $X = \$20.30$

Breakeven Selling Price $X = \$20.30$ per gallon

8-9 Solution: Continued

Case 4, Before-tax Acquisition Cost Analysis. (A breakeven cost analysis assuming the acquisition cost will be treated like a patent cost for tax purposes and amortized over 5 yrs.)

Cash Flows from Part 1A are:

Year	0	1	2	3	4	5
Cash Flow	-542	-47	669	397	240	182

Net Present Value from Part 1A is $412

This NPV represents additional after-tax acquisition cost that can be incurred and still give the investor a 15% DCFROR. Let the before-tax acquisition cost equal "X" and be subject to 5 year amortization. The tax savings generated from the additional amortization deductions above those associated with the $100,000 patent rights fee are calculated as follows:

	Before-Tax Value	Tax Savings
Year 0	X(1/5) = .20X	.20X(.4) = .08X
Year 1	X(1/5) = .20X	.20X(.4) = .08X
Year 2	X(1/5) = .20X	.20X(.4) = .08X
Year 3	X(1/5) = .20X	.20X(.4) = .08X
Year 4	X(1/5) = .20X	.20X(.4) = .08X

$$X = 412 + 0.08X + 0.08X(P/A_{15,4})$$
$$2.855\phantom{_{15,4})}$$

Therefore, X = $596 is the before-tax breakeven acquisition cost that could be incurred and still have the project earn the desired 15% after-tax minimum rate of return.

CHAPTER 8 PROBLEM SOLUTIONS

8-10 Solution:

Petroleum Project, Costs ($) and Production (Bbl) are in Thousands

Year	0	1	2	3	4	5
Production, (Bbls)		62	53	35	24	17
Intangibles, (IDC's)	750	250				
Tangible (Completion)		670				
Mineral Rights. Acq.	100					
Operating Costs		175	193	212	233	256
Price, ($/Bbl)		26.0	26.0	26.0	27.3	28.7

Integrated Producer, Case 1A, Expense Cash Flows

Year	0	1	2	3	4	5
Gross Revenue		1,612	1,378	910	655	488
-Royalties		-226	-193	-127	-92	-68
Net Revenue		1,386	1,185	783	563	420
-Oper Costs		-175	-193	-212	-233	-256
-Intangible	-525	-175				
-Depreciation		-96	-164	-117	-84	-60
-Deprec Writeoff						-149
-Amortization		-45	-60	-60	-60	-60	-15
-Cost Depln		-32	-28	-18	-13	-9
Taxable Income	-570	848	740	376	173	-69
-Tax @ 40%	228	-339	-296	-150	-70	27
Net Income	-342	509	444	226	103	-42
+Deprec/Writeoff		96	164	117	84	209
+Depletion		32	28	18	13	9
+Amortization	45	60	60	60	60	15
-Capital Costs	-325*	-745**				
Cash Flow	-622	-48	696	421	260	191

* Capital cost includes $100 mineral rights acquisition and 30% of $750 IDC's that must be amortized over 60 months.

** Capital cost includes $670 tangible cost and 30% of $250 IDC's.

PW Eq: $0 = -622 - 48(P/F_{i,1}) + 696(P/F_{i,2}) + 421(P/F_{i,3}) + 260(P/F_{i,4})$

$+ 191(P/F_{i,5})$, i = DCFROR = 36.3% > i^* of 15%, accept

NPV @ 15% = $-622 - \overset{.8696}{48}(P/F_{15,1}) + \overset{.7561}{696}(P/F_{15,2}) + \overset{.6575}{421}(P/F_{15,3}) + \overset{.5718}{260}(P/F_{15,4})$

$+ \overset{.4972}{191}(P/F_{15,5}) = +383 > 0$, accept

PVR = $383 / \{622 + 48(P/F_{15,1})\} = 0.58 > 0$, accept

8-10 Solution: Continued

Integrated Producer, Case 1B, Stand Alone Cash Flows

Year	0	1	2	3	4	5
Gross Revenue		1,612	1,378	910	655	488
-Royalties		-226	-193	-127	-92	-68
Net Revenue		1,386	1,185	783	563	420
-Oper Costs		-175	-193	-212	-233	-256
-Intangible	-525	-175				
-Depreciation		-96	-164	-117	-84	-60
-Deprec Writeoff						-149
-Amortization	-45	-60	-60	-60	-60	-15
-Cost Depletion		-32	-28	-18	-13	-9
-Loss Forward		-570				
Taxable Income	-570	278	740	376	173	-69
-Tax @ 40%		-111	-296	-150	-70	27
Net Income	-570	167	444	226	103	-42
+Deprec/Writeoff		96	164	117	84	209
+Cost Depletion		32	28	18	13	9
+Amortization	45	60	60	60	60	15
+Loss Forward		570				
-Capital Costs	-325*	-745**				
Cash Flow	-850	180	696	421	260	191

* Capital cost includes $100 mineral rights acquisition and 30% of $750 IDC's that must be amortized over 60 months.

** Capital cost includes $670 tangible cost and 30% of $250 IDC's.

PW Eq: $0 = -850 + 180(P/F_{i,1}) + 696(P/F_{i,2}) + 421(P/F_{i,3}) + 260(P/F_{i,4}) + 191(P/F_{i,5})$, i = DCFROR = 32.1% > i^* of 15%, accept

NPV @ 15% = $-850 + 180(P/F_{15,1}) + 696(P/F_{15,2}) + 421(P/F_{15,3}) + 260(P/F_{15,4}) + 191(P/F_{15,5})$ = +353 > 0, accept

PVR = 353 / 850 = 0.42 > 0, accept

CHAPTER 8 PROBLEM SOLUTIONS

8-10 Solution: Continued

Integrated Producer, Case 2, Risk Adjust Case 1A Cash Flows

Non-Risk Adjusted Cash Flows

Cash Flow	-622	p=0.40	-48	696	421	260	191
Year	0		1	2	3	4	5

p=0.60

```
-Abandonment Cost        -70
-30% Unamortized IDC    -180   } writeoffs
-Cost Depl Writeoff     -100
Taxable Income          -350
-Tax @ 40%               140
Net Income              -210
+ Writeoffs              280
Failure Cash Flow        +70
```

Risk Adjusted Cash Flows (40% Probability of Success)

Expected Value Cash Flows	-622	23*	278	168	104	76
Year	0	1	2	3	4	5

* Cash Flow = -48(0.4) + 70(0.6) = +23

Expected Discounted Cash Flow Rate of Return:

PW Eq: $0 = -622 + 23(P/F_{i,1}) + 278(P/F_{i,2}) + 168(P/F_{i,3}) + 104(P/F_{i,4}) + 76(P/F_{i,5})$, i = Expected DCFROR = 1.5% < i^* of 15%, reject

Expected Net Present Value:

ENPV @ 15% = $-622 + 23(P/F_{15,1}) + 278(P/F_{15,2}) + 168(P/F_{15,3}) + 104(P/F_{15,4}) + 76(P/F_{15,5})$ = -184.1 < 0, reject

Expected Present Value Ratio:

EPVR = -184.1 / 622 = -0.296 < 0, reject

8-10 Solution: Continued

(Independent > 1,000 Bbls), Case 3, Expense Cash Flows

Year	Time 0	1	2	3	4	5	Salv
Production		62	53	35	24	17	
Gross Revenue		1,612	1,378	910	655	488	
-Royalties		-226	-193	-127	-92	-68	
Net Revenue		1,386	1,185	783	563	420	
-Operating Costs		-175	-193	-212	-233	-256	
-Intangible Drilling	-750	-250					
-Depreciation		-96	-164	-117	-84	-60	-149
-Cost Depletion		-32	-28	-18	-13	-9	
Taxable Income	-750	833	800	435	234	95	-149
-Tax Due @ 40%	300	-333	-320	-174	-94	-38	60
Net Income	-450	500	480	261	141	57	-89
+Depreciation		96	164	117	84	60	149
+Cost Depletion		32	28	18	13	9	
-Capital Costs*	-100*	-670*					
Cash Flow	-550	-42	672	397	237	126	60

*The year 0 capital cost equals the $100 mineral rights acquisition. Year 1 capital cost is the $670 tangible cost.

PW Eq: $0 = -550 - 42(P/F_{i,1}) + 672(P/F_{i,2}) + 397(P/F_{i,3}) + 237(P/F_{i,4}) + 186(P/F_{i,5})$, i = DCFROR = 40.3% > i^* of 15%, accept

NPV @ 15% = $-550 - 42\underset{.8696}{(P/F_{15,1})} + 672\underset{.7561}{(P/F_{15,2})} + 397\underset{.6575}{(P/F_{15,3})} + 237\underset{.5718}{(P/F_{15,4})} + 186\underset{.4972}{(P/F_{15,5})}$ = +$410 > 0, accept

PVR = $410 / \{550 + 42\underset{.8696}{(P/F_{15,1})}\}$ = +0.70 > 0, accept

CHAPTER 8 PROBLEM SOLUTIONS

8-10 Solution: Continued

(Independent > 1,000 Bbls), Case 3, Stand Alone Cash Flows

Year	Time 0	1	2	3	4	5	Salvage
Production		62	53	35	24	17	
Gross Revenue		1,612	1,378	910	655	488	
-Royalties		-226	-193	-127	-92	-68	
Net Revenue		1,386	1,185	783	563	420	
-Operating Costs		-175	-193	-212	-233	-256	
-Intangible Drilling	-750	-250					
-Depreciation		-96	-164	-117	-84	-60	-149
-Cost Depletion		-32	-28	-18	-13	-9	
-Loss Forward		-750					
Taxable	-750	83	800	435	234	95	-149
-Tax Due		-33	-320	-174	-94	-38	60
Net Income	-750	50	480	261	141	57	-89
+Depreciation		96	164	117	84	60	149
+Cost Depletion		32	28	18	13	9	
+Loss Forward		750					
-Capital Costs	-100*	-670*					
Cash Flow	-850	258	672	397	237	126	60

*The year 0 capital cost equals the $100 mineral rights acquisition. Year 1 capital cost is the $670 tangible cost.

PW Eq: $0 = -850 + 258(P/F_{i,1}) + 672(P/F_{i,2}) + 397(P/F_{i,3}) + 237(P/F_{i,4})$
$+ 186(P/F_{i,5})$, i = DCFROR = 33.9% > i* of 15%, accept

NPV @ 15% = $-850 + 258 \overset{.8696}{(P/F_{15,1})} + 672 \overset{.7561}{(P/F_{15,2})} + 397 \overset{.6575}{(P/F_{15,3})}$
$+ 237 \overset{.5718}{(P/F_{15,4})} + 186 \overset{.4972}{(P/F_{15,5})} = +\$371 > 0$, accept

PVR = 371 / 850 = +0.44 > 0, accept

8-10 Solution: Continued

(Independent > 1,000 Bbls), Case 3, Risk Analysis

Non-Risk Adjusted Cash Flows

Cash Flow	-550	p=0.40 -42	672	397	237	186
Year	0	1	2	3	4	5

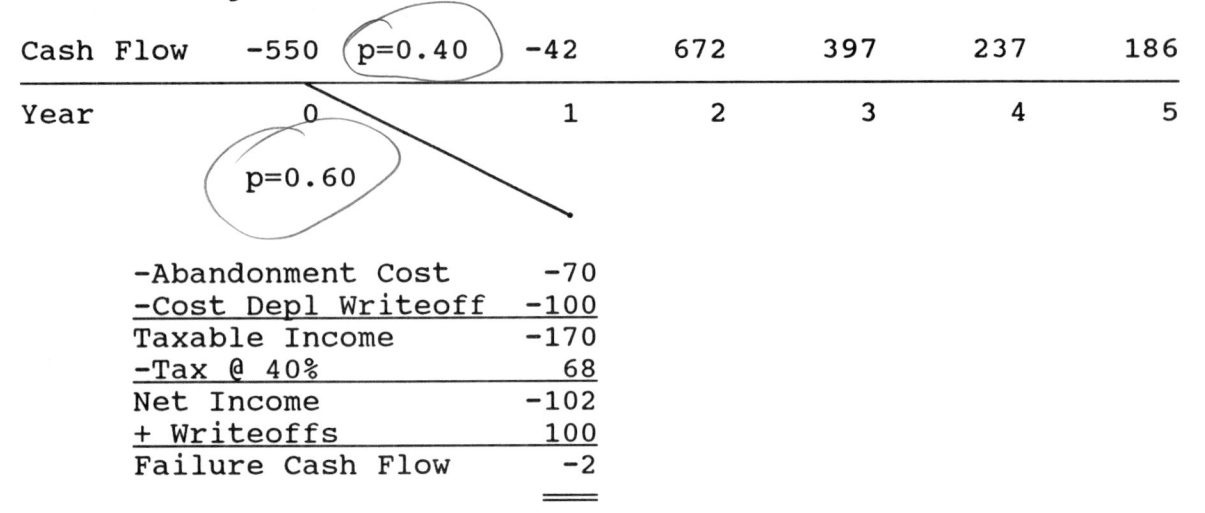

p=0.60

```
-Abandonment Cost    -70
-Cost Depl Writeoff -100
Taxable Income      -170
-Tax @ 40%            68
Net Income          -102
+ Writeoffs          100
Failure Cash Flow    -2
```

Risk Adjusted Cash Flows (40% Probability of Success)

Expected Value Cash Flows	-550	-18*	269	159	95	74
Year	0	1	2	3	4	5

* Cash Flow = -42(.4) - 2(.6) = -18

Expected Discounted Cash Flow Rate of Return

PW Eq: $0 = -550 - 18(P/F_{i,1}) + 269(P/F_{i,2}) + 159(P/F_{i,3}) + 95(P/F_{i,4}) + 74(P/F_{i,5})$, i = Expected DCFROR = 1.7% < i^* of 15%, reject

Expected Net Present Value

ENPV @ 15% = $-550 - 18(P/F_{15,1}) + 269(P/F_{15,2}) + 159(P/F_{15,3}) + 95(P/F_{15,4}) + 74(P/F_{15,5})$ = -167 < 0, reject

Expected Present Value Ratio

EPVR = -167 / [550 + 18(P/F$_{15,1}$)] = -0.30 < 0, reject

(.8696 above P/F$_{15,1}$)

CHAPTER 8 PROBLEM SOLUTIONS

8-10 Solution: Continued

(Independent < 1,000 Bbls), Case 4, Expense Cash Flows

Year	0	1	2	3	4	5	5 Salv
Gross Revenue		1,612	1,378	910	655	488	
-Royalties		-226	-193	-127	-92	-68	
Net Revenue		1,386	1,185	783	563	420	
-Oper Costs		-175	-193	-212	-233	-256	
-Intangible	-750	-250					
-Depreciation		-96	-164	-117	-84	-60	
-Deprec Writeoff							-149
Before Depln	-750	866	828	453	247	104	-149
-100% Limit		866	828	453	247	104	
-Percent Depln		-208	-178	-117	-85	-63	
-Cost Depln		-32					
Taxable Income	-750	658	650	336	162	41	-149
-Tax @ 40%	300	-263	-260	-134	-65	-16	60
Net Income	-450	395	390	202	97	25	-89
+Depreciation		96	164	117	84	60	149
+Depletion		208	178	117	85	63	
-Capital Costs	-100*	-670**					
Cash Flow	-550	28	732	436	266	148	60

* Capital cost is the $100 mineral rights acquisition cost.
** Capital cost is the $670 tangible equipment cost.

PW Eq: $0 = -550 + 28(P/F_{i,1}) + 732(P/F_{i,2}) + 436(P/F_{i,3}) + 266(P/F_{i,4}) + 208(P/F_{i,5})$, i = DCFROR = 50.3% > i* of 15%, accept

NPV @ 15% = $-550 + 28(P/F_{15,1}) + 732(P/F_{15,2}) + 436(P/F_{15,3}) + 266(P/F_{15,4}) + 208(P/F_{15,5})$ = 570.0 > 0, accept

PVR = 570 / 550 = 1.04 > 0, accept

8-10 Solution: Continued

(Independent < 1,000 Bbls), Case 4, Stand Alone Cash Flows

Year	0	1	2	3	4	5	5 Salv
Gross Revenue		1,612	1,378	910	655	488	
-Royalties		-226	-193	-127	-92	-68	
Net Revenue		1,386	1,185	783	563	420	
-Oper Costs		-175	-193	-212	-233	-256	
-Intangible	-750	-250					
-Depreciation		-96	-164	-117	-84	-60	
-Deprec Writeoff							-149
Before Depltn	-750	866	828	453	247	104	-149
-100% Limit		866	828	453	247	104	
-Percent Depl		-208	-178	-117	-85	-63	
-Cost Depltn		32					
-Loss Forward		-750	-92				
Taxable Income	-750	-92	558	336	162	41	-149
-Tax @ 40%			-223	-134	-65	-16	60
Net Income	-750	-92	335	202	97	25	-89
+Depreciation		96	164	117	84	60	149
+Depletion		208	178	117	85	63	
+Loss Forward		750	92				
-Capital Costs	-100*	-670**					
Cash Flow	-850	291	769	436	266	148	60

208 (sum of year 5 cash flow and salvage)

* Capital cost is the $100 mineral rights acquisition cost.
** Capital cost is the $670 tangible equipment cost.

PW Eq: $0 = -850 + 291(P/F_{i,1}) + 769(P/F_{i,2}) + 436(P/F_{i,3}) + 266(P/F_{i,4}) + 208(P/F_{i,5})$, i = DCFROR = 41.25% > i^* of 15%, accept

NPV @ 15% = $-850 + 291(P/F_{15,1}) + 769(P/F_{15,2}) + 436(P/F_{15,3}) + 266(P/F_{15,4}) + 208(P/F_{15,5})$ = +526.7 > 0, accept

PVR = 526.7 / 850 = 0.62 > 0 accept

CHAPTER 8 PROBLEM SOLUTIONS

8-10 Solution: Continued

(Independent < 1,000 Bbls), Case 4, Risk Analysis

Non-Risk Adjusted Cash Flows

Cash Flow	-550	p=0.40	28	732	436	266	208
Year	0		1	2	3	4	5

p=0.60

```
-Abandonment Cost      -70
-Cost Depl Writeoff   -100
Taxable Income        -170
-Tax @ 40%              68
Net Income            -102
+ Writeoffs            100
Failure Cash Flow       -2
```

Risk Adjusted Cash Flows

Expected Value Cash Flows	-550	10*	293	174	106	83
Year	0	1	2	3	4	5

* $28(0.4) - 2(0.6) = +10$

Expected Discounted Cash Flow Rate of Return:

PW Eq: $0 = -550 + 10(P/F_{i,1}) + 293(P/F_{i,2}) + 174(P/F_{i,3}) + 106(P/F_{i,4})$
$+ 83(P/F_{i,5})$, i = Expected DCFROR = 6.8% < i^* of 15%, reject

Expected Net Present Value:

ENPV @ 15% = $-550 + 10(P/F_{15,1}) + 293(P/F_{15,2}) + 174(P/F_{15,3})$
$+ 106(P/F_{15,4}) + 83(P/F_{15,5}) = -103 < 0$, reject

Expected Present Value Ratio:

EPVR = -103 / 550 = -0.19 < 0, reject

8-10 Solution: Continued

Integrated, Case 5, Expense, Breakeven Crude Oil Price Analysis

Cash Flows

Year	0	1	2	3	4	5
Net Revenue		.86X(62)	.86X(53)	.86X(35)	.86X(24)	.86X(17)
-Oper Costs		-175	-193	-212	-233	-256
-Intangible	-525	-175				
-Depreciation		-96	-164	-117	-84	-60
-Deprec Writeoff						-149
-Amortization	-45	-60	-60	-60	-60	-15
-Cost Depletion		-32	-28	-18	-13	-9
Taxable Income	-570	53X-538	46X-445	30X-408	21X-389	15X-489
-Tax @ 40%	228	-21X+215	-18X+178	-12X+163	-8X+156	-6X+196
Net Income	-342	32X-323	28X-267	18X-245	13X-234	9X-294
+Depreciation		96	164	117	84	209
+Cost Depletion		32	28	18	13	9
+Amortization	45	60	60	60	60	15
-Capital Costs	-325	-745				
Cash Flow	-622	32X-880	28X-15	18X-49	13X-77	9X-60

$$0 = -622 + (32X-880)(P/F_{15,1})^{.8696} + (28X-15)(P/F_{15,2})^{.7561} + (18X-49)(P/F_{15,3})^{.6575}$$

$$+ (13X-77)(P/F_{15,4})^{.5718} + (9X-60)(P/F_{15,5})^{.4972}$$

$0 = 72.74X - 1{,}504.63$, therefore, $X = \$20.69$

Breakeven Selling Price Per Unit = $20.69 per barrel

CHAPTER 8 PROBLEM SOLUTIONS

8-10 Solution: Continued

Case 6, Integrated Company Acquisition Breakeven Cost

Cash Flows from Part 1A are:

Year	0	1	2	3	4	5
Cash Flow	-622	-48	696	421	261	191

Net Present Value from Part 1A is $383.54

This NPV represents additional after-tax acquisition cost that can be incurred and still give the investor a 15% DCFROR. Let the before-tax acquisition cost equal "X" and be subject to cost depletion. The tax savings generated from the additional cost depletion deductions above those associated with the $100,000 acquisition fee are calculated as follows:

	Before-Tax Value	Tax Savings
Year 1	X(62/191) = .32X	.32X(.4) = .13X
Year 2	.68X(53/129) = .28X	.28X(.4) = .11X
Year 3	.40X(35/76) = .18X	.18X(.4) = .07X
Year 4	.22X(24/41) = .13X	.13X(.4) = .05X
Year 5	.09X(17/17) = .09X	.09X(.4) = .04X

$$0 = .13X(P/F_{15,1}) \overset{.8696}{} + .11X(P/F_{15,2}) \overset{.7561}{} + .07X(P/F_{15,3}) \overset{.6575}{}$$

$$+ .05X(P/F_{15,4}) \overset{.5718}{} + .04X(P/F_{15,5}) \overset{.4972}{} = .2907X$$

X - .2907X = 383.54 NPV, therefore, X = $540.73

An integrated producer who can expense deductions against other income could invest $540,730 to acquire the mineral rights to this project and still have the project earn a 15% DCFROR.

8-11 Solution: Mining Project, Costs ($) and Production in Thousands

Year	0	1	2	3	4	5
Production in Tons		62	53	35	24	17
Mineral Development	750	250				
Mining Equipment		670				
Mineral Rights. Acq.	100					
Operating Costs		175	193	212	233	256
Price, $ Per Ton		26.0	26.0	26.0	27.3	28.7

Corporate Mining, Case 1A, Expense Cash Flows

Year	0	1	2	3	4	5	Salv
Gross Revenue		1,612	1,378	910	655	488	
-Royalties		-226	-193	-127	-92	-68	
Net Revenue		1,386	1,185	783	563	420	
-Oper Costs		-175	-193	-212	-233	-256	
-Development	-525	-175					
-Depreciation		-96	-164	-117	-84	-60	
-Deprec Writeoff							-149
-Amortization	-45	-60	-60	-60	-60	-15	
Before Depln	-570	881	768	393	187	89	-149
50% Limit		440	384	197	93	-45	
-Percent Depl		-208	-178	-117	-85	63	
-Cost Depltn		32					
Taxable Income	-570	673	590	276	102	44	-149
-Tax @ 40%	228	-269	-236	-110	-41	-18	60
Net Income	-342	404	354	166	61	26	-89
+Depreciation		96	164	117	84	60	149
+Depletion Taken		208	178	117	85	45	
+Amortization	45	60	60	60	60	15	
-Capital Costs	-325*	-745**					
Cash Flow	-622	22	756	460	290	146	60
						206	

* Capital cost includes $100 mineral rights acquisition and 30% of $750 development that must be amortized over 60 months.
** Capital cost includes $670 equipment cost and 30% of $250 development cost.

PW Eq: $0 = -622 + 22(P/F_{i,1}) + 756(P/F_{i,2}) + 460(P/F_{i,3}) + 290(P/F_{i,4})$

$+ 206(P/F_{i,5})$ $i = DCFROR = 45.1\%$

NPV @ 15% $= -622 + 22(P/F_{15,1}) + 756(P/F_{15,2}) + 460(P/F_{15,3}) + 290(P/F_{15,4})$

$+ 206(P/F_{15,5}) = +539$

PVR = 539 / 622 = 0.87

CHAPTER 8 PROBLEM SOLUTIONS

8-11 Solution: Continued

Corporate Mining, Case 1B, Stand Alone Cash Flows

Year	0	1	2	3	4	5	Salv
Gross Revenue		1,612	1,378	910	655	488	
-Royalties		-226	-193	-127	-92	-68	
Net Revenue		1,386	1,185	783	563	420	
-Oper Costs		-175	-193	-212	-233	-256	
-Development	-525	-175					
-Depreciation		-96	-164	-117	-84	-60	
-Deprec Writeoffs							-149
-Amortization	-45	-60	-60	-60	-60	-15	
Before Depln	-570	881	768	393	187	89	-149
-50% Limit		440	384	197	93	-45	
-Percent Depln		-208	-178	-117	-85	63	
-Cost Depln		32					
-Loss Forward		-570					
Taxable Income	-570	103	590	276	102	44	-149
-Tax @ 40%		-41	-236	-110	-41	-18	60
Net Income	-570	62	354	166	61	26	-89
+Depreciation		96	164	117	84	60	149
+Depletion Taken		208	178	117	85	45	
+Amortization	45	60	60	60	60	15	
+Loss Forward		570					
-Capital Costs	-325*	-745**					
Cash Flow	-850	250	756	460	290	146	60
						206	

* Capital cost includes $100 mineral rights acquisition and 30% of $750 development that must be amortized over 60 months.

** Capital cost includes $670 equipment cost and 30% of $250 development cost.

$$0 = -850 + 250(P/F_{i,1}) + 756(P/F_{i,2}) + 460(P/F_{i,3}) + 290(P/F_{i,4})$$
$$+ 206(P/F_{i,5}) \quad i = DCFROR = 39.7\%$$

$$NPV @ 15\% = -850 + 250(P/F_{15,1}) + 756(P/F_{15,2}) + 460(P/F_{15,3})$$
$$+ 290(P/F_{15,4}) + 206(P/F_{15,5}) = +\$510$$

PVR = 510 / 850 = .60

8-11 Solution: Continued

Corporate Mining, Case 2 Risk Adjustment Based on Case 1A

Non-Risk Adjusted Cash Flows

Cash Flow	-622 p=0.40	22	756	460	290	206
Year	0	1	2	3	4	5

p=0.60

-Abandonment Cost	-70
-30% Unamortized Develop.	-180
-Cost Depl Writeoff	-100
Taxable Income	-350
-Tax @ 40%	140
Net Income	-210
+ Writeoffs	280
Failure Cash Flow	+70

Risk Adjusted Cash Flows

Cash Flows	-622	51*	302	184	116	82
Year	0	1	2	3	4	5

* $22(.4) + 70(.6) = +51$

Expected Discounted Cash Flow Rate of Return

PW Eq: $0 = -622 + 51(P/F_{i,1}) + 302(P/F_{i,2}) + 184(P/F_{i,3}) + 116(P/F_{i,4})$
$+ 82(P/F_{i,5})$ i = Expected DCFROR = 6.1% < i^* of 15%, reject

Expected Net Present Value

ENPV @ 15% = $-622 + 51(P/F_{15,1}) + 302(P/F_{15,2}) + 184(P/F_{15,3})$
$+ 116(P/F_{15,4}) + 75(P/F_{15,5}) = -121 < 0$, reject

Expected Present Value Ratio

EPVR = -121 / 622 = -0.195 < 0, reject

CHAPTER 8 PROBLEM SOLUTIONS

8-11 Solution: Continued

Individual, Case 3, Expense Cash Flows

Year	0	1	2	3	4	5	Salv
Gross Revenue		1,612	1,378	910	655	488	
-Royalties		-226	-193	-127	-92	-68	
Net Revenue		1,386	1,185	783	563	420	
-Oper Costs		-175	-193	-212	-233	-256	
-Development	-750	-250					
-Depreciation		-96	-164	-117	-84	-60	
-Deprec Writeoff							-149
Before Depln	-750	866	828	453	247	104	-149
-50% Limit		433	414	227	123	-52	
-Percent Depln		-208	-178	-117	-85	63	
-Cost Depletion		32					
Taxable Income	-750	658	650	336	162	52	-149
-Tax @ 40%	300	-263	-260	-134	-65	-21	60
Net Income	-450	395	390	202	97	31	-89
+Depreciation		96	164	117	84	60	
+Writeoff							149
+Depletion Taken		208	178	117	85	52	
-Capital Costs	-100*	-670**					
Cash Flow	-550	28	732	436	266	143	60

203

* Capital cost is the $100 mineral rights acquisition cost.
** Capital cost is the $670 equipment cost.

$$0 = -550 + 28(P/F_{i,1}) + 732(P/F_{i,2}) + 436(P/F_{i,3}) + 266(P/F_{i,4})$$
$$+ 203(P/F_{i,5}) \quad i = DCFROR = 50.3\% > 15\%, \text{ accept}$$

$$NPV @ 15\% = -550 + 28(P/F_{15,1}) + 732(P/F_{15,2}) + 436(P/F_{15,3}) + 266(P/F_{15,4})$$
$$+ 203(P/F_{15,5}) = 567.5 > 0, \text{ accept}$$

PVR = 567.5 / 550 = 1.03 > 0, accept

8-11 Solution: Continued

Individual, Case 3, Stand Alone Cash Flows

Year	0	1	2	3	4	5	Salv
Gross Revenue		1,612	1,378	910	655	488	
-Royalties		-226	-193	-127	-92	-68	
Net Revenue		1,386	1,185	783	563	420	
-Oper Costs		-175	-193	-212	-233	-256	
-Development	-750	-250					
-Depreciation		-96	-164	-117	-84	-60	
-Deprec Writeoff							-149
Before Depltn	-750	866	828	453	247	104	
-50% Limit		433	414	227	123	-52	
-Percent Depl		-208	-178	-117	-85	63	
-Cost Depltn		32					
-Loss Forward		-750	-92				
Taxable Income	-750	-92	558	336	162	52	-149
-Tax @ 40%			-223	-134	-65	-21	60
Net Income	-750	-92	335	202	97	31	-89
+Depreciation		96	164	117	84	60	149
+Depletion Taken		208	178	117	85	52	
+Loss Forward		750	92				
-Capital Costs	-100*	-670**					
Cash Flow	-850	291	769	436	266	143	60
						203	

* Capital cost is the $100 mineral rights acquisition cost.
** Capital cost is the $670 equipment cost.

PW Eq: $0 = -850 + 291(P/F_{i,1}) + 769(P/F_{i,2}) + 436(P/F_{i,3}) + 266(P/F_{i,4})$
$+ 203(P/F_{i,5})$, i = DCFROR = 41.2% > 15%, accept

NPV @ 15% = $-850 + 291(P/F_{15,1}) + 769(P/F_{15,2}) + 436(P/F_{15,3})$
$+ 266(P/F_{15,4}) + 203(P/F_{15,5}) = +524.2 > 0$, accept

PVR = 524.2 / 850 = 0.62 > 0, accept

CHAPTER 8 PROBLEM SOLUTIONS

8-11 Solution: Continued

Individual, Case 3, Risk Adjustment Based on "Expense" Cash Flows

Non-Risk Adjusted Cash Flows

Cash Flow	-550	p=0.40	28	732	436	266	203
Year	0		1	2	3	4	5

p=0.60

-Abandonment Cost	-70
-Cost Depl Writeoff	-100
Taxable Income	-170
-Tax @ 40%	68
Net Income	-102
+ Writeoffs	100
Failure Cash Flow	-2

Risk Adjusted Cash Flows

Expected Value Cash Flows	-550	10*	293	174	106	80
Year	0	1	2	3	4	5

* $28(.4) - 2(.6) = +10$

Expected DCFROR

PW Eq: $0 = -550 + 10(P/F_{i,1}) + 293(P/F_{i,2}) + 174(P/F_{i,3}) + 106(P/F_{i,4})$
$\quad\quad + 80(P/F_{i,5})$ i = Expected DCFROR = 6.67% < i^* of 15%, reject

Expected Net Present Value

ENPV @ 15% = $-550 + 10(P/F_{15,1}) + 293(P/F_{15,2}) + 174(P/F_{15,3})$
$\quad\quad + 106(P/F_{15,4}) + 80(P/F_{15,5}) = -105 < 0$, reject

Expected Present Value Ratio

PVR = -105 / 550 = -0.19 < 0, reject

8-11 Solution: Continued

Corporate Mining, Case 4, Breakeven Selling Price Analysis

Year	Time 0	1	2	3	4	5	Salv
Total Production		62	53	35	24	17	
Net Production (86%)		53	46	30	21	15	
Net Revenue		53X	46X	30X	21X	15X	
-Operating Costs		-175	-193	-212	-233	-256	
-Development	-525	-175					
-Depreciation		-96	-164	-117	-84	-60	
-Deprec Writeoff							-149
-Amortization	-45	-60	-60	-60	-60	-15	
Before Depletion	-570	53X-506	46X-417	30X-389	21X-377	15X-331	-149
-50% Limit		27X-253	23X-208	15X-195	0*	0	
-Percent (15%)		-8X	-7X	-5X			
-Cost Depletion		32					
Taxable Income	-570	45X-506	39X-417	25X-389	21X-377	15X-331	-149
-Tax @ 40%	228	-18X+202	-16X+167	-10X+156	-8X+151	-6X+132	60
Net Income	-342	27X-304	23X-250	15X-233	13X-226	9X-199	-89
+Depreciation		96	164	117	84	60	149
+Depletion Taken		8X	7X	5X			
+Amortization	45	60	60	60	60	15	
-Capital Costs	-325	-745					
Cash Flow	-622	35X-893	30X-26	20X-56	13X-82	9X-124	60
						9X-64	

* By iterative calculations, percentage depletion is the largest depletion deduction in years 1, 2 & 3 and the 50% limit is zero or near zero in years 4 and 5. Since the cost depletion basis is recovered by the year 1 percent depletion, no depletion exists in years 4 and 5.

$$0 = -622 + (35X-893)(P/F_{15,1})^{.8696} + (30X-26)(P/F_{15,2})^{.7561} + (20X-56)(P/F_{15,3})^{.6575}$$
$$+ (13X-82)(P/F_{15,4})^{.5718} + (9X-64)(P/F_{15,5})^{.4972}$$

$0 = 78.18X - 1,533.71$, therefore, $X = \$19.62$

Breakeven Selling Price Per Unit = $19.62 per ton

# CHAPTER 8 PROBLEM SOLUTIONS 123

8-11 Solution: Continued

Corporate Mining, Case 5, Acquisition Breakeven Cost Analysis

Year	0	1	2	3	4	5	Salv
Revenue		1,612	1,378	910	655	488	
-Royalties		-226	-193	-127	-92	-68	
Net Revenue		1,386	1,185	783	563	420	
-Oper Costs		-175	-193	-212	-233	-256	
-Development	-525	-175					
-Depreciation		-96	-164	-117	-84	-60	
-Deprec Writeoff							-149
-Amortization	-45	-60	-60	-60	-60	-15	
Before Depltn	-570	881	768	393	187	89	-149
-50% Limit		440	384	197	93	-45	
-Percent Depl		-208	-178	-117	-85	63	
-Cost Depltn		32					
Taxable	-570	673	590	276	102	44	-149
-Tax @ 40%	228	-269	-236	-110	-41	-18	60
Net Income	-342	404	354	166	61	26	-89
+Depreciation		96	164	117	84	60	149
+Depletion		208	178	117	85	45	
+Amortization	45	60	60	60	60	15	
-Capital Costs	-325	-745					
Cash Flow	-622	22	756	460	290	146	60
						206	

Net Present Value $539

Since percentage depletion is allowed for all mineral producers, if we assume percentage depletion deductions will continue to be larger than the new cost depletion deductions, the before-tax value we could afford to pay for the property is the same as the after-tax net present value of $539,000. Checking this assumption, additional mineral rights cost of $539,000 added to the $100,000 in the analysis statement gives $639,000 total acquisition cost. The first year cost depletion would be $639,000(62/191) = $207,420 which is less than year 1 percentage depletion of $208,000 so percent depletion would still be taken. The additional mineral rights acquisition cost would not affect the depletion deduction so $539,000 is the incremental breakeven acquisition cost.

CHAPTER 9 PROBLEM SOLUTIONS

9-1 Solution: Before-Tax Time Diagrams in Actual Dollars

```
                    525,000(.259)   470,000(.259)   460,000(.259)
                    OC =135,980       =121,730        =119,140
OLD     ─────────────────────────────────────────────────────────
        0               1               2               3

                    C=8,000
                    525,000(.183)   470,000(.183)   460,000(.183)
        C=39,000    OC=96,080         = 86,010        = 84,180
NEW     ─────────────────────────────────────────────────────────
        0               1               2               3

                    C=8,000
                    525,000(.076)   470,000(.076)   460,000(.076)
NEW     C=39,000    Savings = 39,900  = 35,720        = 34,960
-OLD    ─────────────────────────────────────────────────────────
        0               1               2               3
```

Incremental Cash Flows in Escalated Dollars

Year	0	1	2	3
Savings		39,900	35,720	34,960
-Development		-8,000		
-Depreciation		-3,900	-7,800	-7,800
-Deprec Writeoff				-19,500
Taxable Income		28,000	27,920	7,660
-Tax @ 40%		-11,200	-11,168	-3,064
Net Income		16,800	16,752	4,596
+Depreciation		3,900	7,800	27,300
-Capital Costs	-39,000			
Cash Flow	-39,000	20,700	24,552	31,896

A) PW Eq: $0 = -39,000 + 20,700(P/F_{i,1}) + 24,552(P/F_{i,2}) + 31,896(P/F_{i,3})$

i = DCFROR = 39.9%

B) Non-Discounted Payback = $1 + (39,000 - 20,700)/24,552 = 1.75$

C) From Equation 5-1: $1 + i = (1 + f)(1 + i')$

Constant $ DCFROR = $i' = \{(1.399)/(1.1)\} - 1 = .2716$ or 27.2%

Alternatively, Constant Dollar Cash Flows:

```
            20,700(P/F_10,1)   24,552(P/F_10,2)   31,896(P/F_10,3)
-39,000     =18,818            =20,290            =23,963
────────────────────────────────────────────────────────────────
  0              1                  2                  3
```

PW Eq: $0 = -39,000 + 18,818(P/F_{i',1}) + 20,290(P/F_{i',2}) + 23,963(P/F_{i',3})$

i' = Constant Dollar DCFROR = 27.2%, the same as from Eq 5-1

CHAPTER 9 PROBLEM SOLUTIONS

9-2 Solution: Abandon or Develop - All Values in Thousands of Dollars.

```
                    ---------- Sunk ----------   Writeoff All Capital Costs
ABANDON             Acq Cost = 400   IDC = 600   Against Other Income at Yr0
Now at Yr 0         ─────────────────────────────────────────────────────────
                         -2              0          0 Now              1

                    ---------- Sunk ----------   C_Tang=200          Rev=420
DEVELOP in          Acq Cost = 400   IDC = 600   C_IDC =100  P=0.6   OC= 35
Month 7 of Yr 0     ─────────────────────────────────────────────────────────
Called Yr 0 Now          -2              0          0 Now              1
                                                              P=0.4 ─┐
```

The $400 year -2 Acquisition Cost and the $600   Yr 1 Abandon
year 0 IDC are sunk along with the tax deduction   Salvage=100
for 70% of the $600 year 0 IDC. These values are not
relevant to our analysis, but the remaining tax effects are relevant.

Depreciation Calculations	Cost Depletion Calculations
Yr 1 200(.1429) = 29	Yr 1 400(25% of Reserves) = 100
Yr 1 Sale Writeoff = 171	Yr 1 Sale Writeoff = 300

Amortization Calculations

Year 0 $600 IDC	Year 1 $100 IDC	Total
Yr 0 180(8/60) = 24		24
Yr 1 180(12/60) = 36	Yr 1 30(6/60) = 3	39
Yr 1 Writeoff = 120	Yr 1 Writeoff = 27	147

| | Abandon | ---- Develop & Succeed ---- | | Fail and |
Year	0 Now	0 Now	1	Yr 1 Sale	Abandon Yr 1
Gross Revenue			420	350	100
-Royalties			-76		
Net Revenue			344	350	100
-Oper Costs			-60		
-Intangible		-70			
-Depreciation			-29	-171	-200
-Amortization	-180 writeoff	-24	-36	-147	-156
-Cost Depletion	-400 writeoff		-100	-300	-400
Taxable Income	-580	-94	119	-268	-656
-Tax @ 40%	232	38	-48	107	262
Net Income	-348	-56	71	-161	-394
+Depreciation			29	171	200
+Cost Depletion	400		100	300	400
+Amortization	180	24	36	147	156
-Capital Costs		-230			
Cash Flow	232	-262	236	457	362

Prob.Success=0.6 Prob.Fail=0.4

$NPV_{Abandon} = +\$232$

$ENPV_{Develop} = -262 + [236(P/F_{20,1}) + 457(P/F_{20,1})](.6) + 362(P/F_{20,1})(.4)$

$\qquad\qquad\;\; = +\$205 < NPV_{Abandon}$, Therefore, Abandon now.

9-3 Solution:

Stripper Well Solution to Determine the Sale Price That Makes Selling a Breakeven With Abandoning the Well. All Values in Thousands of Dollars.

SELL Cash Flow Calculation

Let X = Sale Value	X
-Book Value Writeoff	-5
Taxable Income	X-5
-Tax @ 40%	-.4X+2
Net Income	.6X-3
+Book Value Writeoff	5
Cash Flow	.6X+2

ABANDON Cash Flow Calculation

Equipment Salvage Value	30
-Abandon Cost	-20
-Book Value Writeoff	-5
Taxable Income	5
-Tax @ 40%	-2
Net Income	3
+Book Value Writeoff	5
Cash Flow	8

Set "Sale Cash Flow" Equal to "Abandon Cash Flow" and Solve for the unknown breakeven sale value "X":

.6X + 2 = 8, Therefore, X = $10

9-4 Solution: Land Acquisition Solution

```
C = $60,000                              Esc $ Sale Value = $X
_____
0                                                      2
```

Sale Value in Esc $	X
-Book Value Writeoff	-60,000
Taxable Income	X-60,000
-Tax @ 30%	-.3X+18,000
Net Income	.7X-42,000
+Book Value Writeoff	60,000
Cash Flow in Esc $	.7X+18,000

Constant Dollar Present Worth Equation:

$60,000 = (.7X+18,000)(P/F_{f=10\%,2})(P/F_{i*'=20\%,2})$

$60,000 = .4017X + 10,330$

X = $123,649

Alternate Solution:

$1 + i = (1 + f)(1 + i')$; so $i^* = (1 + .10)(1 + .20) - 1 = .32$ or 32%

$i^* = 32\%$ is equivalent to $i^{*'} = 20\%$ for 10%/yr inflation, f.

Escalated Dollar Present Worth Equation:

$60,000 = (.7X+18,000)(P/F_{32,2})$ therefore X = $123,649

CHAPTER 9 PROBLEM SOLUTIONS

9-5 Solution:

Property Acquisition Analysis, Solution in Thousands of Dollars.

```
              C=500                CF=-1,500  P=0.6   1,000  1,800  1,200   800   400
DEVELOP      ──────(Sunk)          ────────────────────────────────────────────────────
              -2                      0                1      2      3      4      5
                                    P=0.4
                                         ╲   CF=0


              C=500                CF=800   (Opportunity Cost if Developed)
SELL         ──────(Sunk)          ────────────────────────────────────────────────────
              -2                      0                1      2      3      4      5
```

Yr 0 Sell Cash Flow

Sale Revenue	1,000
-Book Value Writeoff	500
Taxable Income	500
-Tax @ 40%	-200
Net Income	300
+Book Value Writeoff	500
Cash Flow	800

Sell CF = Sell NPV = +$800, Develop ENPV = +$495 as calculated below.

Therefore, select the maximum NPV and Sell.

Development Expected NPV for $i^* = 20\%$:

$$ENPV = -1{,}500 + [1{,}000(P/F_{20,1}) + 1{,}800(P/F_{20,2}) + 1{,}200(P/F_{20,3})$$
$$+ 800(P/F_{20,4}) + 400(P/F_{20,5})](0.6) = +\$495$$

Incremental ENPV generates the same economic conclusion:

$ENPV_{Develop-Sell} = 495 - 800 = -\$305$, so reject the develop alternative.

Breakeven Probability of Occurence Analysis

Let "X" equal the breakeven probability of success, which is the value of "X" that makes the $ENPV_{DEV} = NPV_{Sell} = +\$800$

$$-1{,}500 + [1{,}000\underset{.8333}{(P/F_{20,1})} + 1{,}800\underset{.6944}{(P/F_{20,2})} + 1{,}200\underset{.5787}{(P/F_{20,3})}$$
$$+ 800\underset{.4823}{(P/F_{20,4})} + 400\underset{.4019}{(P/F_{20,5})}](X) = 800$$

$X(3{,}324.3) - 1{,}500 = 800$

Therefore, X = 0.69 or 69% is the breakeven probability of success.

9-6 Solution: Investment Analysis, in Actual Dollars

Depreciable Costs	100,000	50,000		
Working Capital	25,000			
Sale Value				250,000
Revenue		200,000	280,000	280,000
Operating Costs		140,000	190,000	190,000
	0	1	2	3

Cash Flow Calculations

Year	0	1	2	3	3 Salv.
Revenue		200,000	280,000	280,000	250,000
−Operating Costs		−140,000	−190,000	−190,000	
−Depreciation		−21,429	−36,735	−26,239	
−Deprec Writeoff					−65,598
−WC Writeoff					−25,000
Taxable Income		38,571	53,265	63,761	159,402
−Tax @ 40%		−15,429	−21,306	−25,504	−63,761
Net Income		23,143	31,959	38,257	95,641
+Depreciation		21,429	36,735	26,239	65,598
+WC Writeoff					25,000
−Capital Costs	−125,000	−50,000			
Cash Flow	−125,000	−5,429	68,694	64,496	186,239
				250,735	

PW Eq: $0 = -125{,}000 - 5{,}429(P/F_{i,1}) + 68{,}694(P/F_{i,2}) + 250{,}735(P/F_{i,3})$

i = DCFROR = 39%

NPV @ i^* = 15% = +$87,084

NPV represents additional after-tax cost (negative cash flow) that may be incurred at time zero (in addition to $125,000) for the project to yield a DCFROR of 15%. If the equivalent before-tax value is deductible as a development cost at time zero, convert after-tax NPV to the equivalent before tax value by dividing NPV by the sum of one minus the tax rate as follows:

87,084 / (1−0.4) = $145,140, This is the before-tax research or development cost that could be incurred in year 0 and still have the project earn a 15% discounted cash flow rate of return.

CHAPTER 9 PROBLEM SOLUTIONS

9-7 Solution: Land Acquisition Solution, Values in Dollars

```
                                          Revenue=250,000
C_Land=100,000    OC=2,500    OC=2,500    OC=2,500
|_____|_____|_____|
0                 1           2           3
```

Cash Flow Calculations

Year	0	1-3	Yr 3 Sale
Revenue			250,000
-Property Taxes		-2,500	
-Writeoff Bk Value			-100,000
Taxable Income		-2,500	150,000
-Tax @ 30%		750	-45,000
Net Income		-1,750	105,000
+Writeoff Bk Value			100,000
-Capital Cost	-100,000		
Cash Flow	-100,000	-1,750	205,000

PW Eq: $0 = -100,000 - 1,750(P/A_{i,3}) + 205,000(P/F_{i,3})$

Escalated Dollar DCFROR, i, = 25.6%

Use Equation 5-1 to convert the escalated dollar DCFROR to the equivalent constant dollar DCFROR as follows: $1+i = (1+f)(1+i')$

Constant Dollar DCFROR for 8% inflation,

$i' = (1.256 / 1.08) - 1 = 0.163$ or 16.3%.

9-8 Solution: Common Stock vs Bonds, All Values in Thousands of Dollars

Alternative #1, Purchase Common Stock

```
C=100
|─────────────────────────────────|      F = 100(F/P_{10,10}) = 259.4
0                                10
```

Taxable Gain = 259.4 - 100 = 159.4
Tax on Gain = 159.4(0.30) = -47.8

Yr 10 After-Tax Cash Flow (Future Value) = 259.4 - 47.8 = $211.6

Alternative #2, Purchase Bond

```
C=100    I=10    I=10    .........   I=10
|─────────────────────────────────────|   L=100
0         1       2     ............ 10
```

Interest Income of ten (10) thousand dollars per year is before-tax and needs to be converted to an after-tax value that represents the actual dollars available to be reinvested at the after-tax money market interest rate of 7.0% (10% - 3%) as follows:

10 - 10(0.3) = 7.0 Net Cash Flow From Bond Dividends Each Year

Therefore, the year 10 after-tax cash flow (future value) from the bond investment is:

Year 10 FW = 7.0(F/A_{7,10})$^{13.816}$ + 100 maturity value = $196.7

Purchase common stock to maximize future value of $211.6 versus $196.7

The required before-tax growth rate for common stock that would make the alternatives economically equivalent is shown below:

Let X = Before-tax common stock sale value at year 10 to give after-tax cash flow of $196.7 which equals the bank investment projected future value.

196.7 = Required after-tax year 10 value
196.7 = X - (X-100)(0.3)
196.7 = X - 0.3X + 30
196.7 = 0.7X + 30

Therefore, 0.7X = 196.7 - 30, so X = $238.1

PW Eq: 100 = 238.1(P/F_{i,10}),   Growth Rate, i = 9.06%

CHAPTER 9 PROBLEM SOLUTIONS

9-9 Solution: Breakeven Sales Solution in Thousands of Dollars

Let X = the breakeven sales revenue required to give the investment a 25% DCFROR.

Year	0	1	2	3	4	5
Revenue		X	X+10	X+20	X+30	X+40
-Operating Costs		-50.0	-60.0	-70.0	-80.0	-90.0
-Depreciation	-71.5	-122.5	-87.5	-62.5	-45.0	-45.0
-Deprec Writeoff						-67.0
Taxable Income	-71.5	X-172.5	X-137.5	X-112.5	X-95.0	X-162.0
-Tax @ 40%	28.6	-.4X+69.0	-.4X+55.0	-.4X+45.0	-.4X+38.0	-.4X+64.8
Net Income	-42.9	.6X-103.5	.6X-82.5	.6X-67.5	.6X-57.0	.6X-97.2
+Depreciation	71.5	122.5	87.5	62.5	45.0	45.0
-Deprec Writeoff						67.0
-Capital Cost	-500.0					
Cash Flow	-471.4	.6X+19.0	.6X+5.0	.6X-5.0	.6X-12.0	.6X+14.8

PW Eq: $0 = -471.4 + (.6X+19)(P/F_{25,1})^{.8000} + (.6X+5)(P/F_{25,2})^{.6400}$
$+ (.6X-5.0)(P/F_{25,3})^{.512} + (.6X-12.0)(P/F_{25,4})^{.4096} + (.6X+14.8)(P/F_{25,5})^{.3277}$

$0 = 1.6136X - 455.63$ Therefore, X = \$282.37

\$282.37 is the year 1 breakeven revenue. This amount will increase by \$10 in each succeeding year.

9-10 Solution: Case A, B, C & D) All Values in Thousands of Dollars

Cash Flows

Year	0	1	2	3	4	5	6
Revenue			900	900	900	900	1,300*
-Operating Costs			-200	-200	-200	-200	-200
-Development	-100	-300					
-Depreciation		-50	-100	-100	-100	-100	-50
-Work Cap Bk Val							-200
Taxable Income	-100	-350	600	600	600	600	850
-Tax @ 40%	40	140	-240	-240	-240	-240	-340
Net Income	-60	-210	360	360	360	360	510
+Depreciation		50	100	100	100	100	50
+Work Cap Bk Val							200
-Capital Costs		-700					
Cash Flow	-60	-860	460	460	460	460	760

* Revenue includes working capital return and salvage.

A) Net Present Value

$NPV = -60 - 860(P/F_{15,1}) + 460(P/A_{15,4})(P/F_{15,1}) + 760(P/F_{15,6}) = +663$

B) Additional Before-Tax Research and Development Cost at Year 0

$NPV / (1-\text{tax rate}) = 663 / (1-0.4) = \$1,105$

$1,105 is the additional before-tax year 0 development cost that can be expensed 100% in year 0 and just increase the year 0 negative cash flow by -663 (which makes the overall project NPV at 15% equal zero).

See the next page for verification of this result.

C) Consider $900,000 Sale Offer at Year 1.

Sale CF = $900 - (900-0)(0.4 \text{ tax rate}) = 540$ after taxes at year 1 = NPV_{Sell}

Yr 1 $NPV_{Dev} = -860 + 460(P/A_{15,4}) + 760(P/F_{15,5}) = 831$

$NPV_{Dev} > NPV_{Sell}$ so select Develop.

D) What sale value at year 1 makes selling a breakeven with developing?

Let X = breakeven before-tax sale price at year 1.

$X - (X-0)(0.4 \text{ tax rate}) = 0.6X = CF_{Sell} = NPV_{Sell} = NPV_{Dev} = 831$

X = $1,385 = Breakeven Selling Price

CHAPTER 9 PROBLEM SOLUTIONS

9-10 Solution: Verification of the Problem 9-10, Part "B" answer

Additional Before-tax research/development cost = NPV / (1-tax rate)
= $663 / (1-0.4) = $1,105. This research/development cost in addition
to the $100 research cost already built into the analysis at year 0
makes NPV equal to zero as the following cash flow and NPV calculations
show.

Year	0	1	2	3	4	5	6
Revenue			900	900	900	900	1,300*
-Operating Costs			-200	-200	-200	-200	-200
-Development	-1,205	-300					
-Depreciation		-50	-100	-100	-100	-100	-50
-Work Cap Bk Val							-200
Taxable Income	-1,205	-350	600	600	600	600	850
-Tax @ 40%	482	140	-240	-240	-240	-240	-340
Net Income	-723	-210	360	360	360	360	510
+Depreciation		50	100	100	100	100	50
+Work Cap Bk Val							200
-Capital Costs		-700					
Cash Flow	-723	-860	460	460	460	460	760

* Revenue includes working capital return and salvage.

PW Eq: $0 = -723 - 860(P/F_{i,1}) + 460(P/A_{i,4})(P/F_{i,1})$
$+ 760(P/F_{i,6})$ $i = DCFROR = 15\%$

$NPV = -723 - 860(P/F_{15,1}) + 460(P/A_{15,4})(P/F_{15,1}) + 760(P/F_{15,6}) = 0$

9-11 Solution: Constant Dollar Analysis of Problem 9-10, Case A

$i^{*'} = (1+i)/(1+f) - 1$, therefore $i^{*'} = (1.15/1.10) - 1 = 4.55\%$

Constant Dollar NPV Equals:

$$NPV = -60 - 860\overset{.9091}{(P/F_{10,1})}\overset{.9565}{(P/F_{4.55,1})} + 460\overset{.8264}{(P/F_{10,2})}\overset{.9149}{(P/F_{4.55,2})}$$

$$+ 460\overset{.7513}{(P/F_{10,3})}\overset{.8750}{(P/F_{4.55,3})} + 460\overset{.6830}{(P/F_{10,4})}\overset{.8370}{(P/F_{4.55,4})}$$

$$+ 460\overset{.6209}{(P/F_{10,5})}\overset{.8005}{(P/F_{4.55,5})} + 760\overset{.5654}{(P/F_{10,6})}\overset{.7657}{(P/F_{4.55,6})}$$

$= +\$663$

If handled properly, constant dollar and escalated dollar NPV results
will always be equivalent within roundoff error of the factors used.

9-11 Solution: Continued

Case B) Additional Before-Tax Research and Development Cost

NPV / (1 - tax rate) = 663 / (1-.4) = $1,105

Cases C and D are calculated similarly and give the same results as in Problem 9-10.

9-12 Solution: Accounting for Risk in Problem 9-10

```
Success Cash Flows   -60  P=0.4  -860   P=0.7   460   460   460   460   760
                      |----------|-------------|-----|-----|-----|-----|
                      0   P=0.6   1   P=0.3    2     3     4     5     6
Failure Cash Flows
                               0              200+500(.4) = 400
```

Case A)

$$\text{ENPV @ 15\%} = -60 + [-860\overset{.8696}{(P/F_{15,1})} + \{460\overset{2.855}{(P/A_{15,4})}\overset{.8696}{(P/F_{15,1})}$$

$$+ 760\overset{.4323}{(P/F_{15,6})}\}(0.7)](0.4) + 400\overset{.7561}{(P/F_{15,2})}(.3)(.4) = +88.92$$

Case B) Additional Before-Tax Research and Development Cost That Could be Incurred on a Risk-Adjusted Analysis Basis:

NPV / (1-tax rate) = 88.92 / (1 - .4) = $148.19

9-13 Solution: Breakeven Before-Tax Revenue Analysis for Problem 9-10A

Year	0	1	2	3	4	5	6
Revenue			X	X	X	X	X+400*
-Operating Costs			-200	-200	-200	-200	-200
-Development	-100	-300					
-Depreciation		-50	-100	-100	-100	-100	-50
-Work Cap Bk Val							-200
Taxable Income	-100	-350	X-300	X-300	X-300	X-300	X-50
-Tax @ 40%	40	140	-.4X+120	-.4X+120	-.4X+120	-.4X+120	-.4X+ 20
Net Income	-60	-210	.6X-180	.6X-180	.6X-180	.6X-180	.6X- 30
+Depreciation		50	100	100	100	100	50
+Work Cap Bk Val							200
-Capital Costs		-700					
Cash Flow	-60	-860	.6X-80	.6X-80	.6X-80	.6X-80	.6X+220

* Revenue includes working capital return and salvage.

CHAPTER 9 PROBLEM SOLUTIONS

9-13 Solution: Continued

Breakeven Before-Tax Revenue Analysis for Problem 9-10A - Continued

$$PW\ Eq:\ 0 = -60 - 860(P/F_{15,1})^{.8696} + (.6X-80)(P/A_{15,4})^{2.855}(P/F_{15,1})^{.8696}$$

$$+ (.6X+220)(P/F_{15,6})^{.4323}$$

$$0 = 1.749X - 911.37,\ \text{Therefore},\ X = \$521.07$$

$$\frac{\$521,070\ \text{breakeven revenue per year}}{10,000\ \text{units produced per year}} = \$52.11/\text{unit breakeven selling price}$$

9-14 Solution: Facility Analysis, Solution in Dollars
R=Revenue, OC=Operating Costs, P=Probability of Occurrence

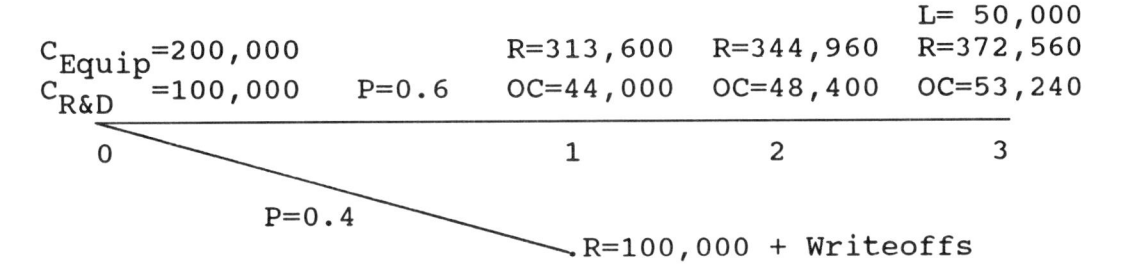

```
                                                  L= 50,000
C_Equip=200,000        R=313,600   R=344,960   R=372,560
C_R&D  =100,000  P=0.6 OC=44,000   OC=48,400   OC=53,240
─────────────────────────────────────────────────────────
0                      1           2           3
      P=0.4
           ↘ R=100,000 + Writeoffs
```

Escalated Dollar Cash Flow Calculations

		60% Probability of Success				40% Prob of Failure
Year	0	1	2	3	Salv	1
Revenue		313,600	344,960	372,560	50,000	100,000
-Oper Costs		-44,000	-48,400	-53,240		
-Develop	-100,000					
-Deprec	-28,571	-48,980	-34,985	-24,990		
-Writeoff					62,474	-171,429
-Loss Forward		-128,571				-128,571
Taxable	-128,571	92,049	261,575	294,330	-12,474	-200,000
-Tax @ 40%		-36,819	-104,630	-117,732	4,990	80,000
Net Income	-128,571	55,228	156,945	176,598	-7,484	-120,000
+Deprec	28,571	48,980	34,985	24,990	62,474	171,429
+Loss Forward		128,571				128,571
-Cap Costs	-200,000					
Cash Flow	-300,000	232,779	191,930	201,588	54,990	180,000
				256,578		

9-14 Solution: Continued

$$\text{Constant \$ ENPV @ 10\%} = -300{,}000 + [232{,}779(P/F_{6,1})^{.9434}(P/F_{10,1})^{.9091}$$

$$+ 191{,}930(P/F_{6,1})^{.9434}(P/F_{8,1})^{.9259}(P/F_{10,2})^{.8264}$$

$$+ 256{,}578(P/F_{6,1})^{.9434}(P/F_{8,1})^{.9259}(P/F_{10,1})^{.9091}(P/F_{10,3})^{.7513}](.6)$$

$$+ 180{,}000(P/F_{6,1})^{.9434}(P/F_{10,1})^{.9091}(.4)$$

$$= +\$56{,}508$$

Using Equation 5-2, it is necessary to calcuate the equivalent escalated dollar minimum rate of return accounting for the various inflation rates each year as follows:

$$i^* = (1+i^{*\prime})(1+f) - 1$$

Yr 1 Escalated \$ Minimum DCFROR = $(1.1)(1.06) - 1 = .1660$ or 16.6%
Yr 2 Escalated \$ Minimum DCFROR = $(1.1)(1.08) - 1 = .1880$ or 18.8%
Yr 3 Escalated \$ Minimum DCFROR = $(1.1)(1.10) - 1 = .2110$ or 21.1%

$$\text{Escalated \$ ENPV} = -300{,}000 + [232{,}779(P/F_{16.6,1})^{.8576}$$

$$+ 191{,}930(P/F_{16.6,1})^{.8576}(P/F_{18.8,1})^{.8418}$$

$$+ 256{,}578(P/F_{16.6,1})^{.8576}(P/F_{18.8,1})^{.8418}(P/F_{21.1,1})^{.8258}](.6)$$

$$+ 180{,}000(P/F_{16.6,1})^{.8576}(.4)$$

$$= +\$56{,}440$$

Factor roundoff error causes the slight difference in this result and the constant dollar result.

9-15 Solution:

Natural Gas Pipeline, Breakeven Analysis With Mid-Period Compounding

Year	0	0.5	1.5	2.5	3.5	4.5	5.5
Revenue		1900X	1440X	1030X	730X	440X	150X
-Oper Costs		-5	-5	-5	-5	-5	-5
-Depreciation		-31	-54	-38	-27	-20	-20
-Depr Writeoff							-30
Taxable Income		1900X-36	1440X-59	1030X-43	730X-32	440X-25	150X-55
-Tax @ 40%		- 760X+14	-576X+23	-412X+17	-292X+12	-176X+10	-60X+22
Net Income		1140X-22	864X-36	618X-26	438X-20	264X-15	90X-33
+Deprec		31	54	38	27	20	50
-Cap Costs	-220						
Cash Flow	-220	1140X+9	864X+18	618X+12	438X+7	264X+5	90X+17

PW Eq: $0 = -220 + (1{,}140X+9)(P/F_{12,0.5})^{.9449} + (864X+18)(P/F_{12,1.5})^{.8437}$

$+ (618X+12)(P/F_{12,2.5})^{.7533} + (438X+7)(P/F_{12,3.5})^{.6726}$

$+ (264X+5)(P/F_{12,4.5})^{.6005} + (90X+17)(P/F_{12,5.5})^{.5362}$

$0 = 2{,}773X - 170.4$, rearranging gives: $170.4 = 2{,}773X$

$X = \$0.06145$ per MCF

Therefore, the breakeven transport charge for a 12% escalated dollar DCFROR on the $220,000 pipeline investment is $0.0614 per MCF based on mid-year values and compounding which treats year 1 values at period n=0.5, year 2 values as occuring at period n=1.5, and so forth.

$P/F_{12,0.5} = (1/1.12)^{0.5} = 0.9449$

$P/F_{12,1.5} = (1/1.12)^{1.5} = 0.8437$

and so forth for n = 2.5, 3.5, etc...

9-16 Solution: Coal Property Solution in Thousands of Dollars

```
Development       = 10,000    Rev = 30,000  33,000  36,300  39,930  43,923
Deprec Equipment  = 15,000    OC  = 12,000  13,200  14,520  15,972  17,569
Working Capital   =  2,000
Salvage (Including Working Capital Return)                            5,000
─────────────────────────────────────────────────────────────────────────
                      0          1       2        3       4       5
```

The $10,000 mineral rights acquisition cost incurred at year -2 is sunk, but remaining tax effects and sale value are not sunk.

Development Cash Flow Calculations

Year	0	1	2	3	4	5	Salv
Gross Revenue		30,000	33,000	36,300	39,930	43,923	5,000
-Royalties		-2,400	-2,640	-2,904	-3,194	-3,514	
Net Revenue		27,600	30,360	33,396	36,736	40,409	5,000
-Oper Costs		-12,000	-13,200	-14,520	-15,972	-17,569	
-Development	-7,000						
-Depreciation	-2,143	-3,673	-2,624	-1,874	-1,340	-1,338	-2,008
-Amortization	-600	-600	-600	-600	-600		
-WC Writeoff							-2,000
Before Depltn	-9,743	11,327	13,936	16,402	18,824	21,502	992
-50% Limit		5,663	6,968	8,201	9,412	10,751	
-Percent Depl		-2,760	-3,036	-3,340	-3,112*	-3,233	
-Cost Depltn		2,000	1,810	1,401	432		
Taxable Income	-9,743	8,567	10,900	13,062	15,712	18,269	992
-Tax @ 40%	3,897	-3,427	-4,360	-5,225	-6,285	-7,308	-397
Net Income	-5,846	5,140	6,540	7,837	9,427	10,961	595
+Depreciation	2,143	3,673	2,624	1,874	1,340	1,338	2,008
+Depletion		2,760	3,036	3,340	3,112	3,233	
+Amortization	600	600	600	600	600		
+WC Writeoff							2,000
-Capital Costs	-20,000**						
Cash Flow	-23,103	12,173	12,800	13,651	14,479	15,532	4,603
						20,135	

* Cumulative percentage depletion in years 1, 2 and 3 = $9,136 so $864 more depletion equals $10,000 mineral rights acquisition cost. $864/0.10 = $8,640 net revenue after royalty is needed for 10% depletion, balance is 8% depletion. 8% depletion revenue = ($36,736-$8,640)(0.08) = $28,096(0.08) = $2,248. Cumulative year 4 percentage depletion = $2,248 + $864 = $3,112.

** Capital cost includes $15,000 for equipment, $2,000 for working capital, $3,000 for 30% of the $10,000 development cost.

CHAPTER 9 PROBLEM SOLUTIONS

9-16 Solution: Continued

Case 1 - Calculating DCFROR and NPV ($10,000 acquisition cost is sunk)

PW Eq: $0 = -23,103 + 12,173(P/F_{i,1}) + 12,800(P/F_{i,2}) + 13,651(P/F_{i,3})$
$+ 14,479(P/F_{i,4}) + 20,135(P/F_{i,5})$ $i = DCFROR = 50.7\%$

NPV $= -23,103 + 12,173(P/F_{20,1}) + 12,800(P/F_{20,2}) + 13,651(P/F_{20,3})$
$+ 14,479(P/F_{20,4}) + 20,135(P/F_{20,5}) = +\$18,904$

After-Tax Cash Flow of Yr 0 Sale Offer:

Before-tax sale value less the tax due from the sale equals the sale cash flow and net present value. At the point of the sale, (time zero) the only cost incurred was 2 years ago. That cost is sunk and not relevant except for remaining tax effects. If we sell the property the remaining book value is deducted from the sale revenue to determine taxable gain as follows:

$20,000-(20,000-10,000)(0.4) = \$16,000 < \$18,904$ Develop NPV, so Develop

Case 2 - Breakeven Sell Price with Developing

In this analysis you are determining the breakeven sale price the makes the sale NPV equal to the develop NPV. This calculation is very similar to the analysis just made except the selling price becomes an unknown variable. Letting "X" equal the breakeven selling price we obtain the following:

$X - (X-10,000)(0.4) = \$18,904$

$0.6X + 4,000 = \$18,904$, therefore, $X = \$14,904/0.6 = \$24,840$

Case 3 - Additional Development Cost that Could be Incurred.

Neglecting sale value opportunity cost considerations, this question asks you to determine the additional development cost (above the current $10,000) that can be incurred and still have the project earn a 20% DCFROR on invested dollars? As in the previous solutions to this problem, if we let "X" be the unknown breakeven development cost, then "X" less the tax savings from deductions on "X" will be equal to the after-tax NPV of development ($18,904). 70% of "X" can be expensed at time zero by a corporate mineral producer with the remaining 30% amortized over 5 years (year 0 to 4).

$X-(0.7)X(0.4 \text{ tax rate})-(0.06)X(0.4)-(0.06)X(0.4)(P/A_{20,4}) = \$18,904$

$X - 0.28X - 0.024X - 0.024X(2.589) = \$18,904$

$0.634X = 18,904$ therefore, $X = \$29,823$

$29,823 is the additional year 0 before-tax development cost that could be incurred and still have the project earn a 20% DCFROR. Opportunity cost is neglected.

9-17 Solution: Case A, 100% Working Interest, 87.5% Net Revenue Interest

Year	0	1	2	3	4
Production,bbls/yr		17,500	9,000	6,500	3,000
Selling Price,$/bbl		$20.00	$20.00	$21.00	$22.05
Operating Cost,$/bbl		$4.00	$4.00	$4.00	$4.00
Intangible Drilling	$250,000				
Tangible Completion	$100,000				
Lease Cost	$0				

Cash Flows:

Year	0	1	2	3	4
Gross Revenue		350,000	180,000	136,500	66,150
-Royalties		-43,750	-22,500	-17,063	-8,269
Net Rev. Interest, 87.5%		306,250	157,500	119,438	57,881
-Operating Expenses		-70,000	-36,000	-26,000	-12,000
-Intangibles (70%)	-175,000	-	-	-	-
-Deprec. (Tangibles)		-14,290	-24,490	-17,490	-43,730
-Amort. (30% Intang.)	-7,500	-15,000	-15,000	-15,000	-22,500
Taxable Income	-167,500	206,960	82,010	60,948	-20,349
-Tax @ 38%	63,650	-78,645	-31,164	-23,160	7,733
Net Income	-103,850	128,315	50,846	37,787	-12,616
+Depreciation		14,290	24,490	17,490	43,730
+Amortization		15,000	15,000	15,000	30,000
-Capital Costs	-175,000				
Cash Flow	-278,850	157,605	90,336	70,277	61,114

$$\text{NPV @ 12\%} = -278{,}850 + 157{,}605(P/F_{12,1})^{.8929} + 90{,}336(P/F_{12,2})^{.7972}$$

$$+ 70{,}277(P/F_{12,3})^{.7118} + 61{,}114(P/F_{12,4})^{.6355} = \$22{,}752$$

PVR = 22,752/278,850 = 0.082

PW Eq: $0 = -278{,}850 + 157{,}605(P/F_{i,1}) + 90{,}336(P/F_{i,2})$

$\qquad\qquad + 70{,}277(P/F_{i,3}) + 61{,}114(P/F_{i,4})$

ROR = 16.6% (by financial calculator)

CHAPTER 9 PROBLEM SOLUTIONS

9-17 Solution: Continued

Case B - 5% Carried Interest, Back in for 25% Working Interest and 21.875% Net Revenue Interest

Payout Calculation Using Production:

When the cumulative value of net revenue (defined here as production times the selling price less royalties and cash operating costs) gives revenue equal to the total dollars invested, the project is at payout. In this case, we know we've spent $350,000, and the price in years 1 and 2 is constant at $20.00 per barrel. Due to the two royalties, the producer only gets 82.5% of each barrel to pay off the investment. Hence, payout in production is calcuated as follows:

Yr 1 Payout Basis $350,000 - [17,500x($20.00(0.825)-$4.00)] = $131,250
Yr 2 Payout Basis $131,250 - [9,000x($20.00(0.825)-$4.00)] = $ 18,750
Yr 3 Payout: $18,750 = (X bbl)($21.00(0.825)-$4.00)   X = 1,407 bbl

So, in year 3, 1,407 barrels would be subject to the over-riding royalty interest of 5.0%, after which (the reversion point), 5,093 barrels are applicable to the 25.0% working interest, and a 21.875% net revenue interest (25.0% adjusted for 12.5% royalties).

Cash Flow Calculations:

Year	0	1	2	3	4
Carried Interest Rev.(5%)		17,500	9,000	1,477	0
Net Revenue Interest(21.875%)		0	0	23,396	14,470
Total Revenue		17,500	9,000	24,873	14,470
-Operating Expense (25%)		0	0	-5,093	-3,000
Taxable Income		17,500	9,000	19,780	11,470
-Tax @ 38%		-6,650	-3,420	-7,517	-4,359
Net Income		10,850	5,580	12,264	7,112
-Capital Costs					
Cash Flow		10,850	5,580	12,264	7,112

NPV @ 12% = $10,850(P/F_{12,1})^{.8929} + 5,580(P/F_{12,2})^{.7972}$

$+ 12,264(P/F_{12,3})^{.7118} + 7,112(P/F_{12,4})^{.6355}$ = **$27,386**   Max. NPV, select Carried Interest

From a purely economic viewpoint, selecting the largest NPV leads to the conclusion to farm out the property. However, from a practical viewpoint the NPV results are very close and effectively a breakeven. This is verified by an appropriate incremental analysis. (see next page)

9-17 Solution: Continued

Incremental Analysis:

```
Incremental Cash Flow    -278,850   146,755   84,756   58,013   54,002
A-B                     ─────────────────────────────────────────────
                            0          1         2        3        4
```

ROR_{A-B} = 11.03% < i*=12%, so reject A, accept B by very slight margin

NPV_{A-B} = 22,752 - 27,386 = -$4,634 < 0, so reject A, accept B

PVR_{A-B} = -4,634/278,850 = -0.017 < 0, so reject A, accept B

The "carried interest farm out" (Case B) has a slight economic advantage with all methods. Since Cases A and B are mutually exclusive alternatives, Case B with maximum total investment NPV of $27,386 is the economic choice. Incremental PVR and ROR lead to the same conclusion.

CHAPTER 9 PROBLEM SOLUTIONS

9-18 Solution:

The following incremental cash flow calculations are based on the before-tax data provided in the problem statement. The in-fill drilling alternative reflects combined adjusted production from both the new and existing wells, versus the current production forecast for the current or existing well. Notice that beginning in year 3 and beyond, the incremental production is negative which translates into reduced revenues, which also implies the company would pay less in royalties and operating costs (the later in year 6 only).

Incremental Cash Flow Calculations:

Year	Time 0	1	2	3	4	5	6
Production	90,000	140,000	45,000	-10,000	-25,000	-30,000	-25,000
Price ($/MCF)	1.25	1.25	1.50	1.75	2.00	2.25	2.50
Revenue	112,500	175,000	67,500	-17,500	-50,000	-67,500	-62,500
-Royalties	-14,063	-21,875	-8,438	2,188	6,250	8,438	7,813
Net Revenue	98,438	153,125	59,063	-15,313	-43,750	-59,063	-54,688
-Op Costs	-1,000	-2,000	-2,000	-2,000	-2,000	-2,000	4,000
-IDC	-88,200						
-Deprec	-6,000	-10,286	-7,347	-5,248	-3,748	-3,748	-5,622
-Amort	-3,780	-7,560	-7,560	-7,560	-7,560	-3,780	
Taxable Inc	-542	133,279	42,156	-30,120	-57,058	-68,591	-56,310
-Tax @ 38%	206	-50,646	-16,019	11,446	21,682	26,065	21,398
Net Income	-336	82,633	26,136	-18,675	-35,376	-42,526	-34,912
+Deprec	6,000	10,286	7,347	5,248	3,748	3,748	5,662
+Amort	3,780	7,560	7,560	7,560	7,560	3,780	
-Cap. Cost	-79,800						
Cash Flow	-70,356	100,479	41,043	-5,867	-24,068	-34,998	-29,290

Depreciation, Tangible Cost = $168,000(0.25) = $42,000
Year 0 42,000(0.1429) = 6,000
Year 1 42,000(0.2449) = 10,286
Year 2 42,000(0.1749) = 7,347
Year 3 42,000(0.1249) = 5,248
Year 4 42,000(0.0893) = 3,748
Year 5 42,000(0.0892) = 3,748
Year 6 42,000(0.0893) = 3,748
Year 6 Book Value   = 1,874   5,622 Yr 6 Total

Amortization Deductions $168,000(0.75)(0.30) = $37,800
Year 0   37,800(6/60) = 3,780
Year 1-4 37,800(12/60) = 7,560
Year 5   37,800(6/60) = 3,780

9-18 Solution: Continued

Present Worth Equation: (Note Cost-Income-Cost in CF's)

$$0 = -70{,}356 + 100{,}479(P/F_{i,1}) + 41{,}043(P/F_{i,2})$$
$$- 5{,}867(P/F_{i,3}) - 24{,}068(P/F_{i,4})$$
$$- 34{,}998(P/F_{i,5}) - 29{,}290(P/F_{i,6})$$

NPV @ 12% = -$2,093, so reject in-fill drilling

Note the incremental project investment payout period is 0.7 per year, but the incremental investment is rejected. This shows payout is a poor economic indicator.

DCFROR analysis of this cash flow stream leads to the dual rate of return problem and requires modifying cash flow streams.

Modified Present Worth Cost ROR Analysis:

$$70{,}356 + 5{,}867\overset{.7118}{(P/F_{12\%,3})} + 24{,}068\overset{.6355}{(P/F_{12\%,4})}$$
$$+ 34{,}998\overset{.5674}{(P/F_{12\%,5})} + 29{,}290\overset{.5066}{(P/F_{12\%,6})} = 124{,}524 = \text{Modified Cost}$$

$$124{,}524 = 100{,}479(P/F_{i\%,1}) + 41{,}043(P/F_{i\%,2})$$

Modified DCFROR = 10.51% < 12.0%, reject in-fill drilling

Present Value Ratio, PVR = -2,093/70,356 = -0.0297 < 0,
reject in-fill drilling

9-19 Solution: Dollar Values in Millions

Escalated Dollar Cash Flows Calculations:

Year	Time 0	1	2	3	4	Salv.	Fail., Yr 1
Revenue		25.00	25.00	25.00	25.00		10.00
-Op. Costs		-10.00	-10.00	-10.00	-10.00		
-Develop	-12.00						
-Deprec		-2.14	-3.67	-2.62	-1.87	-4.69	-15.00
-Amort		-0.50	-0.50	-0.50	-0.50	-0.50	-2.50
Taxable Inc	-12.00	12.36	10.83	11.88	12.63	-5.19	-7.50
-Tax @ 38%	4.56	-4.70	-4.11	-4.51	-4.80	1.97	2.85
Net Income	-7.44	7.66	6.71	7.36	7.83	-3.22	-4.65
+Deprec		2.14	3.67	2.62	1.87	4.69	15.00
+Amort		0.50	0.50	0.50	0.50	0.50	2.50
-Cap Cost	-15.00						
Cash Flow	-22.44	10.30	10.89	10.49	10.20	1.97	12.85

CHAPTER 9 PROBLEM SOLUTIONS

9-19 Solution: Continued

Depreciation, Equipment Cost = $15 Million
Year 1   15(0.1429) = 2.14
Year 2   15(0.2449) = 3.67
Year 3   15(0.1749) = 2.62
Year 4   15(0.1249) = 1.87
Year 4   Book Value = 4.69

Amortization Deductions on $2.5 Million Patent Cost
Year 1-4   2.5(1/5) = 0.50
Writeoff   2.5(1/5) = 0.50

Year 0 Sell CF
Revenue   4.50
-Bk Value   -2.50
Taxable   2.00
-Tax @ 38% -0.76
Net Income   1.24
+Bk Value   2.50
Cash Flow$_0$ 3.74

(A) Escalated Dollar Expected Net Present Value @ 15%:

$$\text{ENPV} = -22.44 + (0.8)[10.30\overset{0.8696}{(P/F_{15\%,1})} + 10.89\overset{0.7561}{(P/F_{15\%,2})}$$

$$+ 10.49\overset{0.6575}{(P/F_{15\%,3})} + 12.17\overset{0.5718}{(P/F_{15\%,4})}]$$

$$+ (0.2)[12.85\overset{0.8696}{(P/F_{15\%,1})}] = +\$4.63 > \$3.74$$

Development is the economically preferred alternative.

(B) Constant Dollar Expected NPV @ i*=15% With 8.7% Inflation:

Using Equation 5-1:

Escalated Equivalent i*' = (1.15)(1.087) - 1 = 0.25 or 25.0%, therefore

$$\text{ENPV} = -22.44 + (0.8)[10.30\overset{0.8000}{(P/F_{25\%,1})} + 10.89\overset{0.6400}{(P/F_{25\%,2})}$$

$$+ 10.49\overset{0.5120}{(P/F_{25\%,3})} + 12.17\overset{0.4096}{(P/F_{25\%,4})}]$$

$$+ (0.2)[12.85\overset{0.8000}{(P/F_{25\%,1})}] = +\$0.07 < \$3.74$$

Selling is the economically preferred alternative.

9-20 Solution:

```
          OC=  75,000
           C=1,000,000      —              —         OC=225,000     —        R=300,000
Purchase  ─────────────────────────────────────────────────────────────────────────────
           0              1              2              3              4              5
```

```
          OC=  75,000
          LP=144,000   LP=288,000    LP=288,000    LP=288,000    LP=288,000   LP=144,000
Lease     ─────────────────────────────────────────────────────────────────────────────
           0              1              2              3              4              5
```

```
          C=1,000,000
          S=  144,000   S=288,000    S=288,000    S=288,000    S=288,000   S=444,000
Purchase
-Lease    ─────────────────────────────────────────────────────────────────────────────
           0              1              2              3              4              5
```

Incremental Cash Flows:

Year	0	1	2	3	4	5
Savings	144,000	288,000	288,000	288,000	288,000	444,000
-Repair				-225,000		
-Depreciation	-142,857	-244,898	-174,927	-124,948	-89,249	-223,121
Taxable Income	1,143	43,102	113,073	-61,948	198,751	220,879
-Tax @40%	-457	-17,241	-45,229	24,779	-79,501	-88,351
Net Income	686	25,861	67,844	-37,169	119,251	132,527
+Depreciation	142,857	244,898	174,927	124,948	89,249	223,121
-Cap. Costs	-1,000,000					
Cash Flow	-856,457	270,759	242,771	87,779	208,499	355,649

PW Eq: $0 = -856{,}457 + 270{,}759(P/F_{i,1}) + 242{,}771(P/F_{i,2})$
$\qquad\qquad + 87{,}779(P/F_{i,3}) + 208{,}499(P/F_{i,4}) + 355{,}649(P/F_{i,5})$

Annual effective discount rate = $(1+0.01)^{12} - 1 = 0.1268$ or 12.68%

ROR = i = 10.87% (by financial calculator) < i*=12.68%, reject purchase

NPV @ 12.68% = -$38,481 < 0, reject purchase

PVR = -38,461 / 856,457 = -0.045 < 0, reject purchase

CHAPTER 9 PROBLEM SOLUTIONS

9-21 Solution:

A) 10 Year Bond Analysis

```
C=$10,000    I=$800 ................. I=$800   Maturity Value
──────────────────────────────────────────────  = $10,000
0            1 ..................... 10 yr
```

Using Eq. 3-2: Before-Tax Yield = 8%

After-Tax Yield = 8%(1-0.38) = 4.96%

Bond market values are based on before-tax yields (interest rates) and therefore are not affected by the investor's tax situation. Bond market value (price) is not identical to the investor's NPV from buying a bond. NPV is dependent upon an investor's tax situation.

at 6% interest, P = 800(P/A$_{6,10}$) + 10,000(P/F$_{6,10}$) = $11,472
                        7.360   .5584

at 10% interest, P = 800(P/A$_{10,10}$) + 10,000(P/F$_{10,10}$) = $8,770
                         6.144   .3855

B) 30 Year Bond Analysis

```
Value=?      I=$800 ..................... I=$800  Maturity Value
──────────────────────────────────────────────── = $10,000
0            1 .......................... 30 yr
```

at 8% interest, P = Value = $10,000

at 6% interest, P = 800(P/A$_{6,30}$) + 10,000(P/F$_{6,30}$) = $12,753
                        13.765   .1741

at 10% interest, P = 800(P/A$_{10,30}$) + 10,000(P/F$_{10,30}$) = $8,115
                         9.427   .0573

C) 30 Year Zero Coupon Bond

```
Value=?      -                            -     Maturity Value
──────────────────────────────────────────────── = $10,000
0            1 .......................... 30 yr
```

at 8% interest, P = Value = 10,000(P/F$_{8,30}$) = $994
                                  .099377

at 6% interest, P = Value = 10,000(P/F$_{6,30}$) = $1,741
                                  .1741

at 10% interest P = Value = 10,000(P/F$_{10,30}$) = $573
                                   .0573

CHAPTER 10 PROBLEM SOLUTIONS

10-1 Solution: Replacement Analysis in Actual Dollars

```
            Deprec Cost=15,000    OC=6,000   OC=7,000   OC=8,000
NEW (Machine A)  ─────────────────────────────────────────────── L=2,000
                 0                 1          2          3
            Deprec Cost=21,000    OC=5,000   OC=5,000   OC=5,000
OLD (Machine B)  ─────────────────────────────────────────────── L=3,000
                 0                 1          2          3
```

Machine "A" Cash Flows

Year	Time 0	1	2	3	Salvage
Revenue					2,000
-Operating Costs		-6,000	-7,000	-8,000	
-Depreciation	-3,000	-4,800	-2,880	-1,728	-2,592
Taxable Income	-3,000	-10,800	-9,880	-9,728	-592
-Tax @ 40%	1,200	4,320	3,952	3,891	237
Net Income	-1,800	-6,480	-5,928	-5,837	-355
+Depreciation	3,000	4,800	2,880	1,728	2,592
-Capital Costs	-15,000				
Cash Flow	-13,800	-1,680	-3,048	-4,109	2,237

PW Cost$_A$ @ 20% = 13,800+1,680(P/F$_{20,1}$)+3,048(P/F$_{20,2}$)+1,872(P/F$_{20,3}$)

= $18,400   Select A with Minimum PW Cost

Breakeven Cost/Unit = 18,400/[(1,000)(250)(P/A$_{20,3}$)(1-.4)] = $0.058/unit

Machine "B" Cash Flows

Year	Time 0	1	2	3	Salvage
Revenue					3,000
-Operating Costs		-5,000	-5,000	-5,000	
-Depreciation	-4,200	-6,720	-4,032	-2,419	-3,629
Taxable Income	-4,200	-11,720	-9,032	-7,419	-629
-Tax @ 40%	1,680	4,688	3,613	2,968	252
Net Income	-2,520	-7,032	-5,419	-4,452	-377
+Depreciation	4,200	6,720	4,032	2,419	3,629
-Capital Costs	-21,000				
Cash Flow	-19,320	-312	-1,387	-2,032	3,252

PW Cost$_B$ @ 20% = 19,320 + 312(P/F$_{20,1}$) + 1,387(P/F$_{20,2}$) - 1,220(P/F$_{20,3}$)

= +$19,838   Reject B, since A has Minimum PW Cost

Breakeven Cost/Unit = 19,838/[(1,000)(250)(P/A$_{20,3}$)(1-.4)] = $0.063/unit

If the additional 500 units of Machine B productivity can be utilized,
PW Cost$_B$ of 1000 units = 19,838(2/3)=13,225 < 18,400 PWCost$_A$. Select B.

CHAPTER 10 PROBLEM SOLUTIONS 149

10-2 Solution: All Values in Actual Dollars

```
                                C=23,000
    C=2,000(.6)=1,200   OC=3,000 OC=4,000 OC=2,000 OC=2,500 OC=3,000
A) ─────────────────────────────────────────────────────────────── L=8,000
        0              1        2        3        4        5

    C=20,000           OC=1,500 OC=2,000 OC=2,500 OC=3,000 OC=3,500
B) ─────────────────────────────────────────────────────────────── L=3,000
        0              1        2        3        4        5
```

Machine "A" Cash Flows

Year	Time 0	1	2	3	4	5	Salvage
Revenue							8,000
-Operating Costs		-3,000	-4,000	-2,000	-2,500	-3,000	
-Depreciation			-3,286	-5,633	-4,023	-2,874	-7,185
Taxable Income		-3,000	-7,286	-7,633	-6,523	-5,874	815
-Tax Due @ 40%		1,200	2,914	3,053	2,609	2,350	-326
Net Income		-1,800	-4,371	-4,580	-3,914	-3,524	489
+Depreciation			3,286	5,633	4,023	2,874	7,185
-Capital Costs	-1,200		-23,000				
Cash Flow	-1,200	-1,800	-24,086	1,053	109	-650	7,674

$$\text{PW Cost}_A = 1{,}200 + 1{,}800(P/F_{15,1}) + 24{,}086(P/F_{15,2}) - 1{,}053(P/F_{15,3})$$
$$- 109(P/F_{15,4}) + 650(P/F_{15,5}) - 7{,}674(P/F_{15,5}) = \$16{,}731$$

Machine "B" Cash Flows

Year	Time 0	1	2	3	4	5	Salvage
Revenue							3,000
-Operating Costs		-1,500	-2,000	-2,500	-3,000	-3,500	
-Depreciation	-2,857	-4,898	-3,499	-2,499	-1,785	-1,785	-2,677
Taxable Income	-2,857	-6,398	-5,499	-4,999	-4,785	-5,285	323
-Tax Due @ 40%	1,143	2,559	2,199	2,000	1,914	2,114	-129
Net Income	-1,714	-3,839	-3,299	-2,999	-2,871	-3,171	194
+Depreciation	2,857	4,898	3,499	2,499	1,785	1,785	2,677
-Capital Costs	-20,000						
Cash Flow	-18,857	1,059	199	-500	-1,086	-1,386	2,871

$$\text{PW Cost}_B = 18{,}857 - 1{,}059(P/F_{15,1}) - 199(P/F_{15,2}) + 500(P/F_{15,3})$$
$$+ 967(P/F_{15,4}) + 1{,}267(P/F_{15,5}) - 2{,}633(P/F_{15,5}) = \$17{,}997$$

Select Machine "A" offering the lowest present worth cost of $16,731

CASE B) If extra Service can be utilized, select machine "B" since 17,997/1.4 = $12,855 is less than the machine "A" present worth cost of $16,731

10-3 Solution: Calculate the Year 0 Opportunity Cost

Salvage Tax = (30,000−21,000)(0.4) = 3,600
Opportunity Cost = 30,000 − 3,600 = 26,400

Year	0	1	2	3
−Repair Cost	−25,000			
−Operating Costs		−15,000	−18,000	−21,000
−Depreciation	−21,000			
Taxable Income	−46,000	−15,000	−18,000	−21,000
−Tax @ 40%	18,400	6,000	7,200	8,400
Net Income	−27,600	−9,000	−10,800	−12,600
+Depreciation	21,000			
−Opportunity Cost	−26,400			
Cash Flow	−33,000	−9,000	−10,800	−12,600

A) Present Worth Cost

$$33,000 + 9,000(P/F_{20,1})^{.8333} + 10,800(P/F_{20,2})^{.6944} + 12,600(P/F_{20,3})^{.5787} = \$55,291$$

B) Annual Cost $55,291(A/P_{20,3})^{.47473} = \$26,248$

C) Breakeven Lease Payments. Let the three uniform and equal beginning of year lease payments equal "X", 40% of "X" goes to tax, so yr 0, 1 and 2 cash flow increases by 0.6X.

PW Eq: $(.6X-33,000) + (.6X-9,000)(P/F_{20,1})^{.8333} + (.6X-10,800)(P/F_{20,2})^{.6944}$

$-12,600(P/F_{20,3})^{.5787} = 0$

1.5168X = 55,291   Therefore, <u>X = 36,455</u>

Alternative Calculation of X:

PW Cost = PW Revenue(1−tax rate) $55,291 = [X + X(P/A_{20,2})](1 - 0.4 \text{ tax rate})$

[55,291/2.528(0.6)] = 36,453 = X at years 0, 1 and 2 which is the beginning of years 1, 2, 3.

Using annual costs would yield the following calculations:

Annual Cost = Annual Revenue(1−tax rate)

26,248 = X(1−0.4 tax rate)   Therefore, X = $43,748 at years 1, 2 and 3.

Convert to beginning of year values as follows:

$43,748(P/F_{20,1})^{.8333} = \underline{\$36,455}$

CHAPTER 10 PROBLEM SOLUTIONS 151

10-4 Solution: Equipment Acquisition Analysis in Thousands of Dollars

```
      C=50      OC=12     OC=15     OC=18     OC=21     OC=24
A) |----------|---------|---------|---------|---------|--------- L=3
   0          1         2         3         4         5

               C=32      C=50
      C=15     OC=20     OC=16    OC=3      OC=4      OC=5
B) |----------|---------|---------|---------|---------|--------- L=25
   0          1         2         3         4         5
```

Machine A Cash Flows

Year	Time 0	1	2	3	4	5	Salvage
Revenue							3.00
-Operating Costs		-12.00	-15.00	-18.00	-21.00	-24.00	
-Depreciation	-7.14	-12.24	-8.75	-6.25	-4.46	-4.46	-6.69
Taxable Income	-7.14	-24.24	-23.75	-24.25	-25.46	-28.46	-3.69
-Tax Due @ 40%	2.86	9.70	9.50	9.70	10.18	11.38	1.48
Net Income	-4.29	-14.55	-14.25	-14.55	-15.28	-17.08	-2.22
+Depreciation	7.14	12.24	8.75	6.25	4.46	4.46	6.69
-Capital Costs	-50.00						
Cash Flow	-47.14	-2.30	-5.50	-8.30	-10.82	-12.62	4.48
						_-8.14_/	

Present Worth Cost @ 15% = $69.0, Select A with slightly lower PW Cost.

Machine B Cash Flows

Year	Time 0	1	2	3	4	5	Salvage
Revenue							25.00
-Operating Costs		-20.00	-16.00	-3.00	-4.00	-5.00	
-Depreciation	-2.14	-3.67	-14.34	-20.08	-14.34	-10.25	-25.61
-Write Off			-6.56				
Taxable Income	-2.14	-23.67	-36.90	-23.08	-18.34	-15.25	-0.61
-Tax Due @ 40%	0.86	9.47	14.76	9.23	7.34	6.10	0.25
Net Income	-1.29	-14.20	-22.14	-13.85	-11.01	-9.15	-0.37
+Depreciation	2.14	3.67	14.34	20.08	14.34	10.25	25.61
+Write Off			6.56				
-Capital Costs	-15.00	-32.00	-50.00				
Cash Flow	-14.14	-42.53	-51.24	6.23	3.34	1.10	25.25
						_26.35_/	

Present Worth Cost @ 15% = $70.8

10-4 Solution: Continued

Incremental Analysis, A-B:

The easiest way to get the incremental cash flows for incremental NPV or DCFROR analysis is to look at the differences in the individual Machine A and B cash flows. Look at the difference so that negative cash flow is followed by positive cash flow, so analyze A-B. However it is impossible to avoid the cost, income, cost dual ROR situation.

```
Machine      -33.00      40.23      45.74     -14.53     -14.16     -34.49
A-B Cash Flow ───────────────────────────────────────────────────────────────
                0          1          2          3          4          5
```

Calculate NPV for a range of discount rates "i" to determine the dual "i" values.

i	NPV
0	-10.2
5	- 4.4
10	- 0.6
15	1.8
20	3.2
30	4.2
40	3.7
50	2.5
60	1.0
70	- 0.6

The 1.80 incremental NPV for i* = 15% equals the difference in the Present Worth Cost of "A" of $69.0 and the Present Worth Cost of "B" of $70.8. Remember that the sign convention is opposite for NPV and PW Cost analyses.

Dual DCFROR's are 11% and 66%, but they are not valid for decision making as ROR results. You must go to a modified ROR analysis, either Growth ROR or Present Worth Cost Modified ROR analysis discussed in Chapter Four.

Present Worth Cost Modified DCFROR Analysis:

$$\text{PW Mod. Cost} = 33.00 + 14.53(P/F_{15,3})^{.6575} + 14.16(P/F_{15,4})^{.5717} + 34.49(P/F_{15,5})^{.4972}$$

$$= 67.79$$

Modifed DCFROR PW Eq: $67.79 = 40.23(P/F_{i,1}) + 45.74(P/F_{i,2})$

i = PW Cost Modified DCFROR = 17.0% > i* = 15%, so accept Machine A, consistent with present worth cost and NPV analysis results.

If you prefer to obtain the incremental Machine A-B after-tax cash flow by taking the difference in the alternatives before-tax and converting the incremental costs and savings to after-tax cash flow, be very careful not to net incremental operating costs and capital costs against one another. Also note that the negative incremental "A-B" capital costs in years 1 and 2 are savings that result in negative depreciation in years 2, 3, 4 and 5 and a negative writeoff at year 5.

CHAPTER 10 PROBLEM SOLUTIONS

10-4 Solution: Continued

Before-Tax Incremental Diagram

```
                    C=-32      C=-50
        C=50-15     OC= -8     OC= -1    OC=15     OC=17     OC=19
A-B) |----------|----------|----------|----------|----------|---------- L=-22
     0          1          2          3          4          5
```

Correct handling of the depreciation calculations is the key to correct incremental cash flow analysis, but it is very easy to make mistakes.

Year	Incremental A-B Depreciation		Net Deprec.	
0	(50-15)(.1429)	= 5.0	Yr 0	5.00
1	(50-15)(.2449)	= 8.57	Yr 1	8.57
2	Writeoff on (-15) =	-9.19		
2	(50)(.1749)	= 8.75		
2	(-82)(.1429)	= -11.72	Yr 2	-12.16
3	(50)(.1249)	= 6.25		
3	(-82)(.2449)	= -20.08	Yr 3	-13.83
4	(50)(.0893)	= 4.46		
4	(-82)(.1749)	= -14.34	Yr 4	-9.88
5	(50)(.0892)	= 4.46		
5	(-82)(.1249)	= -10.25	Yr 5	-5.79
5	writeoff on 50	= 6.69		
5	writeoff on (-82)	= -25.62	Yr 5	-18.92

Incremental Cash Flow Calculations

Year	0	1	2	3	4	5
Savings/Salvage		8.00	1.00			-22.00
-Oper Costs				-15.00	-17.00	-19.00
-Deprec/Writeoff	-5.00	-8.57	12.16	13.83	9.88	24.71
Taxable Income	-5.00	-0.57	13.16	-1.17	-7.12	-16.29
-Tax @ 40%	2.00	0.23	-5.26	0.47	2.85	6.52
Net Income	-3.00	-0.34	7.90	-0.70	-4.27	-9.77
+Deprec/Writeoff	5.00	8.57	-12.16	-13.83	-9.88	-24.71
-Capital Costs	-35.00	32.00	50.00			
Cash Flow	-33.00	40.23	45.74	-14.53	-14.15	-34.48

Within roundoff error these incremental A-B after-tax cash flows are the same as those from analyzing the difference in the total investment cash flows.

10-5 Solution: Replacement Analysis, Old D9 vs New D9L
Values in Thousands of Dollars

Old D9

Case 1	Case 2	Case 3 (Accounting
C=90-36 tax if D9 sold	C=90	C=0 Viewpoint)
Yr 0 Bk Value = 0	Yr 0 Bk Value = 0	Yr 0 Bk Value = 0

Valued at after tax cash flow

New D9L

C=460	C=460+36 tax old sale	C=460+36 tax-90 sale
Yr 0 Bk Value = 460	Yr 0 Bk Value = 460	Yr 0 Bk Value = 460

Since the same relative differences exist between the New and Old D9's for all 3 cases (incremental cost of $406 for each), you must get the same economic conclusions using any of the 3 cases. However, do not mix the cases.

Present worth cost analysis results are presented. You can convert present worth cost results to equivalent annual cost by multiplying present worth cost times $A/P_{15,5}$, giving the same economic conclusions.

CASE A) Assumes the New and Old assets give the same service.

Old D9 Cash Flow Calculations

Year	--------- 0 ----------			1	2	3	4	5
Yr 0 Case#	1	2	3					
-Op Costs	-100.0	-100.0	-100.0	-150.0	-237.0	-184.0	-290.0	-156.0
Taxable	-100.0	-100.0	-100.0	-150.0	-237.0	-184.0	-290.0	-156.0
-Tax @ 40%	40.0	40.0	40.0	60.0	94.8	73.6	116.0	62.4
Net Income	-60.0	-60.0	-60.0	-90.0	-142.2	-110.4	-174.0	-93.6
-Cap Costs	-54.0	-90.0						
Cash Flow	-114.0	-150.0	-60.0	-90.0	-142.2	-110.4	-174.0	-93.6

Present Worth Cost for Year 0, Case 1

$$\text{PW Cost Eq: } 114.0 + 90.0(P/F_{15,1})^{.8696} + 142.2(P/F_{15,2})^{.7561} + 110.4(P/F_{15,3})^{.6575}$$

$$+ 174.0(P/F_{15,4})^{.5718} + 93.6(P/F_{15,5})^{.4972}$$

Present Worth Cost, Case 1 .... $518.4
Present Worth Cost, Case 2 .... $554.4
Present Worth Cost, Case 3 .... $464.4

CHAPTER 10 PROBLEM SOLUTIONS

10-5 Solution: Continued

New D9L Cash Flow Calculations

Year	--------- 0 ---------			1	2	3	4	5
Yr 0 Case#	1	2	3					
Revenue								140.0
−Oper Cost				−88.0	−221.0	−108.0	−274.0	−140.0
−Deprec	−65.7	−65.7	−65.7	−112.7	−80.5	−57.5	−41.0	−41.0
−Writeoff								−61.6
Taxable Inc	−65.7	−65.7	−65.7	−200.7	−301.5	−165.5	−315.0	−102.6
−Tax @ 40%	26.3	26.3	26.3	80.3	120.6	66.2	126.0	+41.0
Net Income	−39.4	−39.4	−39.4	−120.4	−180.9	−99.3	−189.0	−61.6
+Deprec	65.7	65.7	65.7	112.7	80.5	57.5	41.0	41.0
+Writeoff								61.6
−Cap Costs	−460.0	−496.0	−406.0					
Cash Flow	−433.7	−469.7	−379.7	−7.7	−100.4	−41.8	−148.0	41.0

Present Worth Cost for Year 0, Case 1:

PW Cost Eq: $433.7 + 7.7(P/F_{15,1})^{.8696} + 100.4(P/F_{15,2})^{.7561} + 41.8(P/F_{15,3})^{.6575}$

$+ 148.0(P/F_{15,4})^{.5718} - 41.0(P/F_{15,5})^{.4972}$

Present Worth Cost, Case 1 ..... $608.0
Present Worth Cost, Case 2 ..... $644.8
Present Worth Cost, Case 3 ..... $554.8

CASE B) If the total productive capacity of the new D9L can be utilized, the Case 1 present worth cost of the new machine would drop to $608/1.3 = $467.7 which makes the New D9L preferable to the Old D9 Case 1 present worth cost of $518.4.

Breakeven Cost Analysis:

Breakeven cost per unit of service analysis is only valid for "Case 1" actual after-tax year 0 costs.

"Old" Breakeven Cost Per Unit of Service Equals:

PW Cost "Old" / PW Production(1-tax rate)

$518,400 / [2,000(P/A_{15,5})^{3.352}(1-0.4)] = \$128.88$ / unit

"New" Breakeven Cost Per Unit of Service Equals:

$608,000 / [2,600(P/A_{15,5})^{3.352}(1-0.4)] = \$116.27$ / unit

Select "New" with the minimum cost per unit.

10-6 Solution:

Lease vs Purchase Analysis, Case A, (Expense Against Other Income)

```
              OC=18    OC=36    OC=36    OC=18
Lease      ─────────────────────────────────────  L=0
              0        1        2        3

              C=100
Purchase   ─────────────────────────────────────  L=30
              0        1        2        3

              OC=-18
Purchase C=100   OC=-36   OC=-36   OC=-18
-Lease     ─────────────────────────────────────  L=30
              0        1        2        3
```

Remember that a negative incremental operating cost is equivalent to positive savings or revenue. Also, do not net incremental capital cost of 100 against the incremental operating cost of -18 in year 0. They are treated differently for tax purposes.

Case A, Incremental Purchase Minus Lease Cash Flows

Year	0	1	2	3	
Savings/Salvage	18,000	36,000	36,000	48,000	(Includes Salvage)
-Depreciation	-20,000	-32,000	-19,200	-11,520	
-Deprec Writeoff				-17,280	
Taxable Income	-2,000	4,000	16,800	19,200	
-Tax @ 40%	800	-1,600	-6,720	-7,680	
Net Income	-1,200	2,400	10,080	11,520	
+Deprec/Writeoff	20,000	32,000	19,200	28,800	
-Capital Costs	-100,000				
Cash Flow	-81,200	34,400	29,280	40,320	

PW Eq: $0 = -81,200 + 34,400(P/F_{i,1}) + 29,280(P/F_{i,2}) + 40,320(P/F_{i,3})$

  i = DCFROR = 13.1% < 15%, so reject purchase

NPV = $-81,200 + 34,400(P/F_{15,1}) + 29,280(P/F_{15,2}) + 40,320(P/F_{15,3})$

  = -2,636

CHAPTER 10 PROBLEM SOLUTIONS

10-6 Solution: Continued

PW Cost of Leasing Cash Flows, Case A

Year	0	1	2	3
Revenue				
-Lease Costs	-18,000	-36,000	-36,000	-18,000
Taxable Income	-18,000	-36,000	-36,000	-18,000
-Tax @ 40%	7,200	14,400	14,400	7,200
Net Income	-10,800	-21,600	-21,600	-10,800
-Capital Costs				
Cash Flow	-10,800	-21,600	-21,600	-10,800

PW Cost = $10,800 + 21,600(P/A_{15,2}) + 10,800(P/F_{15,3}) = \$53,016$

PW Cost of Purchasing Cash Flows, Case A

Year	0	1	2	3
Revenue				30,000
-Depreciation	-20,000	-32,000	-19,200	-11,520
-Deprec Writeoff				-17,280
Taxable Income	-20,000	-32,000	-19,200	1,200
-Tax @ 40%	8,000	12,800	7,680	-480
Net Income	-12,000	-19,200	-11,520	720
+Depreciation	20,000	32,000	19,200	28,800
-Capital Costs	-100,000			
Cash Flow	-92,000	12,800	7,680	29,520

PW Cost = $92,000 - 12,800(P/F_{15,1}) - 7,680(P/F_{15,2}) - 29,520(P/F_{15,3})$

$= \$55,652$

Select leasing with the lowest present worth cost.

Case B, Uniform Annual Equivalent Revenue Required

UAERR = Annual Cost / (1-tax rate)

$\text{UAERR}_{\text{Lease}} = \$53,016(A/P_{15,3})^{.43798} / (1-.4) = \$23,220 / (1-.4) = \$38,700$

$\text{UAERR}_{\text{Purch}} = \$55,652(A/P_{15,3})^{.43798} / (1-.4) = \$24,375 / (1-.4) = \$40,624$

10-6 Solution: Continued

Lease/Purchase Analysis, Case C, Carry Losses Forward (Stand Alone)

Leasing Cash Flows

Year	0	1	2	3
Revenue				
−Lease Costs	−18,000	−36,000	−36,000	−18,000
−Loss Forward		−18,000	−54,000	−90,000
Taxable Income	−18,000	−54,000	−90,000	−108,000
−Tax @ 40%	0	0	0	43,200
Net Income	−18,000	−54,000	−90,000	−64,800
+Loss Forward		18,000	54,000	90,000
−Capital Costs				
Cash Flow	−18,000	−36,000	−36,000	25,200

PW Cost = 18,000 + 36,000(P/A$_{15,2}$) − 25,200(P/F$_{15,3}$) = $59,956

Purchase Cash Flows

Year	0	1	2	3
Revenue				30,000
−Depreciation	−20,000	−32,000	−19,200	−11,520
−Writeoff				−17,280
−Loss Forward		−20,000	−52,000	−71,200
Taxable Income	−20,000	−52,000	−71,200	−70,000
−Tax @ 40%	0	0	0	28,000
Net Income	−20,000	−52,000	−71,200	−42,000
+Deprec/Writeoff	20,000	32,000	19,200	28,800
+Loss Forward		20,000	52,000	71,200
−Capital Costs	−100,000			
Cash Flow	−100,000	0	0	58,000

PW Cost = 100,000 − 58,000(P/F$_{15,3}$) = $61,864

Select Leasing with the lowest present worth cost. Carrying losses forward versus expensing against other income has little effect on lease versus purchase analysis because cumulative tax deductions are similar for both.

CHAPTER 10 PROBLEM SOLUTIONS

10-7 Solution: Replacement Analysis, All Values in Thousands of Dollars

```
         C=240-96(Tax)        OC=360         OC=390        OC=420
Old      ─────────────────────────────────────────────────────────  L=0
         0                    1              2             3

         C=1,000              OC=120         OC=160        OC=200
New      ─────────────────────────────────────────────────────────  L=240
         0                    1              2             3
```

Opportunity Cost = 240 - 96(tax) = 144 for 3 Old Machines

Three (3) Old Machine Cash Flows:

Year	0	1	2	3
Revenue				
-Operating Costs		-360	-390	-420
Taxable Income		-360	-390	-420
-Tax @ 40%		144	156	168
Net Income		-216	-234	-252
-Capital Costs	-144			
Cash Flow	-144	-216	-234	-252

$$AC_{Old} = [144 + 216(P/F_{15,1})^{.8696} + 234(P/F_{15,2})^{.7561} + 252(P/F_{15,3})^{.6575}](A/P_{15,3})^{.43798} = 295.4$$

UAERR = 295.4 / (1-0.4) = $492.33 for 3 Old Machines,

or $164.1 per Old Machine

Two (2) New Machine Cash Flows:

Year	0	1	2	3
Revenue				250
-Operating Costs		-120	-160	-200
-Deprec/Writeoff	-200	-320	-192	-288
Taxable Income	-200	-440	-352	-238
-Tax @ 40%	80	176	141	95
Net Income	-120	-264	-211	-143
+Depreciation	200	320	192	288
-Capital Costs	-1,000			
Cash Flow	-920	56	-19	145

$$AC_{New} = [920 - 56(P/F_{15,1})^{.8696} + 19(P/F_{15,2})^{.7561} - 145(P/F_{15,3})^{.6575}](A/P_{15,3})^{.43798} = 346$$

$UAERR_{New}$ = 346/(1-.4) = 577 for 2 New Machines, or 288.5 per New Machine

Replacement of the Old Machines is not indicated to be economically desirable with either annual cost or UAERR analysis.

10-8 Solution: Purchase vs Leasing a Plant
All Values in Thousands of Dollars.
Assume other income exists against which to use deductions in any year.

```
                    Rev/yr=800              800    800
        C=1,000     OC/yr=200               200    200
Purchase ─────────────────────────────────────────────  L=400
        0           1  ................      9     10

                    Rev/yr=800              800    800
        OC=200      OC/yr=400               400    200
Lease   ─────────────────────────────────────────────  L=0
        0           1  ................      9     10

        C=1,000
Purchase OC=-200    OC/yr=-200             -200     0
- Lease ─────────────────────────────────────────────  L=400
        0           1  ................      9     10
```

Purchase Plant Cash Flows

Year	0	1-9	10	Salv
Revenue		800	800	400
-Oper Costs		-200	-200	
-Deprec	-50	-100	-50	
Taxable Inc	-50	500	550	400
-Tax @ 40%	20	-200	-220	-160
Net Income	-30	300	330	240
+Deprec	50	100	50	
-Cap Cost	-1,000			
Cash Flow	-980	400	380	240
			620	

Lease Plant Cash Flows

Year	0	1-9	10
Revenue		800	800
-Oper Costs	-200	-400	-200
-Deprec			
Taxable Inc	-200	400	600
-Tax @ 40%	80	-160	-240
Net Income	-120	240	360
+Depreciation			
-Capital Costs			
Cash Flow	-120	240	360

Purchase PW EQ:

$0 = -980 + 400(P/A_{i,9}) + 620(P/F_{i,10})$

$i = \text{DCFROR} = 39.7\%$
NPV @ 10% = +$1,563

Lease PW Eq:

$0 = -120 + 240(P/A_{i,9}) + 360(P/F_{i,10})$

$i = \text{DCFROR} = 200\%$
NPV @ 10% = +$1,401

Mutually exclusive alternative analysis requires incremental analysis, Incremental Purchase - Lease Cash Flows

```
CF=-860     CF=+160  ............  CF=+160   CF=+260
─────────────────────────────────────────────────────
   0           1  ..................   9        10
```

Incremental PW Eq: $0 = -860 + 160(P/A_{i,9}) + 260(P/F_{i,10})$,

$i = \text{Incremental DCFROR} = 14\% > 10\%$, so purchase

Incremental NPV = 1,563 - 1,401 = +$162 > 0, so purchase

CHAPTER 10 PROBLEM SOLUTIONS

10-8 Solution: Continued

Cost Analysis of Purchase vs Lease Alternatives. Leave the revenues out of this analysis since they are projected to be the same whether purchase or lease is selected.

Purchase New Plant Cash Flows for Cost Analysis

Year	0	1-9	10	Salv
Revenue				400
-Operating Costs		-200	-200	
-Depreciation	-50	-100	-50	
Taxable Income	-50	-300	-250	400
-Tax @ 40%	20	120	100	-160
Net Income	-30	-180	-150	240
+Depreciation	50	100	50	
-Capital Costs	-1,000			
Cash Flow	-980	-80	-100	240

Year 10 combined: 140

PW Cost @ 10% = $980 + 80(P/A_{10,9}) - 140(P/F_{10,10}) = \$1,386.75$

AW Cost @ 10% = $1,386.75(A/P_{10,10}) = \$225.69$

Lease Plant Cash Flows for Cost Analysis

Year	0	1-9	10
Revenue			
-Oper Costs	-200	-400	-200
Taxable Income	-200	-400	-200
-Tax @ 40%	80	160	80
Net Income	-120	-240	-120
Cash Flow	-120	-240	-120

PW Cost @ 10% = $120 + 240(P/A_{10,9}) + 120(P/F_{10,10}) = \$1,548.43$

AW Cost @ 10% = $1,548.43(A/P_{10,10}) = \$252.00$

Select Purchase to minimize both present worth and annual worth cost. The same economic conclusion (select Purchase) has been reached with all techniques of analysis.

10-9 Solution: Standard Cost of Service for a D9L Dozer.

Let "X" Equal the Before Tax Standard Cost Per Hour Necessary to receive a 15% DCFROR on invested capital. Revenues are separated from costs for illustration and sensitivity analysis purposes. You may also obtain the same solutions by combining both into one cash flow calculation and solving for the standard cost of service/hr X. That solution is left to the reader.

Cash Flows for Breakeven Revenues

Year	0	1	2	3	4	5
Revenue		4,000X	4,000X	3,000X	2,000X	2,000X
Taxable Income		4,000X	4,000X	3,000X	2,000X	2,000X
-Tax @ 40%		-1,600X	-1,600X	-1,200X	-800X	-800X
Cash Flow		2,400X	2,400X	1,800X	1,200X	1,800X

PW of Revenues = $(2,400X)(P/F_{15,1}) + (2,400X)(P/F_{15,2}) + (1,800X)(P/F_{15,3})$

$\qquad + (1,200X)(P/F_{15,4}) + (1,200X)(P/F_{15,5}) = 6,368X$

Cash Flows for Cost of Service

Year	0	1	2	3	4	5
Salvage Revenue						136,298
-Oper Costs		-27,948	-125,364	-100,441	-150,384	-45,499
-Deprec	-69,512	-119,164	-85,117	-60,798	-43,452	-43,403
-Writeoff						-65,154
Taxable Inc	-69,512	-147,112	-210,481	-161,239	-193,836	-17,758
-Tax @ 40%	27,805	58,845	84,192	64,496	77,534	7,103
Net Income	-41,707	-88,267	-126,289	-96,743	-116,302	-10,655
+Deprec	69,512	119,164	85,117	60,798	43,452	43,403
+Writeoff						65,154
-Cap Cost	-486,585					
Cash Flow	-458,780	30,897	-41,172	-35,945	-72,850	97,902

PW Cost = $458,780 - 30,897(P/F_{15,1}) + 41,172(P/F_{15,2}) + 35,945(P/F_{15,3})$

$\qquad + 72,850(P/F_{15,4}) - 97,902(P/F_{15,5}) = \$479,657$

By setting present worth revenues equal to present worth costs we can determine the breakeven standard cost of service per hour X, as follows:

$479,657 = X(6,368 \text{ hours})$, Therefore, X = $75.32 per hour

CHAPTER 10 PROBLEM SOLUTIONS

10-9 Solution: Standard Cost of Service for a D9L Dozer - Continued

For the alternate hours per year, calculate the after-tax discounted revenues and again, set equal to the present worth cost to determine X. Before-tax hours of service are 3,000 hours per year, therefore, the discounted after-tax revenues may be expressed as:

$1,800X(P/A_{15,5}) = 6,034X$

Breakeven Standard Cost of Service is Equal to:

$479,657 = X(6,034 \text{ hours})$ Therefore, X = \$79.46 per hour

It becomes apparent that the faster equipment hours of operation, or production, occur over asset life, the more cost competitive equipment becomes. This happens because equipment productivity is related to product revenue generation and the faster revenues are generated, the better the economics of projects become.

10-10 Solution: Annual Lease vs Purchase, Values in Thousands of Dollars

C=Capital Cost,   OC=Operating Cost,   LP=Lease Payment,   L=Salvage

```
              C=200
            OC= 18         OC=39          OC=45         OC=24
Purchase    ─────────────────────────────────────────────────── L=50
              0              1              2             3

            LP=36          LP=72          LP=72         LP=36
Lease       OC=18          OC=39          OC=45         OC=24
            ───────────────────────────────────────────────────
              0              1              2             3
```

Depreciation Starts in Year 0 with 5 year MACRS. Write off the remaining balance at the end of year 3. The effective state and federal tax rate is 40%. Assume other income exists against which to use deductions from negative taxable income in any year. The minimum DCFROR is 15.0%. Calculate the PW Cost of Purchasing, PW Cost of Leasing and the Incremental DCFROR for Purchase-Leasing.

Purchase Cash Flows (Cost Analysis)

Year	Time 0	1	2	3	Salvage
Revenue					50.00
-Operating Costs	-18.00	-39.00	-45.00	-24.00	
-Depreciation	-40.00	-64.00	-38.40	-23.04	-34.56
Taxable Income	-58.00	-103.00	-83.40	-47.04	15.44
-Tax Due @ 40%	23.20	41.20	33.36	18.82	-6.18
Net Income	-34.80	-61.80	-50.04	-28.22	9.26
+Depreciation	40.00	64.00	38.40	23.04	34.56
-Capital Costs	-200.00				
Cash Flow	-194.80	2.20	-11.64	-5.18	43.82

Present Worth Cost @ 15% = \$176.28

10-10 Solution: Annual Analysis - Lease vs Purchase

Leasing Cash Flows (Cost Analysis)

Year	Time 0	1	2	3
-Operating Costs	-18.00	-39.00	-45.00	-24.00
-Lease Payments	-36.00	-72.00	-72.00	-36.00
Taxable Income	-54.00	-111.00	-117.00	-60.00
-Tax Due @ 40%	21.60	44.40	46.80	24.00
Net Income	-32.40	-66.60	-70.20	-36.00
Cash Flow	-32.40	-66.60	-70.20	-36.00

Present Worth Cost @ 15% = $167.06

Selecting the alternative with the least present worth cost suggests that leasing is the economic choice.

Incremental Analysis (Purchase-Lease), Before-tax Diagram, S=Savings

```
                C=200
                S=36      S=72          S=72          S=36
Purchase-Lease  ─────────────────────────────────────────── L=50
                0         1             2             3
```

Incremental Cash Flows

Year	Time 0	1	2	3	Salvage
Savings	36.00	72.00	72.00	36.00	50.00
-Depreciation	-40.00	-64.00	-38.40	-23.04	-34.56
Taxable Income	-4.00	8.00	33.60	12.96	15.44
-Tax Due @ 40%	1.60	-3.20	-13.44	-5.18	-6.18
Net Income	-2.40	4.80	20.16	7.78	9.26
+Depreciation	40.00	64.00	38.40	23.04	34.56
-Capital Costs	-200.00				
Cash Flow	-162.40	68.80	58.56	30.82	43.82

Incremental NPV @ 15% = -$9.2 < 0 so reject purchase
Incremental DCFROR   = 11.6% < 15% so reject purchase

CHAPTER 10 PROBLEM SOLUTIONS 165

10-10 Solution: Continued - Monthly Analysis, Lease vs Purchase

```
             C=200
             OC=3.0   OC=3.0   OC=3.0   OC=3.5   OC=3.5   OC=4.0   OC=4.0   -
Purchase  ───────────────────────────────────────────────────────────────────── L=50
             0        1 ..... 11       12 ..... 23       24 ..... 35       36

             LP=6.0   LP=6.0   LP=6.0   LP=6.0   LP=6.0   LP=6.0   LP=6.0
             OC=3.0   OC=3.0   OC=3.0   OC=3.5   OC=3.5   OC=4.0   OC=4.0   -
Lease     ───────────────────────────────────────────────────────────────────── L=0
             0        1 ..... 11       12 ..... 23       24 ..... 35       36
```

Purchase Cash Flow Calculations, Monthly Periods

Year 0 depreciation is spread over months 0 to 5, Year 1 depreciation is spread uniformly over months 6 to 17, Year 2 depreciation spread uniformly over months 18 to 29 and year 3 depreciation is spread over months 30 to 35.

Month	0	1-5	6-11	12-17	18-23	24-29	30-35	36
Revenue								50.00
-Op Cost	-3.00	-3.00	-3.00	-3.50	-3.50	-4.00	-4.00	
-Deprec	-6.67	-6.67	-5.33	-5.33	-3.20	-3.20	-3.84	
-Writeoff								-34.56
Taxable	-9.67	-9.67	-8.33	-8.83	-6.70	-7.20	-7.84	15.44
-Tax @ 40%	3.87	3.87	3.33	3.53	2.68	2.88	3.14	-6.18
Net Income	-5.80	-5.80	-5.00	-5.30	-4.02	-4.32	-4.70	9.26
+Deprec	6.67	6.67	5.33	5.33	3.20	3.20	3.84	
+Writeoff								34.56
-Cap Cost	-200.00							
Cash Flow	-200.87	0.87	0.33	0.03	-0.82	-1.12	-0.86	43.82

Effective Annual Discount Rate, $E = 0.15 = (1+i)^{12} - 1$

By trial and error, the monthly interest rate $i = 0.0117$ or 1.17%

PW Cost Purchase

$= 200.87 - 0.87(P/A_{1.17\%,5}) - 0.33(P/A_{1.17\%,12})(P/F_{1.17\%,5}) \ldots = \$178.2$

Note that the monthly period analysis present worth cost of $178.2 is very close to the annual period analysis present worth cost of $176.3 Use of equivalent monthly period and annual period discount rates in the two analyses together with proper timing of the costs in the annual analysis is the key to obtaining equivalent results.

10-10 Solution: Continued - Monthly Analysis, Lease vs Purchase

Lease Cash Flow Calculations, Monthly Periods

Month	0	1-5	6-11	12-17	18-23	24-29	30-35
-Op Cost	-3.00	-3.00	-3.00	-3.50	-3.50	-4.00	-4.00
-Lease Pmt	-6.00	-6.00	-6.00	-6.00	-6.00	-6.00	-6.00
Taxable Inc	-9.00	-9.00	-9.00	-9.50	-9.50	-10.00	-10.00
-Tax @ 40%	3.60	3.60	3.60	3.80	3.80	4.00	4.00
Net Income	-5.40	-5.40	-5.40	-5.70	-5.70	-6.00	-6.00
Cash Flow	-5.40	-5.40	-5.40	-5.70	-5.70	-6.00	-6.00

PW Cost Leasing:

$5.40 + 5.40(P/A_{1.17\%,11}) + 5.70(P/A_{1.17\%,12})(P/F_{1.17\%,11})$

$+6.00(P/A_{1.17\%,12})(P/F_{1.17\%,23}) = \$167.8$

Selecting the alternative with the least present worth cost suggests that leasing is the economic choice, consistent with the annual period evaluation.

Incremental Purchase-Lease

Cash Flows	-195.47	6.27	5.73	5.73	4.88	4.88	5.14	43.82
Month	0	1-5	6-11	12-17	18-23	24-29	30-35	36

PW Eq: $0 = -195.47 + 6.27(P/A_{i\%,5}) + 5.73(P/A_{i\%,12})(P/F_{i\%,5})$

$\quad\quad\quad\quad + 4.88(P/A_{i\%,12})(P/F_{i\%,17}) + 5.14(P/A_{i\%,6})(P/F_{i\%,29})$

$\quad\quad\quad\quad + 36(P/F_{i\%,36})$

Incremental NPV @ 15% annually (or 1.17% per month) = -$10.44 < 0
so reject purchase

Incremental DCFROR per month = 0.88% < i* = 1.17%

Nominal Rate DCFROR is calculated as follows:

12(0.88%) = 10.56% per year, compounded monthly.

To evaluate the incremental investment using annual DCFROR, the monthly DCFROR should be converted to the equivalent effective discrete annual DCFROR rate. The effective discrete annual rate is calculated as follows:

$E = (1+.0088)^{12} - 1 = 0.1109$ or 11.09% < i* = 15%, reject purchase

CHAPTER 10 PROBLEM SOLUTIONS

10-11 Solution: Service Analysis, Values in Thousands of Dollars

```
                      OC= 100        OC=200      OC=200      OC=100
Capital               C=1,000          -            -           -
Intensive, "A"       ├──────────────────────────────────────────────  L=300
                      0              1            2            3

Less Capital          OC=275         OC=550       OC=550       OC=275
Intensive, "B"       ├──────────────────────────────────────────────  L=0
                      0              1            2            3

                     Savings=175     S=350        S=350        S=175
"A-B"                C=1,000           -            -            -
Incremental          ├──────────────────────────────────────────────  L=300
                      0              1            2            3
```

"A-B" Incremental Analysis

Year	0	1	2	3
Savings	175	350	350	475
-Depr/Writeoff	-200	-320	-192	-288
Taxable Income	-25	30	158	187
-Tax @ 40%	10	-12	-63.2	-74.8
Net Income	-15	18	94.8	112.2
+Depr/Writeoff	200	320	192	288
-Capital Cost	-1,000	-	-	-
Cash Flow	-815	338	286.8	400.2

PW Eq: $0 = -815 + 338(P/F_{i,1}) + 286.8(P/F_{i,2}) + 400.2(P/F_{i,3})$

i = Incremental DCFROR = 12% < i*=15% so reject "A", select "B"

Incremental NPV @ 15% = $-815+338\underset{.8696}{(P/F_{15,1})}+286.8\underset{.7561}{(P/F_{15,2})}+400.2\underset{.6575}{(P/F_{15,3})}$

= -$41.09 < 0 so reject "A", select "B"

10-11 Solution: Continued

Cost Analyses

Alternative "A" (Capital Intensive):

Year	0	1	2	3
Revenue	-	-	-	300
-Operating Costs	-100	-200	-200	-100
-Depr/Writeoff	-200	-320	-192	-288
Taxable Income	-300	-520	-392	-88
-Tax @ 40%	+120	+208	+156.8	+35.2
Net Income	-180	-312	-235.2	-52.8
+Depr/Writeoff	200	320	192	288
-Capital Cost	-1,000	-	-	-
Cash Flow	-980	8	-43.2	235.2

$$\text{PW Cost @ 15\%} = 980 - 8(P/F_{15,1})^{.8696} + 43.2(P/F_{15,2})^{.7561} - 235.2(P/F_{15,3})^{.6575}$$

$$= \$851.06$$

$$\text{End-of-Period Equivalent AC} = 851.06(A/P_{15,3})^{.43798} = \$372.75$$

$$\text{Beginning-of-Period Equivalent AC} = 372.75(P/F_{15,1})^{.8696} = \$324.14$$

Alternative "B" (Less Capital Intensive):

Year	0	1	2	3
Revenue	-	-	-	-
-Operating Costs	-275	-550	-550	-275
Taxable Income	-275	-550	-550	-275
-Tax @ 40%	+110	+220	+220	+110
Net Income	-165	-330	-330	-165
-Capital Cost	-	-	-	-
Cash Flow	-165	-330	-330	-165

CHAPTER 10 PROBLEM SOLUTIONS

10-11 Solution: Continued

Alternative "B":

$$\text{PW Cost @ 15\%} = 165 + 330\underset{.8696}{(P/F_{15,1})} + 330\underset{.7561}{(P/F_{15,2})} + 165\underset{.6575}{(P/F_{15,3})}$$

$$= \$809.97 < \$851.06, \text{ so select less capital intensive "B"}$$

End-of-Period Equivalent AC = $809.97\underset{.43798}{(A/P_{15,3})}$ = \$354.75 < \$372.75
Select "B"

Beginning-of-Period Equiv. AC = $354.75\underset{.8696}{(P/F_{15,1})}$ = \$308.49 < \$324.14
Select "B"

In the above analyses, the less capital-intensive alternative "B" is preferred. However, alternative "B" may be treated as an option to lease the equipment. In this case, the problem becomes a lease vs. purchase analysis. Assume, then, that a hypothetical 6% minimum discount rate, that reflects the after-tax cost of borrowing funds to finance the purchase of the asset, is used. Many companies do this. In that case, purchasing seems preferable to leasing. But is it really?

Should the appropriate minimum discount rate be affected by whether the analysis is described as lease vs purchase, or as an old asset compared to a new asset, or as labor compared to automated equipment? It seems evident the answer is "no," unless unique borrowed money financing that does not affect other capital budgets is available for purchasing instead of leasing. In general, if you can borrow to purchase an asset instead of leasing, then you probably can borrow money to acquire automated equipment to replace labor, or to finance any investment being evaluated. However, regardless of the financing source, the economic analysis objective is to make optimum use of available investment dollars from any source. Opportunity cost of capital as a minimum discount rate enables us to achieve that objective. If unique financing exists that creates no impact on available investment dollars to invest elsewhere, then, and only then, opportunity cost of capital equals the after-tax cost of borrowed money.

CHAPTER 11 PROBLEM SOLUTIONS

11-1 Solution: Land Acquisition Analysis, All Values in Dollars

CASE A, Cash Investment

Before-Tax Diagram

```
   C=60,000
   |————————————————————————— L = 150,000
   0      1 ................. 5
```

Tax on gain = (150,000-60,000)(.4 tax rate) = 36,000

After-Tax Diagram

```
   CF=-60,000
   |————————————————————————— CF = 114,000
   0      1 ................. 5
```

PW Eq: $0 = 60,000 - 114,000(P/F_{i,5})$, i=DCFROR=13.7% by trial and error.

CASE B, Leveraged Investment

Before-Tax Diagram

```
            Int= 5,000 Int=4,000 Int=3,000 Int=2,000 Int=1,000
  C=10,000  C=10,000   C=10,000  C=10,000  C=10,000  C=10,000
  |————————————————————————————————————————————————————— L = 150,000
  0         1          2         3         4         5
```

Every dollar of interest saves $0.40 in tax at a 40% effective tax rate.

After-Tax Diagram

```
            Int= 3,000 Int=2,400 Int=1,800 Int=1,200 Int=600
  C=10,000  C=10,000   C=10,000  C=10,000  C=10,000  C=10,000
  |————————————————————————————————————————————————————— CF=114,000
  0         1          2         3         4         5
Net CF=-10,000 -13,000 -12,400   -11,800   -11,200   -10,600
```

Costs vary by a constant gradient of $600 for years 1 to 5.

PW Eq: $0 = -10,000 - [13,000 - 600(A/G_{i,5})](P/A_{i,5}) + 114,000(P/F_{i,5})$

$i = DCFROR = 19.9\%$

The after-tax cost of borrowed money is 10%(1-.4 tax rate) or 6.0% which is less than the cash investment DCFROR of 13.7% so borrowed money leverage works for the investor and the leveraged investment DCFROR of 19.9% is greater than the cash investment DCFROR of 13.7%.

CHAPTER 11 PROBLEM SOLUTIONS 171

11-2 Solution: Develop vs Sell Now Leveraged Analysis

Cash Investment Diagram:

```
                    C_Bldgs=30      Income/Yr =  65      70      75
C_Land=1 (Sunk)     C_Equip= 5      OpCost/Yr =  25      30      35
─────────────────────────────────────────────────────────────────────
    -2                  0 (Now)                   1       2       3
```

Leveraged Develop Cash Flows:

Year	0	1	2	3	3 Salv
Revenue		65.00	70.00	75.00	40.00
-Operating Costs		-25.00	-30.00	-35.00	
-Deprec/Writeoff		-1.63	-2.18	-1.83	-30.37*
-Interest		-3.60	-3.03	-2.40	
Taxable Income		34.77	34.79	35.77	9.63
-Tax @ 35%		-12.17	-12.18	-12.52	-3.37
Net Income		22.60	22.61	23.25	6.26
+Deprec/Writeoff		1.63	2.18	1.83	30.37*
-Principal		-4.72	-5.29	-19.99	
-Cap. Costs	-35.00				
+Borrowed $	30.00				
Cash Flow	-5.00	19.51	19.50	5.09	36.53
				___41.72___	

Year	0
Sale Value	7.0
-Book Writeoff	-1.0
Taxable	6.0
-Tax (35%)	-2.1
Net Income	3.9
+Book Writeoff	1.0
Cash Flow	4.9

*Includes land and depreciable assets.

Depreciation Calculations

Yr 1 5(0.1429)	= 0.72
Yr 1 30(1/31.5)(11.5/12)	= 0.91
Yr 2 5(0.2449)	= 1.23
Yr 2 30(1/31.5)	= 0.95
Yr 3 5(0.1749)	= 0.88
Yr 3 30(1/31.5)	= 0.95
Yr 3 Writeoff on 5	= 2.18
Yr 3 Writeoff on 30	= 27.19
Yr 3 Land Writeoff	= 1.00

Mortgage Payment: $30(A/P_{12,5}) = 8.32$

Year	1	2	3
Principal	30.00	25.28	19.99
Interest	3.60	3.03	2.40
Princ. Pd	4.72	5.29	19.99

$$\text{NPV @ 20\%} = -5.00 + 19.51(P/F_{20,1})^{.8333} + 19.50(P/F_{20,2})^{.6944} + 41.72(P/F_{20,3})^{.5787} = +\$48.94$$

DCFROR = 401%, "i" value that makes NPV equal to zero

Since these projects are mutually exclusive we select the project with the largest NPV which is the "Develop" alternative with an NPV of +48.7 This can be verified by examining the incremental cash flows and computing incremental NPV or by examining the incremental difference in the NPV results as follows:

$NPV_{Develop} - NPV_{Sell\ Now} = 48.9 - 4.9 = +44.0$ which is > 0, accept develop

11-3 Solution: Petroleum Property Evaluation

Develop (Before-Tax) Time Diagram

```
                              Rev=7.0
                IDC=2.0        OC=1.2
                Tang=1.5       IDC=2.0     Rev=11.0    Rev=9.0
Acq=3.0 (Sunk)  Borrow=4.0     Tang=1.0     OC=2.5      OC=2.1
                                                                  L=6.5
-----------------------------------------------------------------------
    -1            0(Now)         1            2            3
```

Develop Cash Flows

Year	0	1	2	3	3 Salv
Revenue		7.00	11.00	9.00	6.50
-Royalties		-1.05	-1.65	-1.35	
Net Revenue		5.95	9.35	7.65	
-Oper Costs		-1.20	-2.50	-2.10	
-Intangible	-1.40	-1.40			
-Depreciation	-0.21	-0.51	-0.51	-0.36	
-Depr Writeoff					-0.91
-Amortization	-0.12	-0.24	-0.24	-0.24	-0.36
-Interest		-0.48	-0.40	-0.32	
-Cost Depletion		-0.30	-0.48	-0.42	-1.80
Taxable Inc	-1.73	1.82	5.22	4.21	3.43
-Tax @ 40%	0.69	-0.73	-2.09	-1.68	-1.37
Net Income	-1.04	1.09	3.13	2.53	2.06
+Depreciation	0.21	0.51	0.51	0.36	0.91
+Depletion		0.30	0.48	0.42	1.80
+Amortization	0.12	0.24	0.24	0.24	0.36
-Principal		-0.63	-0.71	-2.66	
-Cap. Costs	-2.10	-1.60			
+Borrowed	4.00				
Cash Flow	1.19	-0.09	3.65	0.89	5.13

Yr 0 Sell Cash Flow

Sale Value	5.0
-Book W.O.	-3.0
Taxable	2.0
-Tax @ 40%	-0.8
Net Income	1.2
+Book W.O.	3.0
Cash Flow	4.2

$NPV_{Sell} = 4.2$

NPV_{Dev} @ 25% = 6.54 > 4.2, Select Develop

Since neither project has any negative cash flow upon which to properly calculate DCFROR, both alternatives offer infinite leveraged DCFROR's on total investment.
Incremental DCFROR analysis is required to make a proper economic decision with DCFROR analysis. The incremental analysis is on the next page.

Loan Payment Schedule:

$4(A/P_{12,5}) = 1.11$

	Princ Bal	Interest	Princ Pd
Yr 1	4	0.48	0.63
Yr 2	3.37	0.40	0.71
Yr 3	2.67	0.32	2.66

Cost Depletion Schedule:

Yr 1 3(0.10) = 0.30
Yr 2 3(0.16) = 0.48 or [0.16X/(X-0.1X)](3-0.3) = 0.48
Yr 3 3(0.14) = 0.42 or [0.14X/(0.9X-0.16X)](3-0.78) = 0.42
Yr Writeoff   = 1.80

CHAPTER 11 PROBLEM SOLUTIONS

11-3 Solution: Continued

Incremental DCFROR Analysis

```
                       1.19    -0.09    3.65    0.89    5.13
Cash Flow "Develop"   ─────────────────────────────────────
                       0        1        2       3       3+

                       4.2
Cash Flow "Sell Now"  ─────────────────────────────────────
                       0        1        2       3       3+

Incremental           -3.01   -0.09    3.65    0.89    5.13
"Develop-Sell Now"    ─────────────────────────────────────
Cash Flows             0        1        2       3       3+
```

Incremental PW Eq: $0 = -3.01 - 0.09(P/F_{i,1}) + 3.65(P/F_{i,2}) + 6.02(P/F_{i,3})$

i = Incremental DCFROR = 56.4% > i^* of 25%, so accept development

Incremental NPV @ 25% = +2.3 > 0, so accept development

The same increm. NPV results from NPV_{Dev} of 6.5 - NPV_{Sell} of 4.2 = 2.3

11-4 Solution: Silver Property, Values in Millions

```
Acq Cost  =2.0        Rev=4.5      Rev=6.0      Rev=7.5
Equipment =3.0        OC  =3.0     OC =3.37     OC =3.75
Borrowed $=4.0        Dev =1.5
                                                            Salv = 6.0
        |—————————————|————————————|————————————|
        0             1            2            3
```

Loan Amortization Schedule:

$4.0(A/P_{10,10}) = 0.65$

Year	Interest	Principal
1	4(0.1) =0.4	0.65-0.4 =0.25
2	3.75(0.1)=0.37	0.65-0.37=0.28
3	3.47(0.1)=0.35	3.47

Cost Depletion Schedule:

Yr 1 2(0.3/3)   = 0.2
Yr 2 (2-0.2)(0.3/2.7)   = 0.2
Yr 3 (1.8-0.71)(0.3/2.4)   = 0.14

Cash Flows

Year	0	1	2	3	3 Salv
Revenue		4.50	6.00	7.50	6.00
-Operating Costs		-3.00	-3.38	-3.75	
-Development		-1.05			
-Depreciation		-0.43	-0.73	-0.52	
-Deprec Writeoff					-1.32
-Amortization		-0.05	-0.09	-0.09	-0.22
-Interest		-0.40	-0.37	-0.35	
Before Depletion		-0.43	1.43	2.79	4.46
-50% Limit		0	-0.71	1.39	
-Percent Depl (15%)		0.68	0.90	-1.13	
-Cost Depletion		-0.20	0.20	0.14	
Taxable Income		-0.63	0.72	1.66	4.46
-Tax @ 40%		0.25	-0.29	-0.67	-1.78
Net Income		-0.38	0.43	1.00	2.68
+Depreciation		0.43	0.73	0.52	1.32
+Depletion		0.20	0.71	1.13	
+Amortization		0.05	0.09	0.09	0.22
-Principal		-0.25	-0.28	-3.47	
-Capital Costs	-5.00	-0.45*			
+Borrowed	4.00				
Cash Flow	-1.00	-0.40	1.68	-0.73	4.22

*30% of development cost to be amortized

PW Eq: $0 = -1.00 - 0.40(P/F_{i,1}) + 1.68(P/F_{i,2}) - 0.73(P/F_{i,3}) + 4.22(P/F_{i,3})$

i = Leveraged DCFROR = 73.25%

This is the "i" value that makes NPV for this leveraged investment NPV equal to zero.

CHAPTER 11 PROBLEM SOLUTIONS

11-5 Solution: Land Acquisition Analysis

Borrowed $ = 160,000
Cost of Land = 200,000

Escalated $ Sale Price = X
Interest = 16,000
Loan Principal Payment = 160,000

```
0                                                    1 year
```

Year	0	1
Escalated $ Sale Revenue		X
-Interest		-16,000
-Book Value (Initial Cost)		-200,000
Taxable Gain		X-216,000
-Tax @ 34%		-.34X+ 73,440
Net Income		.66X-142,560
+Book Value		+200,000
-Capital Cost	-200,000	
+Borrowed $	160,000	-160,000
Cash Flow	-40,000	.66X-102,560

For a 30% constant dollar DCFROR and 10% inflation per year, the equivalent escalated dollar DCFROR is calculated as follows:

$i = (1+0.10)(1+0.30) - 1 = 0.430$ or 43.0%

PW Eq: $0 = -40,000 + (0.66X-102,560)(P/F_{43,1})$; $(P/F) = .6993$

$40,000 = 0.46X - 71,720$

X = $242,870 = the escalated dollar sale price to give a 30% constant dollar DCFROR on leveraged equity investment.

11-6 Solution: Rental Machinery Analysis, All Values in Thousands of Dollars

```
Working Capital = 10      Rev/yr =  150    180    210
Deprec Equip.   = 150     OC/yr  =   50     70     90
                                                        Salv = 50
                          0         1       2       3   Including WC
                                                        Return
```

Escalated Dollar Cash Flow Calculations

Year	0	1	2	3	3 Salv
Revenue		150.00	180.00	210.00	50.00
-Oper Costs		-50.00	-70.00	-90.00	
-Depreciation	-21.43	-36.73	-26.24	-18.74	-46.86
-Interest		-12.00	-8.00	-4.00	
-Writeoffs					-10.00
Taxable Income	-21.43	51.27	75.76	97.26	-6.86
-Tax @ 40%	8.57	-20.51	-30.30	-38.90	2.74
Net Income	-12.86	30.76	45.46	58.35	-4.12
+Depreciation	21.43	36.73	26.24	18.74	46.86
-Principal		-40.00	-40.00	-40.00	
+Writeoffs					10.00
-Capital Costs	-160.00				
+Borrowed $	120.00				
Cash Flow	-31.43	27.49	31.70	37.10	52.74
				89.84	

Leveraged Escalated Dollar PW Eq:

$$0 = -31.43 + 27.49(P/F_{i,1}) + 31.7(P/F_{i,2}) + 89.84(P/F_{i,3})$$

i = Leveraged Escalated $ DCFROR = 104.8%

NPV @ 20% = +$65.48

Constant Dollar Equivalent Cash Flows

Year 0	Year 1	Year 2	Year 3
-31.43	$27.49(P/F_{10,1})=24.99$	$31.7(P/F_{10,2})=26.2$	$89.84(P/F_{10,3})=67.5$

Leveraged Constant Dollar PW Eq:

$$0 = -31.43 + 24.99(P/F_{i,1}) + 26.2(P/F_{i,2}) + 67.5(P/F_{i,3})$$

i = Leveraged Constant $ DCFROR = 86.2%

Using Equation 5-1 we can check the results:

(1+i) = (1+f)(1+i)

(1 + 1.048) = (1.1)(1.862) = 2.048, so answers are equivalent.

CHAPTER 11 PROBLEM SOLUTIONS

11-7 Solution: Depreciable Investment Analysis (in Thousands of Dollars)

```
Deprec Equip  = 100
Development   =  10      Revenues/yr = 150              150
Work Capital  =  30      Op Costs/yr = 118              118    WC Return
                                                               = 30
                  0                       1 .............. 5
```

Cash Investment Analysis

Year	0	1	2	3	4	5	5 Salv
Revenue		150.0	150.0	150.0	150.0	150.0	30.0
-Oper Costs		-118.0	-118.0	-118.0	-118.0	-118.0	
-Development	-10.0						
-Depreciation	-10.0	-20.0	-20.0	-20.0	-20.0	-10.0	
-Writeoffs							-30.0
Taxable Income	-20.0	12.0	12.0	12.0	12.0	22.0	
-Tax @ 40%	8.0	-4.8	-4.8	-4.8	-4.8	-8.8	
Net Income	-12.0	7.2	7.2	7.2	7.2	13.2	
+Depreciation	10.0	20.0	20.0	20.0	20.0	10.0	
+Writeoffs							30.0
-Capital Costs	-130.0						
Cash Flow	-132.0	27.2	27.2	27.2	27.2	23.2	30.0
						53.2	

Cash PW Eq: $0 = -132 + 27.2(P/A_{i,4}) + 53.2(P/F_{i,5})$

i = Cash Investment DCFROR = 6.5%

Leveraged Investment Cash Flows

Year	0	1	2	3	4	5	5 Salv
Revenue		150.0	150.0	150.0	150.0	150.0	30.0
-Oper Costs		-118.0	-118.0	-118.0	-118.0	-118.0	
-Development	-10.0						
-Depreciation	-10.0	-20.0	-20.0	-20.0	-20.0	-10.0	
-Interest		-12.0	-9.6	-7.2	-4.8	-2.4	
-Writeoffs							-30.0
Taxable Income	-20.0	0.0	2.4	4.8	7.2	19.6	0.0
-Tax @ 40%	8.0	0.0	-1.0	-1.9	-2.9	-7.8	0.0
Net Income	-12.0	0.0	1.4	2.9	4.3	11.8	
+Depreciation	10.0	20.0	20.0	20.0	20.0	10.0	
-Principal		-20.0	-20.0	-20.0	-20.0	-20.0	
+Writeoffs							30.0
-Capital Costs	-130.0						
+Borrowed $	100.0						
Cash Flow	-32.0	0.0	1.4	2.9	4.3	1.8	30.0
						31.8	

11-7 Solution: Continued - Depreciable Investment Analysis, In Thousands of Dollars

Lev. PW Eq: $0 = -32.0 + 1.4(P/F_{i,2}) + 2.9(P/F_{i,3}) + 4.3(P/F_{i,4}) + 31.8(P/F_{i,5})$

i = Leveraged Investment DCFROR = 5.2%

Results for leveraged analysis are less attractive because the after-tax cost of borrowed money (7.2%) exceeds the project cash investment DCFROR, hence leverage works against the investor.

11-8 Solution: Leveraged Evaluation of Problem 10-10

Purchase Cash Flows (Cost Analysis)

Year	Time 0	1	2	3	Salvage
Revenue					50
-Operating Costs	-18	-39	-45	-24	
-Interest Payment		-15	-10	-5	
-Depreciation	-40	-64	-38	-23	-35
Taxable Income	-58	-118	-93	-52	15
-Tax @ 40%	23	47	37	21	-6
Net Income	-35	-71	-56	-31	9
+Depreciation	40	64	38	23	35
-Princ. Paid		-50	-50	-50	
+Loan Income	150				
-Capital Costs	-200				
Cash Flow	-45	-57	-68	-58	44

Present Worth Cost @ 15% = $154.8
Present Worth Cost @ 25% = $141.3

Leasing Cash Flows (Cost Analysis)

Year	Time 0	1	2	3
-Operating Costs	-18.00	-39.00	-45.00	-24.00
-Lease Payments	-36.00	-72.00	-72.00	-36.00
Taxable Income	-54.00	-111.00	-117.00	-60.00
-Tax Due @ 40%	21.60	44.40	46.80	24.00
Net Income	-32.40	-66.60	-70.20	-36.00
Cash Flow	-32.40	-66.60	-70.20	-36.00

Present Worth Cost @ 15% = $167.1
Present Worth Cost @ 25% = $149.0

Selecting the alternative with the least present worth cost suggests that purchasing the equipment is now the economic choice. This was not the choice in evaluating the alternatives from a 100% cash equity analysis.

CHAPTER 11 PROBLEM SOLUTIONS

11-9 Solution:

Uniform mortgage payments over 3 years, at 12% annual interest:

$500,000(A/P_{12,3}) = $208,175

	Year 1	Year 2	Year 3
Before-Tax Interest	60,000	42,219	23,304
Principal Payment	148,175	165,955	185,870

Leveraged Cash Flows:

Year	0	1	2	3
Cash Investment CF	-800,000	400,000	500,000	550,000
-Loan Principal Pmt.	-	-148,175	-165,955	-185,870
-After-Tax Interest*	-	-36,000	-25,331	-13,382
+Borrowed Dollars	+500,000	-	-	-
Leveraged CF	-300,000	215,825	308,714	350,748

*After-Tax Interest = (1-tax rate)(interest)

A) PW Eq: $0 = -300,000 + 215,825(P/F_{i,1}) + 308,714(P/F_{i,2}) + 350,748(P/F_{i,3})$

NPV@ 72% = -$1,238
NPV@ 70% = $5,169

i = Leveraged DCFROR = 70% + (72%-70%)(5,169-0)/(5,169+1,238) = 71.61%

B) Calculate the NPV at i* = 25%

NPV = $-300,000 + 215,825(P/F_{25,1}) + 308,714(P/F_{25,2}) + 350,748(P/F_{25,3})$

= +$249,820

Let the acquisition cost in year 0 = X

X/3 is the annual amortization deduction

(X/3)(0.4) = 0.133X = tax savings per year

$X - 0.133X(P/A_{25,3})^{1.952} = 249,820$

X = $337,419 = acquisition cost to give a 25% DCFROR

AUXILIARY PROBLEMS

1. You have been asked to evaluate whether it is economically better to use a submersible centrifugal pump system or a rod pump system to lift crude oil 4000 feet in a well with an estimated producing life of 12 years. The submersible pump system initially will have an installed cost of $100,000 including tubing, wiring and surface gear while the installed rod pump cost, including sucker rods and surface gear will be $135,000. It is estimated that the submersible pump will need to be replaced every 3 years with a similar refurbished used pump for a cost of $35,000 at year 3, $45,000 at year 6 and $55,000 at year 9. Year 12 salvage value of the submersible pump is $50,000. The down-hole positive displacement rod pump is estimated to need replacing every 4 years for costs of $8,000 at year 4 and $12,000 at year 8. Due to corrosion, the salvage value of the rod pump system at year 12 is estimated to be 0. The minimum ROR is 15%. Use Present Worth Cost analysis to determine which pumping system is economically better. Verify your conclusion with ROR analysis.

2.

	I=100	I=250	I=375	I=500	I=500	L=100 I=400
C=100	C=500	C=100	C=125	C=150	C=150	C=200
0	1	2	3	4	5	6

A project has costs and revenues as shown on the diagram in thousands of dollars. Calculate the project rate of return. Then, assume the minimum rate of return is 15% and calculate the growth rate of return, NPV and PVR for the project using a 6 year evaluation life.

3. A loader is being considered to tram coal from a stockpile to a coal load-out facility. The cost of the machine is estimated to be $900,000 with an estimated salvage of $225,000 at the end of 7 years from now. Operating costs are estimated to be $200,000 per year with major repairs of $150,000 and $100,000 required at the end of the 3rd and 5th years respectively. Given the required tram distance, it is estimated the machine can move 2,400 ton of coal per day, 250 days per year. For a desired minimum rate of return of 12%, calculate the present and annual cost of operating this machine over the next 7 years. Then calculate the breakeven cost per ton of coal being trammed.

4. Rank these non-mutually exclusive alternatives for a 20% opportunity cost of capital. Values are given in thousands of dollars.

		C=100 I=100	C=100 I=150				
A)	C=100	C=200	C=250	I=300	I=300	I=300	I=300
	0	1	2	3	4	5	6

			I=50 I=200			
B)	—	C=300	C=150	I=250	I=250	I=250
	0	1	2	3	4	5

C)	C=200	I=170	C=200	I=350	I=350	I=350	C=100
	0	1	2	3	4	5	6

5. A manager is trying to evaluate the economics of purchasing or leasing a natural gas processing facility. It may be purchased and installed on company land for $1,000,000 or leased for $250,000 per year with beginning of year lease payments. With either alternative, the annual revenue to the plant for natural gas liquids is expected to be $1,500,000 with $800,000 annual operating costs. The life of the plant is estimated to be 8 years. Net salvage value of the plant at the end of the 8th year is estimated to be $150,000 if you purchase. For a 15% minimum rate of return, determine whether the manager should purchase or lease the processing facility. Reinforce your economic conclusion by making a second evaluation using a different analysis.

AUXILIARY PROBLEMS

6. Evaluate the economic potential of purchasing a gold property now (at year 0) for a $2 million mineral rights acquisition cost. Mining equipment costs of $3 million will be incurred at year 0. Mineral development costs of $1 million will be incurred at year 0, and mineral development costs of $1.5 million will be incurred at year 1. Production is expected to start in year 1 with 150,000 tons of gold ore. Production in years 2, 3, and 4 is estimated to be 250,000 tons per year. Gold ore reserves are estimated to be depleted at the end of year 4. Reclamation costs (treated as operating expenses) of $0.5 million will be incurred at year 5. Equipment will be sold at year 5 for $1 million. All gold ore is estimated to contain 0.1 ounce of gold per ton of ore, and metallurgical recovery is estimated to be 90%. The price of gold is forecasted to be $300 per ounce in year 1, escalating 15% in year 2, 20% in year 3, and 10% in year 4. Operating costs are estimated to be $20 per ton of ore produced in year 1, escalating 8% per year thereafter. Make before-tax ROR, NPV, PVR, and Growth ROR analyses for a minimum ROR of 15%.

7. Consideration is currently being given to determine whether a D9N bulldozer should be purchased or leased for necessary service over the next five years. If the machine is purchased, the year 0 purchase price for the D9N is $750,000. Maintenance costs are estimated to be $50,000 at year 0, $100,000 at year 1 (with that amount increasing by 10.0% per year at years 2,3, and 4), and $70,000 at year 5. Major repairs of $180,000 at the end of year 2, and $160,000 at the end of year 4 are also estimated to be required. The end-of-year 5 salvage is estimated to be $50,000. The alternative to purchasing is to lease the machine for $82.50 per hour. It is assumed the machine will operate 18 hours per day, 26 days per month, 12 months per year. An $82.50 per hour lease rate applies for the first three years, then the lease cost is expected to increase by 10.0% to $90.75 per hour for years 4 and 5. The hourly lease rate includes all maintenance and repair costs. Allocate the value of the lease payments for the first 6 months to year 0. Allocate months 7 through 18 lease payments at year 1 and so forth (with months 43 through 54 at year 4) and allocate the final six months of payments (55 through 60) at month 60 to best account for the time value of money. Assume the before-tax minimum rate of return is 20%. Calculate the before-tax present worth costs for each alternative and the incremental net present value (NPV) to determine which of these two alternatives is the economic choice. Then, determine the lease cost per hour that would make leasing breakeven with purchasing.

8. Make the same analyses asked for in Auxiliary Problem #7 on an after-tax basis. Assume that if you purchase, the machine will be depreciated over 7 years using modified ACRS depreciation with the half-year convention, beginning in year one. Expense all maintenance and repair costs in the year incurred assuming other income exists to utilize all deductions in the year they are realized. Write off the remaining book value at the end of year 5. If the machine is leased, assume it is an operating lease so all lease payments will be 100% deductible in the year they are realized. The effective income tax rate is estimated to be 38.0%. Assume the after-tax minimum DCFROR is 20.0%. Calculate the after-tax present worth costs for each alternative and the incremental after-tax NPV to determine which of these two alternatives is the economic choice. Then, determine the lease cost per hour that would make leasing breakeven with purchasing.

9. Development of a natural gas property is projected to involve production, costs and prices as follows with costs expressed in thousands of dollars and production and price in units as noted. Mcf = Thousand Cubic Feet, MMcf = Million Cubic Feet and M$ = Thousands of Dollars.

Year	0	1	2	3	4
Production, (MMcf/Yr)		300	700	500	150
Price, $/Mcf		2.00	2.25	2.50	$2.75
Royalties, 15% of Revenues		15%	15%	15%	15%
Intangible Well Cost, M$	600	300			
Tangible Well Cost, M$		400			
Tangible Pipeline Cost, M$		200			
Mineral Acquisition Cost, M$	100				
Operating Costs, M$		60	70	80	90

A) Calculate the annual before-tax cash flow, then calculate ROR, NPV, PVR and Growth ROR for a 15% minimum ROR, assuming the investor has a 100% working interest in the property and salvage is zero.

B) Assume this project is in a U.S. wilderness area so a $600,000 reclamation cost must be incurred at year 5, then calculate a valid project ROR.

10. A mutually exclusive alternative variation of the development described in Auxiliary Problem #9A is to delay the start of development until four years after year 0 to take advantage of sharply escalating natural gas prices expected to occur four to eight years from now. The four year development delay would make the start of new development year 0 equal to year 4 in problem #9A. Assume the mineral rights acquisition cost is incurred at year 0 and all other costs given in problem #9A will escalate 5% per year over the four year delay period and that year 5 to 8 production rates for the delayed project will be the same as in years 1 to 4 of problem #9. The natural gas selling price of $2.75 per Mcf in year 4 of problem #9A is estimated to escalate 20% per year over the following four years. Is it better to develop now for the development scenario described in problem #9A, or to delay the development for four years as described in this problem statement? Use the analysis method of your choice for a minimum rate of return of 15%.

11. Two used machines can be acquired for $60,000 per machine to provide necessary service for the next two years. The salvage of these machines is estimated to be $20,000 per machine at year two when the old machines will be replaced with one new machine capable of providing the same total service. The new machine would cost $350,000 at year 2. Instead of buying the old machines and replacing them at year 2, a new machine can be purchased today at year 0 for a cost of $300,000 to provide the necessary service. Service with either the old or new machines is needed for the next four years, so a four year evaluation life should be used. It is estimated that purchasing a new machine at year 0 will give it a salvage value of $80,000 at year 4 while purchasing a new machine at year 2 will give it a salvage value of $170,000 at year 4. Operating costs per machine with the used machines are estimated to be $60,000 at year 1 and $70,000 at year 2. Operating costs with a new machine purchased at year 0 are estimated to be $75,000 at year 1, $80,000 at year 2, $85,000 at year 3 and $90,000 at year 4. Operating costs with a new machine purchased at year 2 are estimated to be $80,000 at year 3 and $85,000 at year 4. Assuming a minimum discount rate of 15%, use present worth cost analysis to determine the most economical alternative for providing the necessary service. Then determine the four equal end of year revenues at years 1 through 4 for each alternative that would cover the cost of service and give the investor a 15% ROR.

AUXILIARY PROBLEMS

12. Two alternative choices exist for you to invest $100,000 as shown on the following time diagrams.

    A) C=$100,000   -   -   -   L=$627,500
       ───
            0   1   2 7

    B) C=$100,000   I=$44,190   I=$44,190 ..... I=$44,190   L=0
       ───
            0   1   2 7

    Assuming a minimum ROR of 15%, determine the economically better choice using A) ROR Analysis, B) NPV Analysis, C) PVR Analysis, D) Growth ROR Analysis and E) Future Value Analysis. Discuss the consistency (or lack of consistency) of results with the different methods of analysis.

13. Investment of $100,000 is projected to generate increasing annual production that gives today's dollar net revenues of $30,000 in year 1, $40,000 in year 2 and $50,000 in year 3 with a $40,000 salvage value at year 3. Net revenues and salvage are projected to escalate 8% in year 1, 6% in year 2 and 4% in year 3. Calculate the escalated dollar ROR and NPV for a minimum escalated dollar ROR of 20%. Then calculate the equivalent constant dollar project ROR and NPV assuming inflation will be 8% in year 1, 10% in year 2 and 12% in year 3.

14. A chemical company wants you to analyze whether it is better economically to sell patent rights to a new chemical process for $300,000 cash now at year 0 or whether it would be better to keep the patent rights and develop them using one of two development scenarios for which projected costs (C) and incomes (I) are given on the following diagrams. All dollar values shown are in thousands of dollars.

                    I=$100   I=$420   I=$420
    A)   C=$700   C=$300   C=$200 ..... C=$200
         ───
           0   1   2 9

                                 I=$670   I=$670
    B)   C=$500   C=$800   C=$250 ..... C=$250
         ───
           0   1   2 9

    Use ROR Analysis to determine whether it is better to sell or develop with the "A" or "B" scenario assuming the minimum ROR is 15%. Verify your results with NPV and PVR Analysis. Using any valid analysis, if the minimum ROR is raised to 25% what is your economic choice?

15. Evaluate the economics of using an ore conveyor system as an economic alternative to haul trucks using present worth cost analysis for a 15 year life and a minimum rate of return of 15%. Consider a cost of $16 million for an ore conveyor system in evaluation year 0 with operating costs of $2.5 million in year 1 and estimated to increase by an arithmetic gradient of $300,000 per year in each year after year 1 for the 15 year estimated mine life. Two major repairs costing $4 million and $6 million are estimated to be required at the end of evaluation years 5 and 10. Salvage value is estimated to be $7 million in evaluation year 15. The alternative to the conveyor system is to use 7 new haul trucks with a 170 ton capacity and a cost of $800,000 per truck in evaluation year 0. The haul trucks would have a 5 year life and salvage values of $100,000 each. Operating costs per truck are estimated to be $400,000 in evaluation year 1 and to increase by an arithmetic gradient of $60,000 per truck year through year 5. In 5 years the 7 trucks would be replaced with new trucks costing an estimated $1,400,00 per truck with salvage values of $150,00 per truck 5 years later in evaluation year 10. Operating costs per truck are estimated to be $550,000 in year 6 and to increase by an arithmetic gradient of $70,000 per truck for evaluation years 7 through 10. In 10 years the 7 trucks would be replaced again with new trucks costing $2,300,000 per truck with salvage of $200,000 per truck 5 years later in evaluation year 15. Operating costs per truck are estimated to be $700,000 in year 11 and to increase by an arithmetic gradient of $80,000 per truck for evaluation years 12 through 15. Verify your result with incremental rate of return.

16. Production of crude oil from a 10,000 foot deep north sea well that has L-80 carbon steel 5" tubing requires down-hole injection of chemicals to control tubing corrosion due to high temperatures and pressures and corrosive chlorides in the crude oil. It is proposed to replace the L-80 carbon steel tubing, which cost $8.50 per foot 1 year ago, with 13% chrome stainless steel tubing that would cost $30 per foot. 10,000 feet of tubing are needed and installation costs are estimated to be $80,000. Annual cost savings in chemicals, labor and chemical injection equipment are projected to be $100,000 in year 1 following the installation of the new tubing with savings escalating 7% per year in succeeding years. Use NPV Analysis for a 15% minimum ROR and 6 year evaluation life with a salvage value of 0 in year 6 to determine if installation of the 13% chrome tubing is economically desirable. Assume the existing L-80 carbon steel tubing has no salvage value at year 0. What physical use life will cause the 13% chrome tubing replacement investment to yield a 15% ROR?

17. An existing mineral operation is expected to generate annual net revenue (revenue minus operating costs) of $100 million per year at each of years 1, 2, 3, and 4. Purchase of mineral reserves contained in an adjacent property for $40 million now (time zero) is being considered with the expectation that $50 million would be spent on development and equipment at year 1, and another $55 million at year 2. This expansion would make the total project net revenue $100 million at year 1, $140 million at year 2, $150 million at year 3, $160 million at year 4, and $65 million in each of years 5 through 10. Equipment is projected to be replaced for a cost of $65 million at the end of year 6, and the salvage value at the end of year 10 is estimated at $40 million. Make before-tax NPV analysis to determine whether the project expansion is economically justifiable, given that the minimum rate of return is 15%. Verify your conclusion using before-tax ROR and PVR analyses.

```
Present    -      R=100   R=100   R=100   R=100    -       -       -  ........   -
           0        1       2       3       4      5       6       7  .......   10

                  R=100   R=140   R=150   R=160   R=65    R=65    R=65  .....  R=65
Expand  C=40      C= 50   C= 55                           C=65                  L=40
           0        1       2       3       4      5       6       7  .......   10
```

18. A mineral property is producing at a rate that will generate $5 million in annual net revenue (revenue minus operating costs) during the next year (assume end-of-year 1). Escalation of operating costs is expected to be offset by sales escalation in future years so that annual end-of-year net revenue will remain constant at $5 million each year until mineral reserves are depleted 10 years from now at the current production rate. Increase of the production rate is being considered by incurring a $2 million development and equipment cost now (year 0) and a $4 million equipment and development cost a year from now (year 1). These expansion costs would permit increasing mineral production to give projected total net revenues of $6 million at year 1 and $8 million per year at year 2 through 8 when reserves will be depleted at the increased production rate. Use net present value analysis to evaluate the economic desirability of the expansion investments for a minimum rate of return of 20%. Verify your results using rate of return analysis and PVR analysis.

```
Present    -      I=5     I=5  .............  I=5     I=5     I=5
           0       1       2  ...............  8       9      10

                  I=6
Expand   C=2      C=4     I=8  .............  I=8      -       -
           0       1       2  ...............  8       9      10
```

AUXILIARY PROBLEMS   185

19. A chemical company has done research in recent years that has resulted in a new process patent. To acquire the patent rights an outside investor has offered to pay $2 million now and another $4 million in two equal deferred payments of $2 million each 4 and 5 years from now. The investor has an excellent credit rating and sufficient assets so that the offer seems financially solid. The company estimates that internal development of a new plant to implement the patent rights would cost $0.5 million now and $4 million a year from now to generate net income (revenue minus operating costs) of $1 million a year from now and $2 million per year 2 and 3 years from now. If the plant is developed internally it is projected that it would be sold for $6 million 3 years from now. Use ROR Analysis to determine if the economics favor internal development or selling, assuming other opportunities exist to invest capital at 15%. Then determine the single lump sum sale value that received now would make the economics of selling and developing equivalent.

20. A deep water-flood project has been on line for 2 years and problems with artificial lift equipment are becoming evident. Engineering calculations indicate that the producing wells are capable of 750 barrels of fluid per day (BFPD), but problems with the existing artificial lift system has limited production capacity to 400 BFPD per well. The project engineer has to decide whether to (1) reduce the injection rates to match the artificial lift capabilities, or (2) maintain injection and redesign the artificial lift equipment to lift larger volumes of fluid (750 BFPD per well). If injection is reduced the reserves will be recovered slower with the "reduced injection" schedule shown below. If the artificial lift system is modified the reserves can be accelerated and recovered according to the "modified lift" schedule. M = Thousand.

Year	Reduced Injection Oil Production (M Bbl)	Modified Lift Oil Production (M Bbl)
1	1200	1500
2	1300	1700
3	1500	2200
4	1700	2150
5	1400	1700
6	1300	1500
7	1200	1300
8	1100	750
9	1000	350
10	750	100
11	400	0

The year 0 cost of the up-graded artificial lift facility is estimated at $7 million (85% tangible) with operating costs of $1.5 million more a year relative to the current operation. Other known information follows: 1) working interest is 100%, 2) net interest is 80% and 3) oil price per barrel is $24.00 (assume escalation of incremental operating expenses exactly offsets escalation of incremental revenues). Is it economically preferable to reduce the injection rates or to redesign and modify the lift system if the minimum acceptable before-tax rate of return is 15%?

21. A mining company is evaluating whether it is economically desirable to pay $5 million now for a partially developed gold mine if another $3 million must be spent a year from now for further development with a 70% probability of success and if successful another $4 million must be spent 2 years from now with a 90% probability of this final investment giving a profitable producing gold mine that will generate profits of $4 million per year for 20 years of production starting 3 years from now, assuming a washout of income and operating costs escalation. Salvage value will be 0 at the end of the project and if failure occurs at years 1 or 2 assume net abandonment costs and salvage values will be 0. If the escalated dollar minimum ROR is 20% is the project economical?

186   Economic Evaluation and Investment Decision Methods

22. A coal mining project has been on line for 2 years. Engineering mine plan calculations indicate that the present mine production can be increased to the accelerated coal mining production schedule shown below by changing the mine plan and acquiring additional new equipment. The project engineer has to decide whether to (1) maintain current production rates, or (2) accelerate production by purchasing additional mining equipment to increase coal production. M = Thousand.

Year	Present Production (M Tons)	Accelerated Production (M Tons)
1	1200	1500
2	1300	1700
3	1500	2200
4	1700	2150
5	1400	1700
6	1300	1500
7	1200	1300
8	1100	750
9	1000	350
10	750	100
11	400	0

The year 0 cost of the accelerated coal mining production equipment is estimated at $7 million with operating costs of $1.5 million more a year relative to the current operation. Other known information follows: 1) working interest is 100%, 2) net revenue interest after royalties is 80% and 3) coal price per ton is $24.00 (assume escalation of incremental operating expenses exactly offsets escalation of incremental revenues). Is it economically desirable to maintain present coal mining production rates or to accelerate coal mining production if the minimum acceptable before-tax rate of return is 15%?

23. C = Capital Cost, OC = Operating Cost, I = Income. Values are in dollars.

```
A)  C=25,000     I=8,000     I=8,500  -> gradient = +500/yr.  L=0
        0           1           2 ................... 9

                 I=8,000     I=18,000                        I=18,00
B)  C=12,000     C=15,000    OC=10,000 ................... OC=10,000
        0           1           2 ......................... 10

                             C=21,000
                 I=18,000    I=19,000    I=22,000            I=22,000
C)  C=20,000 OC=10,000   OC=10,000   OC=10,000 ................... OC=10,000
        0         1           2           3 ....................... 11
```

If alternatives A, B, and C are mutually exclusive, which alternative (if any) would be the economic choice if the minimum acceptable rate of return is 20%. If alternative A, B, and C are non-mutually exclusive, rank them in their order of economic desirability using PVR.

24. A prospect consists of two parallel structures on opposite sides of a fault. Both structures are long and narrow and must be drilled separately. Structure A has two potentially productive zones while structure B has only one potentially productive zone. Total Area is 6400 acres, 65% in Structure A and 35% in Structure B. Zone 1 has a geologic chance factor (probability of success) of 9.0% in Structure A and 25% in Structure B. Zone 2, found only in Structure A, has a geologic chance factor of 5.0%. Zone 2 is 500 feet deeper than Zone 1.

Assume development can only occur in the following cases:

1) All zones are productive.
2) Zone 2 of Structure A and Zone 1 of Structure B are both productive.
3) Zones 1 and 2 of Structure A are productive.

Draw the decision tree for this problem and label each branch with the appropriate probability of occurrence.

AUXILIARY PROBLEMS

25. Make expected NPV and expected PVR analysis of the following petroleum exploration and production investment situation assuming the minimum rate of return is 15%. Acquisition of mineral rights at time zero will cost $200,000 and exploration drilling at time zero is expected to cost $800,000 with a 20% probability of success. Exploration drilling failure will require incurring a $50,000 year 1 abandonment cost. If logs from the exploration well indicate success, well completion, producing equipment, tank battery and pipeline costs of $700,000 will be incurred at year 1 with an estimated 100% probability of successfully bringing the well into production. Year 1 net revenue (revenue minus operating expenses) of $300,000 and year 2 through 10 net revenue of $400,000 per year are projected to be realized over the well producing life with declining production assumed to be offset by increased selling prices of crude oil and natural gas to simplify the analysis calculations. If the exploration well is successful, 2 development wells will be drilled simultaneously at year 1 for an estimated cost of $600,000 per well and an 80% probability of success. Development drilling failure will require incurring a $50,000 per well year 2 abandonment cost. Successful wells will be completed at year 2 for a cost of $500,000 per well with year 2 development well net revenues of $300,000 per well and year 3 through 11 net revenues of $500,000 per well per year projected to be realized.

26. A gold project is currently under economic consideration. It is estimated that $1,000,000 would be spent on defining reserves and acquiring the rights and necessary permitting for the property in year 0. The acquisition cost would be followed by the investment of $5,000,000 in mine development, $7,000,000 in mine equipment, and $2,000,000 in working capital for spare parts and product inventories, etc. All three costs (development, equipment, and working capital) are allocated to the end of year 1. Working capital is assumed to be liquidated at the end of year 8 when the project is terminated. Treat the revenue from working capital as regular income at year 8.

    The property is expected to generate 6,000 tons of ore per day for 150 days per year starting in year 2. Mining is limited to 150 days per year due to weather considerations. The ore is expected to have an average grade of 0.05 ounces of gold per ton with an anticipated recovery rate of 0.85. Assume the average selling price of gold is $330 per ounce per year, and operating costs are $210 per ounce per year. Escalation of price and operating costs each year is a "washout," meaning that before-tax profits are constant each year at $120 per ounce ($330/oz minus $210/oz). In acquiring the property, the company has agreed to pay a 6.0% royalty on "net profits" until the project pays out. Net profits are defined as gross revenue less operating costs. After payout, the royalty changes to 30% of net profits for the remainder of the project. Payout of the cumulative, undiscounted year 0 and 1 capital costs of $15,000,000 is based on "undiscounted net profits minus the 6% royalty."

    Calculate the ROR, NPV, and PVR for the mine development investor and also for the royalty recipient, assuming the before-tax, escalated dollar minimum rate of return is 15.0%. Then determine what before-tax dollars could be invested in a reclamation cost at year 9 to give the development investor a 15% ROR.

27. Make the analysis asked for in Auxiliary Problem #26 on an after-tax basis. Assume the year 0 $1,000,000 acquisition cost will be deducted for tax purposes by cost depletion. The $7,000,000 year 1 equipment cost will be deducted by 7 year life MACRS depreciation starting in year 1 with the half-year convention. 70% of the year 1 mining development cost of $5,000,000 will be expensed at year 1, and the remaining 30% will be amortized over 60 months with a full 12 month deduction at year 1. Assume the effective income tax rate is 40%. Calculate the DCFROR, NPV, and PVR for the mine development investor and also for the royalty recipient, assuming the after-tax, escalated dollar minimum ROR is 15.0%. Then determine what before-tax dollars could be invested in a reclamation cost at year 9 to give the development investor a 15% after-tax DCFROR. Assume the cost would be 100% deductible at year 9. Finally, neglecting the reclamation cost and prior to incurring any year 0 costs, what is the before-tax acquisition cost (at year 0) to acquire the rights to develop this property that just gives the development investor a 15% after-tax DCFROR?

188   Economic Evaluation and Investment Decision Methods

28. An investor has paid $100,000 for a machine today (time 0) that is estimated to have a 70% probability of successfully producing 5000 product units per year for each of the next 3 years, when the machine is estimated to be obsolete with a zero salvage value. The product price is the unknown to be calculated, so it is estimated to be $X per unit in year 1 escalated dollars and to increase 10% per year in year 2 and 6% in year 3. Total operating costs are estimated to be $8000 in year 1 escalated dollars and to increase by 15% in year 2 and 8% in year 3. The annual inflation rate is estimated to be 7%. What must be the year 1, 2 and 3 escalated dollar product selling price if the investor is to receive a 12% annually compounded constant dollar expected DCFROR on invested dollars? Use modified ACRS depreciation rates for a 5 year depreciation life starting depreciation in year 0 with the half year convention. Write off the remaining book value at the end of year 3. Other taxable income is assumed to exist against which to use year 0 negative taxable income. Assume a 40% income tax rate. Consider zero net cash flow to be realized the 30% of the time the project fails. This assumes that after-tax equipment dismantlement costs will exactly offset the tax writeoff and salvage value benefits.

29. A non-mineral project has been analyzed to have the following cash investment after-tax cash flow stream:

−$800,000	+$400,000	+$500,000	+$550,000
0	1	2	3

Convert the cash investment cash flow to leveraged cash flow assuming $500,000 is borrowed at year 0 for 12% interest per year with the loan to be paid off with three uniform and equal mortgage payments at years 1, 2 and 3. Assume a 40% effective ordinary income tax rate.

A) Calculate the leveraged project DCFROR.
B) How much could be paid at year 0 to acquire the rights to develop the leveraged project and achieve a 25% leveraged DCFROR on equity dollars if the acquisition cost is amortizable over 3 years (years 1, 2 and 3)?

30. Consider the following "today's dollar" cash flows for years 1 and 2:

		Rev=600
C=100	C=200	OC=100
0	1	2

For an escalated dollar minimum ROR of 15%: A) Calculate the project escalated dollar NPV if revenue escalates at 10% per year, and all costs escalate at 6% per year. B) Calculate the project constant dollar NPV if inflation is 5% per year and escalation of costs and revenues is the same as in Case A.
C) Calculate the project escalated dollar NPV assuming today's dollar values equal escalated dollar values. State the explicit cost and revenue escalation assumption built into this analysis. D) Calculate the project constant dollar NPV assuming today's dollar values equal constant dollar values. State the explicit cost and revenue escalation assumption built into this analysis.

31. You are to determine the investment DCFROR that an investor who pays $400,000 for an office building at year 0 would realize on equity investment based on the following data. 90% of the acquisition cost will be for the building which goes into service in the first month of year 1 (business buildings are real property, depreciable straight line over 31.5 years). 10% of the acquisition cost is for land, deductible only against the terminal sale value estimated to be $500,000 at the end of year 2. Any sale gain would be taxed as individual ordinary income. $320,000 of the acquisition cost will be borrowed at year 0 at 10% annual interest with the loan set up to be paid off over 5 years with uniform and equal mortgage payments. Assume unpaid loan principal will be paid off at the end of year 2 when the property is sold. Revenues are projected to be $80,000 in year 1 and $85,000 in year 2 with operating costs of $30,000 in year 1 and $35,000 in year 2. The effective ordinary income tax rate is 30% and other income exists against which to use deductions in any year that negative taxable income exists.

AUXILIARY PROBLEMS

A) Calculate the leveraged investment DCFROR.
B) Determine the maximum investment price that could be paid to give the investor a 15% leveraged DCFROR on his equity invested dollars assuming the investment is 10% land and 90% office building.
C) Calculate the cash investment DCFROR that corresponds to the leveraged DCFROR calculated in part A for the $400,000 investment price. Then determine the maximum investment price that would give the investor a 15.0% cash equity investment DCFROR if it is 10% land and 90% office building.

32. A project manager is evaluating whether it is economical to develop a project requiring expenditures at time zero of $20,000 for land, $30,000 for inventory working capital, $80,000 for a business building, $240,000 for equipment and $60,000 for vehicles. Starting in year 1 he estimates that production will generate annual end-of-year escalated revenue of $500,000 with escalated operating costs of $300,000. In the following years it is estimated that operating costs and revenue will both escalate at 10% per year. At the end of year 4, it is estimated that all the assets and working capital can be sold for an escalated terminal revenue of $600,000. Determine the investment DCFROR assuming a 40% effective income tax rate. Use straight line depreciation over 31.5 years for the building cost starting in year 1, assuming 12 months of service in year 1; MACRS depreciation for a 7 year life for the equipment cost starting at year 1 with the half-year convention; and MACRS depreciation for a 5 year life for the vehicle cost starting at year 1 with the half-year convention. Assume the terminal value gain is taxed as ordinary income. Take a writeoff on all of the remaining tax book values at the end of year 4. For an after-tax escalated dollar minimum rate of return of 15%, determine NPV and PVR in addition to the previously requested DCFROR analysis.

33. A corporation has requested that you evaluate the economic potential of purchasing a gold property now (at year 0) for $2 million mineral rights acquisition cost. Mining equipment costs of $3 million will be incurred at year 0 and the equipment will be placed into service at year 0 when depreciation starts using modified ACRS 7 year life depreciation with the half year convention at year 0. Writeoff the remaining book value at year 5. Mineral development costs of $1 million will be incurred at month 1 of year 0 and mineral development costs of $1.5 million will be incurred at month 1 of year 1. Production is projected to start in year 1 with the mining of 150,000 tons of gold ore, with uniform production of 250,000 tons of gold ore per year in each of years 2, 3 and 4. Gold ore reserves are estimated to be depleted at the end of year 4. Reclamation costs (treat as operating expenses) of $0.5 million in escalated dollars will be incurred at year 5 when escalated $1 million is projected to be realized from equipment salvage value. All gold ore is estimated to contain 0.1 ounce of gold per ton of ore and metallurgical recovery is estimated to be 90%. The price of gold is estimated to be $300 per ounce in year 1 and to escalate 15% in year 2, 20% in year 3 and 10% in year 4. Operating costs are estimated to be $20 per ton of ore produced in year 1 and to escalate 8% per year. Assume other income exists against which to use negative taxable income in any year. The effective income tax rate is 40%.

A) Calculate the cash investment DCFROR and NPV for a minimum escalated dollar DCFROR of 15%.
B) If it is considered likely that after acquiring the property and before spending money on development and equipment the company can generate a cash offer of $5 million for the property with the execution of the sale agreement and cash payment to be at year 1, is it economically better for the company to sell or keep and develop the property?
C) What sale value at year 1 makes the economics of selling breakeven with development for the assumptions of part B?
D) If development is partially financed with $5 million borrowed at 10% annual interest at year 0 to be paid off with 4 equal mortgage payments at years 1 through 4, calculate the leveraged investment DCFROR and NPV for a leveraged minimum escalated dollar DCFROR of 15%.
E) What sale value at year 1 makes the economics of selling breakeven with development using borrowed money for the sale assumptions of part B?

190 Economic Evaluation and Investment Decision Methods

34. A pipeline to transport natural gas from a new gas well to an existing trunk line is estimated to cost $200,000 at year 0 with escalated dollar operating costs estimated to be $9,000 per year at each of production years 1 through 4. It is expected that the gas well will be shut-in at the end of year 4 and that the pipeline salvage value will be zero. Projected natural gas production to be handled by the pipeline follows:

Year	0	1	2	3	4
Average Annual Production (MMcf)		2,000	1,500	1,000	500

where MMcf equals million cubic feet and Mcf equals thousand cubic feet. The pipeline cost of $200,000 would be depreciated over a 7 year life using MACRS depreciation starting in year 1 with the half year convention. A writeoff on remaining book value would be taken at year 4. The effective income tax rate is 40%. Calculate the uniform transportation price per Mcf of natural gas transported that would give the pipeline investor:

A) A 15% escalated dollar DCFROR on invested capital.
B) A 15% constant dollar DCFROR on invested capital for inflation of 8% per year over the project life.

35. A conveyor to transport coal (or mineral concentrate) from a loading point to a shipping facility is estimated to cost $200,000 at year 0 with escalated dollar operating costs estimated to be $9,000 per year at each of production years 1 through 4. It is expected that use of the conveyor will terminate at the end of year 4, and that the salvage value will be zero. Projected coal (or mineral concentrate) production to be handled by the conveyor follows:

Year	0	1	2	3	4
Average Annual Production (M tons)		2,000	1,500	1,000	500

where "M tons" = thousand tons.

The conveyor cost of $200,000 would be depreciated over a 7 year life using MACRS depreciation, starting in year 1 with the half-year convention. A writeoff on remaining book value would be taken at year 4. The effective income tax rate is 40%. Calculate the uniform transportation price per ton of coal (or mineral concentrate) that would give the investor:

A) A 15% escalated dollar DCFROR on invested capital.

B) A 15% constant dollar DCFROR on invested capital for inflation of 8% per year over the project life.